AS ABOVE, SO BELOW

SUN, MOON & STARS

JULIE LOAR

Capella Press

17 Lofty Court, Pagosa Springs, CO 81147

www.JulieLoar.com

Cover Design: Sue Andra Lion

ISBN 9781792336812

Manufactured in the United States of America

10 9 8 7 6 5 4 3 2 1

❀ Created with Vellum

For my sister, Fran.
Your gift was the spark that lit the flame.
This one's for you.

~

CONTENTS

WHAT OTHERS ARE SAYING

Ancient Sky Watchers and *As Above, So Below* are a two-volume series from *Atlantis Rising's* award-winning astrology columnist. For many years, Julie's column was the clearest, most reliable, and most readable source of ancient sky lore to be found in print or on the web. Her thoughtful presentation of historical and mythical detail, informed by extensive in-depth personal research into classic astrology, made her an authority not only to the astrologically minded, but to anyone interested in the forgotten riches of our ancient, and little understood, past.

Doug Kenyon, Publisher, *Atlantis Rising*

"There is no one who writes about astrology, symbols, mythology, and lore like Julie Loar. No one! She is like a *Joseph Campbell* in her ability to make real for the modern mind all of the intrigue, romance, and inner knowing that was once so much a part of everyone's life. Astrologers in days of yore were every bit a seer in their ability to understand the rhythms of the Great Breath, the universe in all its glory. Our Julie is one of them. A typical "reading" for her is a glimpse at balance and rhythm, that which connects, explores, and unveils at the same time. I consider it an honor to speak up for her, and let everyone know, here is a special genius who can see beyond sight. Consider yourself lucky to have any of her work, her articles, her books."

P. M. H. Atwater, L.H.D., one of the original researchers in the field of near-death studies and author of 18 books, her latest *The Forever Angels: Near-Death Experiences in Childhood and Their Lifelong Impact.*

"Well Julie, it looks like you have another award-winning book on your hands . . . it's a polished and many-faceted jewel."

Ted Denmark PhD, Astrologer and award-winning author of *Winged Messengers.*

This volume of essays by esoteric scholar Julie Loar is an astonishing and thought-provoking collection of articles about spirituality, astrology, the cosmos, and our world. Each one is well-researched and written in a short and highly digestible format that makes them as delicious as a spy novel, and even more engrossing. This collection will surprise and delight you with its pithy observations, depth of information, and the fascinating presentation of Loar's material. You may find yourself binge-reading these lovely essays and coming back for more.

Karen Stuth, author, *The Wisdom of Tula* **card deck and** *Quintangled: A Game of Strategy, Change & Destiny*

"*Ancient Sky Watchers and Mythic Themes* is a treasure chest of knowledge that is critical to our time, even as it was to those who walked our Earth long ago. Julie is a wise keeper of the ancient wisdom, which she so generously and lovingly shares with us all. It is a joy to lose myself in the depth of her writings, magnetized by the infinite layers of meaning beneath the words. This is a book I will return to again and again."

Catherine Grace Landry, author of *The Way of the Simple Soul, The Way of the Lightkeeper.*

"Julie Loar has an uncanny ability to discuss ancient phenomena and relate it to modern times in an articulate and approachable way. Her thorough understanding of astrology, the patterns of the sun, moon, and stars, and her depth of knowledge of ancient cultures makes this a fascinating dive into the pool of venerable sky watchers. Now there is an e-book that I can take with me when I travel - what could be better."

Susan Andra Lion, Author and Illustrator of *Night Threads, A Weaving of Soul Stories from the Dreamtime* **and** *How the Trees Got Their Voices.*

INTRODUCTION TO
VOLUME TWO

The forty articles contained in this volume, and the forty that preceded in the first volume, *Ancient Sky Watchers & Mythic Themes*, originally appeared in *Atlantis Rising* magazine from 2001 until 2019. They are reproduced here with full permission from J. Douglas Kenyon, Publisher of *Atlantis Rising*. Although the printed version of the magazine was suspended in 2019, a new completely online form of *Atlantis Rising*, with access to legacy content and new information, is now available online at

https://atlantisrising.com

The articles in this two-volume anthology have been arranged by category, or topic, and do not appear chronologically as they first appeared in *Atlantis Rising* over the span of two decades. The only changes I made were small syntax items like commas, spaces, or other minor items that were missed at the time of original publication. I also added a few parenthetical remarks where a new discovery or development might have altered either my original opinion based on available data or information that was known at the time of original writing. Otherwise, the content of the articles has not been changed or altered, and I hope you will agree that the material has stood the test of time.

Images used in this volume were either taken by the author, Wikipedia's Creative Commons, public domain, or http://www. Snappygoat.com with much gratitude.

Cover photo: Artist Serge Nivens, 166939040, Adobe Stock

Julie Loar http://www.JulieLoar.com

PREFACE TO VOLUME TWO

This two-volume Anthology contains a collection of my articles on astrology, astronomy, and mythology that were published in *Atlantis Rising* magazine, spanning two decades of contributions. Edited and published by J. Douglas Kenyon *Atlantis Rising* was described by many as the best "hardcopy" magazine dealing with ancient mysteries, unexplained anomalies, and future science. I was always proud to be associated with Doug and the magazine.

Family, friends, and clients have urged me for some time to examine the decades of writing these articles represent and to compile the "best of the best." Since I feel a measure of pride in this long-term accomplishment I agreed. It feels like a worthy and empowering endeavor to bring a measure of immortality to a body of one's work.

Eighty of these articles appear in two volumes. Volume I -- *Ancient Sky Watchers & Mythic Themes* contains forty articles covering the topics of ancient astronomy, mythology, prophecy, zodiacs of antiquity, and closes with recent discoveries in astrophysics. Volume II – *As Above, So Below: Sun, Moon, and Stars* has forty articles that span the topics of stars, planets, dwarf planets. Book Two also explores other fascinating objects in our Solar System and their possible symbolic significance.

I was a charter subscriber to *Atlantis Rising* after I acquired my copy of the first issue, which I still have. I submitted my first piece titled *The*

Lore of a Shaman after returning from an amazing journey to South Africa in the late 90s where I had two audiences with renowned Zulu shaman Credo Mutwa, author of *Song of the Stars*. The article appeared in Issue 23 (Chapter 11 in this volume) and examined his star knowledge and my visit to the amazing site of the Timbavati game preserve inside Krueger National Park. Subsequently, Doug Kenyon invited me to contribute a regular astrology feature to the magazine. I readily agreed, and that began a long relationship. What followed were regular feature articles in every issue from February 2001 until Doug stopped printing in spring of 2019 and decided the time had come to turn his attention to other efforts and a new online incarnation of *Atlantis Rising*. http://www.AtlantisRising.com

My articles ranged from traditional astrological reports to a broader range of astronomy and myth. I appreciated the scope I was able to explore and the challenges some topics offered in terms of research and synthesis. Doug gave me incredible freedom under the wide umbrella of astrology, and I explored topics that fascinated me. I wrote about blue moons, Pluto's moons, moon phases, dwarf planets, Egyptian astronomy, and ancient astronomer priests to name a few. One article on the *Bible & Astrology* was featured on the cover and another article titled *Nemesis & Tyche: Does Our Sun Have a Sister?* in issue #90 won first place in a prestigious national writing contest. Ironically, my Saturn-Pluto conjunction article that was slated to appear in Issue #136, and which counseled letting go of forms whose time has come, presaged the suspension of the printed magazine.

I discovered I had written 108 articles over two decades and was astonished by the power of the symbolism. 108 is considered a sacred number in Hinduism, Buddhism, and yogic tradition that symbolizes spiritual completion. 108 is the number of beads on a *mala*, "garland" in Sanskrit, which is a string of beads used in prayer and meditation and is like a rosary. There are also 108 letters in the Sanskrit alphabet. Vedic mathematicians calculate the Sun's diameter to be 108 times larger than the diameter of the Earth, and measure the distance between the Sun and Earth to be 108 times the Sun's diameter. It feels like a significant confirmation of this effort, especially since the articles themselves form a garland. Seen in this way, it is a thrill to envision each article as a pearl on a strand that forms a sacred circle.

I hope this compilation will reconnect with the audience who enjoyed these articles the first time and that a new group of readers interested in these topics will be drawn to these books. My deep respect and gratitude go to Doug Kenyon for years of holding the torch of wisdom high and bright so others might awaken to the truth in its light. Doug gave me a voice to express the timeless wisdom of astrology and myth and to spread the wings of my writing. I also owe a special debt to *Atlantis Rising* since my now husband Ted Denmark, a long-time subscriber, fellow astrologer and writer, reached out to me a decade ago after having read my articles for years. And thanks to everyone whose encouragement prompted me to compile this collection of articles. It's been a labor of love, pride, and humility to see these pieces come together in this way.

Julie Loar www.JulieLoar.com

Pagosa Springs, Colorado

Spring 2020

PART I

SUN & STARS

1. NEMESIS OR TYCHE: DOES OUR SUN HAVE A SISTER?

"We acquire friends, and we make enemies, but our sisters come with the territory."

Evelyn Loeb, author

Image taken by Kepler telescope

A storm of controversy swirls around this subject. The recent excitement began with a science news story that went viral on the Internet, announcing that scientists J. J. Matese and Daniel Whitmire had found a "jovian mass companion" to our Sun in the outer Solar System. If proved, the scenario is breathtaking and would be the biggest news in astronomy since Copernicus informed us that the Earth orbits the Sun. What would this discovery mean to our notion of the Solar System, and what might the impact be to astrology?

Actually, the idea is not new. As far back as the discovery of Neptune in 1846 astronomers have suspected that "something" was affecting the orbits of the outer planets. Although some believe those anomalies were the result of inaccurate measurements at the time, modern astronomers have noticed that comets entering the inner Solar System seem to have been mysteriously kicked out of their orbits and sent hurtling toward the Sun.

Astronomers first postulated the hypothesis for this still-theoretical object in 1987 to account for cycles of mass extinctions that appear in the geological record. In 1984 paleontologists David Raup and Jack Sepkoski examined 250 million years of fossil records and observed that massive species extinction occurred at 65 million year intervals. They could not identify a cause, although it was speculated that the reason was not terrestrial. Two independent teams of astronomers, Davis, Hut and Miller, and Whitmire and Jackson, examined the data and suggested that the Sun had an as yet undetected companion star in a highly elliptical orbit.

The Kuiper Belt, where Pluto orbits, is a band of rocky debris outside the orbit of Neptune. At the far reaches of the Solar System is a sphere of rocky material known as the Oort Cloud that extends to the boundary of the Sun's gravitational field. Long period comets are thought to originate there. Astronomers believe that the object in question periodically disturbs the orbits of comets in the Oort cloud, deflecting them inward toward the Sun, causing enormous devastation if they impact Earth. This theory became known as the Nemesis, or Death Star, hypothesis. Nemesis is a Greek goddess whose name means "due enactment," or "to give what is due." She was seen as the sinister and inescapable agent of divine retribution, punishing people for misdeeds.

The Nemesis theory fulfills all the requirements prescribed by the Raup and Sepkoski mass extinction timetable. Astrophysicist Richard A. Muller believes that Nemesis is a Red Dwarf, a relatively small and "cool" low mass star. It's believed that Red Dwarfs are the most plentiful stars, accounting for roughly 75% of all the stars in the Milky Way. Muller imagines that Nemesis would be less than a third the size of the Sun, of magnitude 7 to 12, and only 1/1000 as bright. As envisioned by Muller, Davis, and Hut, Nemesis might travel in a long elliptical orbit that at its perihelion (closest point), brings it within a half light year of the Sun (one light year is about six trillion miles), and into the midst of the Oort Cloud. The Sun's closest known neighbor, Proxima Centauri, is about 4.25 light years distant.

He thinks Nemesis might be right under our noses, visible with a pair of binoculars, if we just knew where to look. "We see no reason to assume the star is invisible," says Muller, "since most of the stars in the sky have never had their distance from us measured." Based on a theoretical orbit derived from original apogees of a number of atypical long period comets that describe an orbital arc meeting the specifications of his theory, Mueller believes Nemesis will be found in the southern constellation of Hydra, the Water Serpent. The ultimate evidence would be finding the Nemesis star, and the WISE telescope (Wide-field Infrared Survey Explorer), will provide an infrared atlas to the whole sky. The data has already been collected and a full report is expected by February of 2012.

Another group of scientists, led by Daniel Whitmire, an astrophysicist with the University of Southwestern Louisiana, and Al Jackson, of the Computer Science Corporation, announced their own theory of a companion star to the Sun in the same 1987 issue of *Nature* as Muller and his colleagues. Although the means of triggering massive extinctions are essentially the same, Whitmire's group believed that the companion star is invisible: either a Brown Dwarf, or even a black hole.

Choosing the opposite mythical identity, Whitmire's team dubbed the object Tyche, goddess of fortune, and the good sister of Nemesis. A Brown Dwarf is a "failed star" that did not attract enough matter to cause compression that would cause the hydrogen atoms at the core to fuse and ignite. Brown Dwarfs cool and fade with time, finally emitting only infrared wavelengths. Currently, Whitmire and J.J. Matese are working at the University of Louisiana at Lafayette and published the recent sensational report. They believe Tyche is a gas giant roughly four times as massive as Jupiter (not bigger). Whitmire has said that Tyche will probably have colorful spots and cloud bands like Jupiter and will likely have moons.

Scientists estimate that more than 60% of stars have one or more companions that orbit each other, so statistically it wouldn't be a surprise to discover that our Sun is a binary--it's even likely. At times both stars are massive enough to achieve fusion, and circle each other around a point called the barycenter. At other times one star achieves enough mass to catch fire. In the case of a Brown Dwarf companion the smaller body radiates heat and emits a dim glow. According to the barycenter theory there is a relationship between the unexpected quiet period of sunspots at a time that is expected to be violent that would be explained by the presence of a massive body in the Solar System that prevents solar disruptions because of magnetic ion emissions from the companion star.

More compelling evidence comes from Mike Brown, head of the team at Caltech who discovered dwarf planet Sedna along with Eris, Haumea, Makemake, and Quaoar. Sedna has an extra-long and unusual elliptical orbit and is one of the most distant objects yet observed, with an orbit ranging between 76 and 975 AU (1 AU is the distance between the Earth and the Sun). Sedna's orbit is estimated to take 10,500-12,000 years.

Brown commented in a *Discover* magazine article, "Sedna shouldn't be there. It never comes close enough to be affected by the Sun, but it never goes far enough away from the Sun to be affected by other stars." He suggested that a massive unseen object is responsible for Sedna's mystifying orbit, and that its gravity keeps Sedna in its far-distant portion of space. Brown further speculated, "Out to about 1,000 AU where Sedna lives, there could be ten or twenty Pluto-sized objects, and a handful of larger things, too. Some of these suspected worlds could be as big as Mercury, or even Mars."

Additional support for a binary companion comes from an unexpected quarter. The Hindu Vedas, the ancient wisdom of India, has revealed advanced knowledge that has informed and inspired some of the world's greatest thinkers. The idea was popularized by Walter Cruttenden, founder of the Binary Research Institute, in his recent award-winning documentary *The Great Year*. Hindu cosmology includes an explanation of the phenomenon of Precession of the Equinoxes, through a cycle of ages called *Yugas*, which are mirrored in the description of the Greek ages. The mechanism for this is a binary companion of the Sun whose periodic appearance ushers in a golden age, and whose disappearance plunges the world into unconsciousness. In this view, the closer our companion gets, the more light and wisdom increases, so the idea of a goddess who brings good fortune is an apt mythical connection. The *Rishis*, Hindu sages, taught that this cycle was about 24,000 years, close to a cycle of Precession, so in this case we would expect the orbit of the star to be smaller than what the scientists now believe.

Ancient Indian astronomers went even further, giving a physical reason for how the dual star or binary motion might allow the rise and fall of human consciousness to occur. They said that as the Sun (with the Earth and other planets) traveled along its set orbital path with its companion star it would cyclically move close to, then away from, a point in space referred to as *Vishnunabhi*, a supposed magnetic center or "grand center." Perhaps this is a black hole. This idea is echoed in other philosophies that refer to a Great Central Sun.

Tyche, whose name means "luck" in Greek presided over providence, prosperity, and the destiny of a city. She was often depicted with a crown that looked like city walls. Holding a rudder, she was the divinity who guided world affairs, and in this respect, she was one of the Greek Fates. Depicted with a ball, she represented the caprice of fortune--unsteady and capable of rolling in any direction. Shown with Ploutos, or the horn of Amalthea, she was the symbol of the plentiful gifts of fortune. Tyche stood on the "wheel of fortune," which was the zodiac, or wheel of the year. She was Nemesis's sister and was the positive side of the equation that balanced the dire dispensations of her sibling.

Is Nemesis or Tyche an ominous dark star, a specter of doom, lurking at the edge of the solar system and making its way toward us, trailing Armageddon in its wake? Or, is this mysterious body a goddess of good fortune, banishing darkness and evil, and bringing the return of a golden age of enlightenment?

The Greeks assigned the heavenly counterpart of Tyche to Virgo, the largest constellation in the sky after the southern constellation of Hydra, the Water Serpent, and Virgo and Hydra share a celestial border. It seems fitting that the largest object orbiting the Sun would be discovered here. If Tyche appears in Virgo by Celestial Longitude, she may ultimately and cyclically reveal the deeper significance of this sign, the "hidden light" taught in Alchemy, which must be awakened through spiritual practice.

Hinting at the same knowledge taught in the Vedas, there is another goddess connected with this part of the sky--her name is Astraea. She was an ancient goddess of justice from a prior golden age who abandoned humanity when the world became too evil. She went to live among the stars, but her myth says she will return when people once again seek her wisdom.

Although the science is still theoretical, if Tyche's existence is confirmed, I believe its astrological significance will be tied to its identity and nature. If it's a Brown Dwarf, Tyche may act like a more expansive Jupiter, a goddess of wisdom and good fortune who brings increasing light and wisdom in a cyclical manner as the Vedas indicate. She might be a "failed star" but her periodic proximity to us nevertheless brings the gift of illumination. If Tyche proves to be a Black Hole, then she may act like a more intense version of Saturn's energy, expressing more in the nature of Nemesis, and bringing tough karmic lessons. And if our star's companion is a Red Dwarf, then the influence will be like a smaller sun, contributing more intense light, and lessons of the heart, as she cyclically reappears in an ages long cycle.

In late August 2011 NASA released a tantalizing report that WISE's highly sensitive infrared vision had detected 100 new Brown Dwarfs. In a provocative hint Michael Cushing, a WISE team member at JPL said, "We may even find a Brown Dwarf closer to us than our closest known star." At a time when the world as we know it seems to be coming apart at the seams, a goddess of good fortune would be welcome indeed. Stay tuned.

Atlantis Rising #90 October 2011

(won first place in *Writer's Digest* national contest 2014)

2. A STAR IS BORN: LIFECYCLE OF A STAR

" A billion stars go spinning through the night, blazing high above your head. But within you is the presence that will be when all the stars are dead."

Rainer Maria Rilke, *Buddha in Glory*

Cassiopeia Supernova (SnappyGoat.com 11180)

In modern, western Astrology the Sun is at the center and looms large in symbolic significance. The Sun is said to govern our individuality and our emerging nature. The Sun indicates the major lessons we have come to learn. But our Sun is after all just one star, and in eastern traditions the Moon is the more important body because she moves through the night sky where the rest of the stars are. In earlier times the influence of other stars, rising or setting at the time of birth, were thought to have enormous impact over the destiny of a life, the fortunate or unlucky nature of the star would bode well or ill for the newborn child's life.

What is the true nature of a star? What about other stars in the night skies? Like everything else we witness in life, stars exist within a spectrum of diversity, ranging in size from one hundred times the mass of our Sun to only one-tenth of its mass. Massive stars, much larger than our Sun, burn hotter, shine brighter, and live shorter lives. Less massive stars emit dimmer light and burn their fuel at a more conservative rate, and live much longer lives as a result. Like people stars range in age from young to vastly old. As with humans so with stars, an ordinary life can be a blessing.

The Sun is our very own star, and its color appears yellow-white. Although often described as typical, our star is in the top five percent in our galaxy in terms of size and brightness. The average star in our galaxy is much smaller and dimmer. Our Sun is a middle aged star, roughly half way through its main sequence stage, and is estimated to be 4.6 billion years old. Each second the Sun converts about five million tons of matter into energy. In another four and a half billion years the Sun will have exhausted its fuel and become a Red Giant.

Another distinguishing characteristic is that our star is solitary--a single parent. Most stars have stellar companions. Double star systems are called binary stars, like paired couples, and the term multiple star system describes any system of companion stars. The companions in multiple star systems are in orbit around one another like a dance. Nearly two-thirds of stars in our sector of the Milky Way are multiple star systems. The majority are binary, but there are also triple and quadruple systems. Although they are rare, there are families of five and six stars, entwined in reciprocal orbits by the compelling force of gravity.

Although the brightness, color, and length of life of a star is a function of its original mass, all stars shine for the same reason. Stars are composed almost entirely of hydrogen gas. Star light results from the energy produced at their cores by nuclear fusion. What emerges from the surface of a star is the light we see, as well as ultraviolet light, X-rays and radio waves. A star's life is a dance of existence, a dynamic tension between the expanding energy of the nuclear furnace at its core and the concentrating pull of gravity created by its mass. As long as the push/pull balance is maintained by the burning of hydrogen at its heart, the force of gravity will be held at bay, and the star will shine.

Main sequence stars like our Sun, in the middle of their lives, burn with constant light for billions of years, slowly consuming their reserves of hydrogen fuel. As the hydrogen is finally consumed, the surface of the star cools and the star becomes a Red Giant in a brilliant swan song. After that transitional phase is complete, the last breath of a dying, low mass star, lasting billions of our years, is called a white dwarf. After this period the dying star becomes a Black Dwarf, a stellar corpse, no longer giving light to the dark space in which it resides but still marking its course due to the force of gravity.

The ultimate fate of a star is determined by its success in the battle against gravity. With fuel to burn, the outward radiating pressure produced by nuclear fusion in its core will maintain the balance against the compressive force of its own gravity. Once the star has exhausted its fuel reserves, gravity takes over and the star begins to contract. A dying star has three alternatives based on its original mass: very massive stars become supergiants; a few Supergiants may explode in the process, going supernova, truly ending their life in a blaze of glory; a supernova may subsequently collapse upon itself and become either a black hole or a neutron star, also called a pulsar.

Astronomers still theorize about what magic combination of available matter, resulting solar mass and its residue, contribute just the right combination of factors to generate a solar system capable of sustaining life as we know it. The consensus today is that stars are born from the raw material of nebulas, interstellar clouds of dust and gas. Astronomers believe that planets form from the leftover material around a new born star. Planet birth seems to be a by-product of star birth.

In recent years planets have been discovered in orbit around other stars. These breakthrough discoveries have revealed huge, Jupiter like planets, orbiting suns in other solar systems. Technology has not developed sufficiently to detect earth size planets, but the evidence is encouraging, and as our abilities to peer into space improves we may discover solar systems similar to our own where a life-giving blue planet orbits a friendly star. (January 2020 NASA reported the first earth-sized planet in a habitable zone).

The first stars to form in a galaxy are known as first-generation stars. They are pure hydrogen and helium because almost no elements heavier than helium were formed in the original Big Bang. If a star is massive enough it will begin to convert helium to heavier elements like oxygen and carbon once it has consumed all the hydrogen fuel at its core. Very massive stars will produce elements as heavy as iron. When extremely massive stars explode as supernovas, they produce even heavier elements like uranium, which is the heaviest natural element. These heavy elements are then ejected into space and become part of the dust and gas clouds that condense into the second generation and further generations of stars. Our Sun is a second generation star, or perhaps later.

Stages of a Star's Life - The life of a star life might be described as potential, coalescence, ignition, radiance, swan song, exhaustion and death; not unlike the stages of a human life.

Interstellar dust cloud - Potential - A star begins its existence in a sea of potential. In the beginning an interstellar dust cloud is in motion in space. Perhaps triggered by collisions of deep space objects in the vicinity, the raw material in the dust cloud moves and shifts, gravitating toward the center.

Protosolar nebula - Coalescence / Attraction - Over a vast period of time the enigmatic force of attraction causes the gases in the cloud to coalesce. The cloud shrinks and compresses due to the force of its own gravitational pull. A center forms which draws larger amounts of dust and gas to itself. As the cloud continues to contract the atoms move faster, heating up until the center reaches a point termed critical density. The center separates from the rest of the material and becomes a Protostar.

Star birth - Ignition - When the temperature becomes hot enough nuclear fusion occurs. Four hydrogen atoms fuse into one helium atom. A tiny portion of the mass in each atom has been converted into energy during this transmutation. Flash point is achieved, and a star is born. The brightness, length of life, and ultimate fate of a star is dependent on its original mass or the raw material available during its original formation.

Main Sequence Stars -- Radiance; Stellar Adulthood - The Main Sequence stage of star life is equivalent to adulthood for humans. Stars settle into a state of steady burn and live out their lives according to their supply of fuel. Stars spend their lives on fire from within, casting life giving radiance into the deep darkness of space. Stars are composed mainly of hydrogen gas. Our sun is ninety-two percent hydrogen, nearly eight percent helium, and a fraction of a percent of heavier elements. Star light is burning hydrogen, converting to helium and releasing energy. Stars burn in the heavens, sometimes creating the perfect conditions for life as here on our home planet Earth. The core of a star becomes rich in helium as it consumes its supply of hydrogen fuel. Stars burn hydrogen at their cores for ninety percent of their life span. Our Sun is about half way through its projected nine billion year life span, or about 4.6 billion years of age in Earth terms.

Red Giant -- Swan Song - The Red Giant stage of star can be quiet and prolonged or sudden and violent, depending on star's initial mass. After the fuel at the star's core is exhausted, the thermonuclear reactions will shift to a shell around the core where a supply of hydrogen remains. The core contracts, heating up the layer of burning hydrogen and speeding up the reactions. This produces more energy, and in the short term, the aging star burns brighter. The star expands in size as more energy is released from the core. At this stage, the core becomes hot enough to burn helium which causes its matter to further expand. The star expands to enormous proportions as both hydrogen and helium are transmuted into heavier elements and energy. The star will become a red giant thousands of times its original rightness.

Old Age -- White Dwarf - After all the fuel is exhausted the star will collapse into a shadow of its former self, radiating white light which results from the energy of compression. The star's interior begins to shrink. The surface of the remaining interior heats to white hot, becoming a white dwarf. A white dwarf is a very dense star; the mass of the Sun compressed to the size of Earth. A teaspoon of matter from such a star would weigh tons. When our Sun consumes its nuclear fuel it will shrink and heat up, becoming a white dwarf. The white dwarf represents old age, although sparkling like a white diamond in the darkness no life could be supported on any cinder like planets remaining in the vicinity.

Planetary Nebula -- Funeral Pyre - The star's interior then begins to shrink. After swelling to many times its original size and consuming its supply of helium, a Red Giant jettisons its outer envelope. Outer matter will drift into space as a brightly colored planetary nebulae. The name is inappropriate and came from early descriptions of these nebula as round and planet-like. These spectacular objects look like colored jewels on black velvet and are among the most beautiful objects viewed through a telescope.

Death -- Black Dwarf - Eventually the white dwarf star will cool and emit no energy. The final corpse of a star like our Sun is a cinder, perhaps the size of Earth. A burnt out corpse, emitting no light or energy, but still held in place in its galactic family by the force of gravity. As far as astrophysicists know, no white dwarf has yet died in our universe, which means they either live an incomprehensibly long time, or our universe is still quite young.

∼

Types of Stars

Red Dwarf -- A Slow Burn - Red dwarfs are small, dim main sequence stars and seem to be the most plentiful. Red dwarfs live long lives because in stellar terms, they simmer their fuel slowly at low temperatures. The furnace at the heart of Red Dwarf Proxima Centauri, our nearest star, will likely radiate at its present output for another two hundred billion years, living twenty times longer than our Sun. Astronomers call these truly average stars Red Dwarfs because of their color and size. Red Dwarfs constitute over half the stellar citizenship of the Milky Way. Astronomers have counted more than one hundred billion red dwarfs, and none of them can be seen without a telescope. Although one-tenth the diameter of our Sun and one-tenth the mass, Proxima Centauri only generates one twenty-thousandth of the light. This would be dense twilight on Earth.

Brown Dwarf -- Unrealized potential - True stars produce energy and light by fusing hydrogen into helium in the nuclear furnaces, burning at their cores. Brown Dwarfs are unable to summon the internal spark to ignite the thermonuclear furnace and therefore only emit a dull glow. Some Brown Dwarfs waver close to the dividing line between star and planet. Because they are still difficult to detect, only a few Brown Dwarfs are known.

Supergiants -- Brilliance - At the other extreme of this spectrum are blue supergiants like Deneb, in Cygnus, and Rigel in Orion. Stars of such enormous mass radiate brilliance fifty thousand times the brightness of our Sun. In the course of their few million year life span their cores fill with helium. This causes the star to become larger and hotter, swelling to enormous proportions. They live hot, fast lives in stellar terms. Very massive stars become supergiants. They draw on energy from nuclear fusion that produces elements as heavy as iron. Such stars could be as large as Jupiter's orbit.

Blaze of Glory -- Supernova - Late in their lives extremely massive supergiant stars become unstable, and a few of them become supernovas, exploding giants which impinge upon the universe like immense lightning bolts. These very massive stars can explode in a cataclysmic death after a few million years, dying young as stars go. Only stars greater than six solar masses have the potential to go supernova. The detonation of a supernova results in a cosmic firecracker a million times hotter than the surface of the Sun. Astronomers believe the catastrophic obliteration of a supergiant is a factor in the birth of new stars and galaxies, perhaps creating the elements required to generate life in the athanor of their violent death. Our own Solar System is believed to be the result of an earlier supernova.

With the advent of electricity and artificial daylight, we have become separated from the magic of the night sky. Light from modern cities blinds us to the stars, but if we escape to a place where artificial light is minimized we can once again thrill to the spectacle of the vault of heaven. Earth orbits our very own star, which in turn inhabits a spiral arm within the Milky Way galaxy. The galaxy in turn is part of what astronomers call the Local Group, containing several dozen galaxies and spanning a distance of ten million light years. Not only are we earthlings not living at the center of creation, we aren't even close to the center of our galaxy. Contemplating our place in the scheme of things engenders a deep sense of humility. It's humbling and empowering to go out on a clear dark night and gaze into Infinity.

Atlantis Rising #29 August 2001

3. ASTROLOGY & THE FIXED STARS: WHAT CAN THE LORE OF FAMOUS STARS REVEAL ABOUT HUMAN NATURE?

"Star light, star bright, the first star I see tonight, I wish I may, I wish I might, have the wish I wish tonight."

Mother Goose Nursery Rhyme

Brocchi's Cluster CR 399 (SnappyGoat.com)

The familiar nursery rhyme quoted above is thought to have
originated in America in the nineteenth century, but the sentiment is as
timeless as the earliest humans gazing at the night sky. The stars hold a
perennial fascination and have served as story board and navigation
guide for thousands of years. Legend says that Persian Magi followed
a bright star from the East in search of a new king and found him in
Bethlehem. Even space age astronauts are taught to navigate by the
stars.

The stars aren't really "fixed." About 4,000 years ago, at the beginning
of the Age of Aries, the stars of the Ram rose before the Sun at Spring
Equinox sunrise, but gradually the phenomenon of Precession has
caused a shift in the stars which rise before the Sun. Now, as we come
to the end of the Age of Pisces, the stars of the Fishes will make way
for Aquarius. Western Astrology still treats Spring Equinox as the
beginning of the "sign" of Aries, and the circle of the astrological

zodiac is one of time which no longer moves in resonance with the constellations themselves.

Although our Sun is a star, and the most important factor in the astrology of our Solar System, few astrologers incorporate the rich lore of other stars into their interpretative mix. Our yellow-white star is often described as typical, but is in the top five percent in our galaxy in terms of size and brightness. The Sun is estimated to be 4.6 billion years old and roughly halfway through its main-sequence stage.

In esoteric astrology the planets influence the personality and life experiences in the perceived reality we call the third dimension. Stars, on the other hand, are thought to stimulate the soul on the path of initiation, aiding the work of evolving the personality into a suitable instrument to serve the greater good.

Constellations are divisions of sky in the same way countries are on Earth, and since 1930 there is international agreement on eighty-eight constellations that include stars and other deep space objects. The names of the constellations are generally Latin, the names of stars are usually Arabic, and the designations of star brightness or place within the constellation are Greek letters and numbers. With a few exceptions the alpha star is the brightest in the constellation.

One measure astronomers use to locate objects in space is Celestial Longitude and Latitude in the same way maps use longitude and latitude to define coordinates on Earth. There are 360 degrees of Celestial Longitude. Zero degrees of this measure is placed at spring equinox, which is also the zero point of the Tropical Zodiac and the beginning of the astrological sign of Aries. So in terms of expressing Celestial Longitude Aries is 0-29, Taurus is 30-59 and so on.

The following stars were selected to allow a star for each zodiac sign based on degrees of Celestial Longitude. These bright stars are not in the zodiac constellation but do align longitudinally like cities on a map which are in different states or provinces but are due north or south of each other. Most of them are among the brightest stars in the sky. What follows are ideas of how these powerful bright stars might have significant connections to the birth chart based on accumulated star lore.

Aries – Alderamin -- Alderamin, which means "shoulder," is the white alpha star in the constellation of Cepheus, the King and resides at 12 Aries 48, the same as Celestial Longitude. The original name of the star was Al Dhira al Yamin, "right arm." One source equates the name of the constellation Cepheus with Cheops of Great Pyramid fame. Alderamin is the western base of the house of the King and will have the honor of being the Pole Star about 5,500 years from now as will its counterparts Beta and Gamma Cepheus sooner. The mythic themes of this star are linked to ideas of sovereignty and enlightened kingship, ruling from a place of wisdom gained from experience.

Taurus – Capella -- Capella, the "Little She Goat" is the yellow alpha star of Auriga, the Charioteer, and is identical with our Sun in spectral composition. Capella is at 21 Taurus 51, or 51 degrees of Celestial Longitude. Although called "little goat" Capella is a giant star, sixteen times larger than our Sun and 150 times more luminous, and is really more like the horse which pulls the Chariot. The Greeks saw Capella as Amalthea, the goat who nursed Zeus as an infant. Norman Lockyer believed at least five Egyptian temples were oriented to Capella, including a temple to Ptah at Memphis a staggering 7,200 years ago. Mythically Capella is auspicious and portends honor and wealth.

Gemini – Betelgeuse -- Betelgeuse, from the Arabic meaning "House of the Twins," is the alpha star in the constellation of Orion, the Hunter. Betelgeuse is an orange supergiant star that is larger than the orbit of Venus. The earliest names referred to the constellation as a Giant. Betelgeuse is at 28 Gemini 45, or 88 degrees of Celestial Longitude. Polaris, our current Pole Star, is at this same degree. The constellation Orion straddles the Celestial Equator and is visible all over the world. Betelgeuse is seen as a fortunate star, offering great success without a lot of struggle, implying perhaps that the rewards were gained in another life.

Cancer – Sirius -- Sirius, the "Shining One," is the alpha star in the constellation of Canis Major, the Big Dog, and is called the "Dog Star." Sirius is brilliant white and the brightest star in the sky from our perspective on Earth. Sirius was the star of Isis, and when Sirius rose with the sun at summer solstice each year that event signaled the onset of the annual Nile flood. Sirius is at 14 Cancer 05 with a Celestial Longitude of 104 degrees. Mysteriously, sources from 2,000 years ago describe this star as "red," "coppery," and fiery." However, since 1,000 CE Sirius is very white with blue tinges. Although it's theorized that Sirius B, it's now-dark companion, was formerly a red supergiant, no residue of gases has been detected to solve the mystery. Sirius confers great power and a child born in ancient Egypt on the day this star rose with the sun would have led a sacred life dedicated to Isis.

Leo – Dubhe -- Dubhe is Arabic for "bear," and is the alpha star in the constellation of Ursa Major, the Great Bear. Dubhe is a yellow star and one of the "pointers" of the Big Dipper asterism that point to the Pole Star. Norman Lockyer found several Egyptians temples aligned to Dubhe. Dubhe is in the "back of the bear" at 15 Leo 11 degrees of the zodiac and 135 degrees of Celestial Longitude. Dubhe seems to embody the idea of courage and if connected to a natal chart is thought to confer a brave heart, but also to give lessons relating to other matters of the heart.

Virgo – Thuban -- Thuban, from Arabic Ath Thuban, "snake," is the alpha star in the constellation of Draco, the Dragon. Thuban lies in the middle of the Dragon's long tail. Pale-yellow Thuban resides at 07 Virgo 26 degrees of the zodiac and 157 degrees of Celestial Longitude. Thuban is not the brightest star in Draco, but it was the Pole Star during the so-called Pyramid Age of Egypt nearly 5,000 ago. There is a sense of guarding something secret and sacred about this star and its stories. Mythically dragons are often depicted as hoarding their treasure, so appropriate revelations and willingness to share the bounty can be the issue here.

Libra – Arcturus -- Arcturus, "guardian of the bear," is the golden-yellow alpha star in the constellation of Bootes, the Herdsman, at 24 Libra 13 and 204 degrees of Celestial Longitude. The name in Greek is

Arktouros. Perhaps Arcturus is also guardian of the north since we use the term arctic to describe the frozen north. Arcturus is like a pathfinder and acts as a guardian, providing lessons of learning, teaching others, and leadership. Arcturus is said to engender a desire to create a better way, and gives the native influenced by this star an innate skill to lead. There is also a sense of watching gateways and portals.

Scorpio - Alpha Centauri -- Alpha Centauri, or Rigil Kentaurus, "Foot of the centaur," is the white alpha star in the constellation of the Centaur, and is at 29 Scorpio 29 and 239 degrees of Celestial Longitude. Alpha Centauri has the distinction of being our closest star. It is also a triple star system, which is fitting as it is sometimes known by a third name, Toliman, from the Arabic for ostriches. This constellation is thought to be Chiron, the wise centaur, unlike the centaur of Sagittarius that represents the process of becoming wise. The old stories depict the starry Centaur as approaching the stars of Ara, the Altar to make an offering. In Greek myth Chiron fashioned the constellations and taught humanity how to read the stars. Healing a deep wound can be the message of this star when it is connected to a chart.

Sagittarius - Ras Algethi -- Ras Algethi, "Kneeler's Head," is the alpha star in the constellation of Hercules, the strong man of Greek myth. Ras Algethi is a beautiful double star that shines at 16 Sagittarius 08, or 256 degrees of Celestial Longitude. One star is red-orange and the other is blue-green. This is an ancient constellation that was commonly seen as a kneeling figure. Long before these stars were Hercules they represented the hero Gilgamesh. Ras Algethi's influence carries the idea of devotion, surrender to a higher power, and humbly offering all we have. The idea of sacrifice is embodied in the hero's journey.

Capricorn – Vega -- Vega, "vulture," is the alpha star in the constellation of Lyra, the Lyre. Blue-white Vega is at 15 Capricorn 19 zodiac degrees and 285 degrees of Celestial Longitude. Vega was the Pole Star 12,000 years ago during the time of fabled Atlantis, and will reclaim that honor in another 12,000 - 14,000 years. In Egypt the vulture star was equated with the goddess Ma'at. Lockyer believed this star marked orientation of temples at Dendara before Gamma Draco and Alpha Ursa Major. In Asia Vega is called the Weaving Princess star. She was once a girl who fell in love with a shepherd, who is Altair, and they neglected their duties. Her father put them on opposite sides of the sky, and now they only meet once a year at midsummer. In myth Vega carries the idea of a potent charisma. The test is how this gift is used.

Aquarius – Altair -- Altair, is the yellowish-white alpha star in Aquila, the Eagle. The star's name derives from the Arabic word for the constellation and represents the wings of an eagle, or perhaps a falcon. Altair forms one corner of a huge triangle known to all navigators. Altair is at 01 Aquarius 46 degrees of the zodiac and 301 degrees of Celestial Longitude. Like its name, Altair carries the significance of flying high where "no one has gone before," blazing new trails and setting lofty goals for those who follow. Mythically this star has a courageous and pioneering quality.

Pisces – Fomalhaut -- Fomalhaut, "mouth of the fish," is the alpha star in Pisces Austrinus, the Southern Fish, and was one of the four Royal Stars of Persia more than 4,000 years ago. Fomalhaut is a blue-white star at 03 Pisces 51 and 333 degrees of Celestial Longitudes. Above the equator Fomalhaut's appearance in the night sky is an annual harbinger of autumn. On celestial maps Aquarius, the Water Bearer seems to be emptying his urn into the mouth of the Southern Fish. The energy of Fomalhaut seems to amplify other energies present in a birth chart and engenders a test of overcoming glamour and a lust for glory.

Ancient wisdom traditions teach that stars are vastly evolved beings whose longs lives and radiance gives life, light and power to aid evolution. Perhaps the ancients understood a form of stellar wisdom that has been lost to history, and we might enrich and empower ourselves by returning to a visceral connection to the sky. As the ancient Egyptians said in texts to the deceased pharaoh, "May you seize the sky."

Atlantis Rising #68 February 2008

4. STAR OF WONDER: WAS THE STAR OF BETHLEHEM A COME, PLANETARY CONJUNCTION, SUPERNOVA, OR SOMETHING ELSE?

"... For we have seen his star in the east, and we have come to worship him."

The Bible, Matthew 2:2

The Three Magi (160632 SnappyGoat.com)

The modern calendar begins with the birth of Christ and refers to subsequent years as AD, meaning *Anno Domini,* the "year of our Lord," and prior years as BC, Before Christ. This reckoning was developed by the monk Dionysius Exiguus and was based on his belief of when Christ was born. Other more politically-correct systems have emerged in academic circles such as BP, Before Present, or BCE, Before Current Era.

Scholars disagree with Dionysius when the actual event occurred and believe that the well-meaning monk made unfortunate errors in his record keeping. Today, the most-agreed upon timeframe for the birth of Christ is between 8 BCE to 4 BCE.

In an effort to solve the calendar controversy, and fix the date of Jesus's birth, astronomers have tried to identify the Star of Bethlehem, using modern science and computers. Two thousand years ago planets were called "wandering stars," so stellar candidates for the Star of Bethlehem include planetary conjunctions of Jupiter and Saturn (7 BCE), Jupiter, Saturn, and Mars (6 BCE), and Jupiter and Venus (5 BCE) as well as a comet and Nova in 5 BCE, and a possible naked-eye spotting of Uranus. Not a bad margin of error, considering the calendar issue. However, no agreement among experts has moved scholars any closer to pinpointing the birth of Jesus.

The story of the Christmas star, and the exotic Magi bearing gifts, appears only in the gospel of Matthew (Matthew 2:2). The idea of Wise Men following a bright star until the miraculous light came to rest over the stable of a newborn king is compelling because of its mythic overtones. Thousands of years ago watching the sky was the domain of astronomer-priests who interpreted comets and conjunctions, reading omens and portents on behalf of king and country.

Magi is plural of Magus, *Magoi* in Greek, and is generally translated as "Wise Men," but also magician, priest, or astrologer. Religious and secular sources agree that the Magi were highly respected for their wisdom and that extensive knowledge of the night sky was their province.

The image of three kings mounted on camels and dressed in exotic clothing, bearing gifts of gold, frankincense ,and myrrh has become cultural icon. Symbolically gold signified kingship or royal status. Frankincense is a resin used for prayer and ceremony, so this gift affirmed his sacred mission. Myrrh is a balm that was used to "embalm" corpses, so this gift foretold his sacrificial death. The Bible makes no mention of the Magi's number, and chroniclers of their journey number their party anywhere from two to twelve. Tradition has settled on three; one for each gift.

Different sources point to different Eastern origins for the Magi. Persian Zororastrian, star priests from Sheba, or Babylonian or Assyrian astronomers have been suggested. Likewise tradition has named them in various ways, the most common being Gaspar, Balthasar, and Melchior. Typically, Gaspar is depicted as a black African, Balthasar a European with a long white beard, and Melchior is shown as "Oriental" or Persian. Perhaps this diversity is intended to suggest the wide-spread expectation and acceptance of the new king's birth and to explain Matthew's political purpose for telling the tale.

If the Biblical account represents a historical event, I believe the country of Sheba, or Saba, home of the famous, dark-skinned queen from southern Arabia who paid Solomon a call, was the most likely origin of the Magi. At the time in question the land was ruled by priest-kings called Sabeans who possessed profound knowledge of the sky. A temple to the moon god Illumqua was discovered by archeologists at Marib, which was once the capital of Sheba. The land of Sheba was also renowned for trade of spices and incense, especially frankincense, as well as gold and jewels.

What is most telling about Matthew's account is that no one but the Magi seems to have noticed the star. In fact, Matthew remarks that when Herod heard the news, "Herod, the king trembled, and all Jerusalem with him." (Matthew 2:3) Given the times, if there had been a dramatic celestial occurrence it seems likely that others would have commented, but the Bible is strangely silent. That suggests that either the knowledge was esoteric, requiring wisdom of the night sky to recognize something extraordinary, or the star was symbolic. If nothing obvious or easy to identify appeared in the night sky around 5 BCE, what drew the Magi to Jerusalem?

Those who watched the sky looked for changes or disasters, literally "disorder in the stars." By observing and passing down patterns that recurred over thousands of years the nature of experience on earth could be predicted. The sky is fairly orderly, moving through predictable cycles of differing lengths, so any change was considered worthy of note. Days, months, and years are short and easy to monitor. Cycles like precession of the equinoxes are much longer and more difficult to track.

Precession is the effect, visible only over time, of the earth's wobble. This motion causes stars that rise in the predawn sky to shift slowly backward at the rate of one degree of arc every 72 years. The visible effect of this motion may not have been noticeable in the course of a single star watcher's lifetime, but in a tradition like the Magi, carefully handed down over long generations, the place where a star rose over a mountain peak or other point on the horizon would be noticed as it moved westward.

In modern times, the Greek astronomer Hipparchus is credited with discovering the phenomenon of precession, but alternative scholars, including the authors of *Hamlet's Mill*, have offered compelling evidence that this knowledge reached much farther back in time and was transmitted through myth.

Precession has two effects from the sky-watching perspective. First, the motion causes the polar axis to shift relative to the night sky and slowly moves a different "pole star" into the northern sky over time. Second, precession causes sunrise to move backward (toward the west), against different constellations. This motion came to be tracked against the familiar constellations that circle the ecliptic, the apparent annual journey of the sun. What evolved over time we now call the astrological ages, as the backward motion of the sun (really the earth's slow wobble) changes at spring equinox. Sometimes known as "grand months" the ages last approximately 2,160 years. Even if the wobble is regular, the constellations are not all the same size, so ages may have varied in length.

We really don't know when the familiar constellations of the zodiac were formed but historically Babylonian astronomers fixed the zodiac at spring equinox in Aries about four thousand years ago. Western astrologers still base the zodiac on the seasons and call spring equinox the zero point of Aries even though the stars no longer line up with that constellation. Western Tropical Astrology analyzes the relative positions of sun, moon, and planets through the temporal divisions of the solar year, beginning with spring equinox.

Through these stellar ages "gods" have embodied the archetype of the age determined by the constellation presiding over spring equinox sunrise. During the age of Taurus, the Bull (circa 4,300 BCE to 2,100 BCE), Minotaurs, Apis bulls, and the Bull of Heaven dominated myth and legend.

Next the march of ages brought the ram-headed god Khnum of Egypt to the stellar throne while the constellation of Aries, the Ram provided staging for the spring equinox sunrise around 2,100 BCE. The onset of the Christian era in approximately 4 BCE began as the spring sun rose against the backdrop of the constellation of Pisces, the Fishes. From then until the present the Fisher of Men has been the Avatar, or god-king, of the age of Pisces. As we approach the much-heralded age of Aquarius, the stars of the Water Bearer will replace those of the Fishes. At some point a new Avatar/archetype for the Aquarian age will emerge, bringing the return of the "once and future king."

Knowledge of precession would have been central to the sacred and secret tradition of the sky-watching Magi. As the Great Wheel slowly turned the Magi would have monitored and anticipated the arrival of a new constellation on the spring equinox horizon, speculating on the character of the new age.

An important change did occur in the predawn sky around 8 BCE - 4 BCE as a new star rose before the sun. Now designated Eta Pisces this fairly-ordinary star ascended due east at spring equinox and displaced the stars of Aries after more than two thousand years. I believe that the "Star in the East" wasn't a flashing comet or brilliant planetary conjunction but a star in the constellation of Pisces, the Fishes, proclaiming the dawn of a new age.

What made the star special that the Magi followed "to Bethlehem, in Judah," was not its outward brilliance or showy display but its position in the sky. Eta Pisces resides on the "border" of Aries and Pisces, and although unnamed some intriguing lore is connected with this star.

In his classic book, *Star Names, Their Lore & Meaning*, R.H. Allen states that another author, the German Orientalist, J. Epping *Astronomisches aus Babylon,* insisted that this star marked the ecliptic point of the first constellation of the Babylonians. Since Eta Pisces was the first to rise after the stars of Aries passed the spring equinox marker in the epoch of 8 BCE -4 BCE, this is strong testimony that this star could have been seen as the announcer of the age of Pisces. Allen also tells us that another name for this star was "Dweller of the Fish." An apt description for the herald of an era symbolized by fish.

Ancient wisdom traditions inform us that each age brings forth a new Avatar, a Divine Incarnation, to intercede on behalf of humanity.

Certainly the advent of such a new "King" would have been anticipated by Magi who lived at the cusp of an age. Whether a literal voyage of homage to Bethlehem occurred or not Matthew's story was based on respected authority from an ancient lineage. A star that beckoned to the Magi and drew them to a humble birthplace bearing kingly gifts would have lent strong justification for the birth of the Messiah.

Whether the story is myth, history, or a poetic combination, as the Lamb of God from the age of Aries was transformed into the Fisher of Men for the age of Pisces I believe the "Star in the East," once called "Dweller of the Fish," marked the point in time of the transition.

Atlantis Rising #49 December 2004

5. SOLAR FIRE: BEYOND SUN SIGNS

"Thou sun, of this great world both eye and soul."

John Milton, *Paradise Lost*

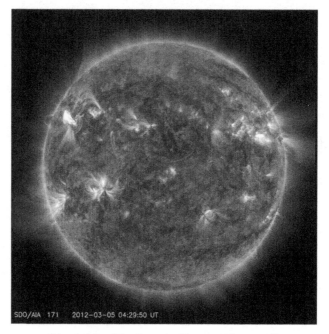

*Solar Activity - Solar Dynamics Observatory (image credit
NASA/SDO/AIA)*

Once regarded by astronomers as a small, and relatively insignificant
star, our chief luminary is now believed to be brighter than 85%, and in
the top 10% by mass, of the hundreds of billions of stars in the Milky
Way galaxy. Most other stars in our galaxy are red dwarfs. Our Sun is a
main-sequence star, about 4.5 billion years old, and contains more than
99.8% of the total mass of the solar system, with Jupiter containing
most of the remainder.

The Sun generates energy by nuclear fusion of hydrogen nuclei into
helium, fusing 430–600 million tons of hydrogen every second. Solar
physicists say it takes a million years for the energy created at the Sun's
core to make its way to the surface where it radiates into space. The
Sun is about 70% hydrogen and 28% helium by mass, and since its
birth, our star has consumed about half of the hydrogen in its heart. It
will continue to radiate for another five billion years, and its
luminosity is expected to nearly double in that time. At the end of the
Sun's life it will expand to become a Red Giant, expelling its outer
layers in a dramatic and glowing planetary nebula.

Although the Sun is a huge ball of gas, it appears to have a sharp edge because the energy radiates from the photosphere, which is a thin layer a couple hundred miles thick, compared with the Sun's overall radius of 432,000 miles (695,000 kilometers). Above this lies the slightly hotter chromosphere, another relatively thin layer that measures between 1,000 and 2,000 miles thick. Above the chromosphere is the corona, a superheated region where temperatures rise to millions of degrees. Because the Sun's gravity isn't strong enough to hold onto such hot gas, the outer atmosphere boils off into space. The corona is invisible in ordinary light, and it is only during a total solar eclipse, when the Moon blocks the much brighter photosphere, that the stunning sight of the corona can be seen.

The Sun is a nearly-perfect sphere, and rotates on its axis. But unlike Earth and other solid objects, the Sun is a giant ball of gas and plasma, so different parts of the Sun spin at different speeds. We know this by observing sunspots. The region of the Sun near its equator rotates once every 25 days. The rotation rate decreases with increasing latitude, so rotation is slowest near the Sun's poles, which rotate once every 36 days.

Sunlight travels to Earth in about eight minutes and nineteen seconds and supports life by photosynthesis, as well as driving Earth's climate and weather. In addition to heat and light, the Sun's hot corona emits a low density stream of charged particles, mostly electrons and protons, known as the solar wind. The bubble in the interstellar medium formed by the solar wind, called the heliosphere, is the largest continuous structure in the solar system, extending well beyond Pluto. The solar wind, and the much higher energy particles ejected by solar flares, can have dramatic effects ranging from power line surges to radio interference, the beautiful aurora borealis, pointing the ionized gas tails of comets away from the Sun, and creating measurable effects on spacecraft trajectories.

The most conspicuous features on the Sun are sunspots. Sunspots are the "cool" regions, and their lower relative temperature makes them look dark by comparison. Sunspots are caused by complicated, and not very well understood, interactions with the Sun's magnetic field. They can last anywhere from a few hours to a few months. Sunspots tend to cluster, with some sunspot groups containing a hundred or more individual spots. These large groups possess powerful magnetic fields and often give rise to flares, the largest explosions in the solar system. A typical flare lasts for five to ten minutes and releases as much energy as a million hydrogen bombs. The biggest flares last for several hours and emit enough energy to power the United States, at its current rate of electric consumption, for 100,000 years.

The Moon circles the Earth, the Earth orbits the Sun, and the Sun in turn orbits the center of the Milky Way galaxy, creating what is called the Cosmic Year. Astronomers have calculated that it takes 225-240 million years for the Sun to orbit the Milky Way, traveling at the astonishing speed of 782,000 km/hour in a circular path. Our Solar System resides in what is called the Orion Arm of the galaxy and is 26,000 light-years from the center. The spiral arms of our great galaxy also twirl through space. The Sun has circled the center of the galaxy about twenty times in its stellar lifetime, and the last time the Sun was in its current position, dinosaurs roamed the Earth. If estimates are accurate, the Sun has thirty more cosmic circuits before it runs out of gas.

The Sun is the largest object in our solar system and is definitely center stage. Our brilliant day star is the source of light and life on Earth and has been revered from time out of mind. Sunrise probably inspired the first prayers as light returned and dissipated the dark uncertainties of night. Human minds seek meaning through allegory and metaphor, and some of humanity's deepest truths have been transmitted through myth--our sacred stories. Myths about the Sun and Moon are at the heart of beliefs about the possible origins of humanity. In part, these stories grew out of a desire to explain the Sun's apparent motion and daily appearance and disappearance.

The most popular symbolic representation of the Sun is an all-seeing eye. A wheel is the next most common theme with the spokes seen as the Sun's rays. Many cultures saw the Sun being drawn across the sky in a chariot pulled by various magical steeds. Scientists claim we are made of star stuff, and mythically the Sun and Moon are always seen as ancestors, heroes or benefactors, but almost always in a parental role. The ancient Persian's believed that the stars were children of the Sun and Moon. The Greeks called the Sun Helios and the Romans called it Sol.

In western culture we are accustomed to think of the Sun as male and the Moon as female, but the Sun has been seen as a goddess as often as a god. In certain belief systems the Sun's heart is seen as feminine and the fiery outer nature as masculine. In the German language the Sun is feminine and the Moon is masculine, but in Romance languages it is the reverse. In Australia the Moon is male and the Sun female. The Intuit believe that the Sun is the older sister of a male Moon. On the Malay Peninsula, both the Sun and Moon are female. American Indians most often see the Sun and Moon as brother and sister, but in some tribes they are mates. The Egyptian Sun god, Ra, was seen as a child at dawn, an adult at noon, and an old man at sunset. Ra traveled across the daytime sky in a boat and navigated the treacherous underworld at night. Other Egyptian gods, such as Amun, were combined with Ra to increase their power. It is intriguing that Polynesians also call their sun god Ra.

Some scholars speculate that prevailing climate conditions may have influenced the perception of gender for the Sun and Moon. In climates where the Sun scorched the day, causing people to seek shelter, the cooler dark of night was seen as more nurturing and therefore feminine. However, in places where the warmth of the Sun was a welcome relief after a bitter winter, the Sun was imagined as a nurturing and feminine influence. One example is the great Sun goddess Saule of the Lithuanian and Baltic peoples who live in harsh northern climes.

Important solar festivals have often been held at the solstices, Latin for "sun stands still," when the Sun appears to stop in the sky before changing direction and shifting its apparent annual motion. These two points in the year are the extremes of light and dark. The symbolic rebirth of the Sun king happens at winter solstice in the northern hemisphere when the length of the day increases again. Many European countries celebrate the festival of Yule at winter solstice. The word comes from yole, or yuul, which means "sun" in several languages. Some linguists suggest it is also the origin of the English word wheel, a popular solar symbol, representing the turning the year.

In astrology the Sun is seen as the character of the individuality and the main focus for the soul's lessons and experiences. From a spiritual perspective, we can view the apparent annual journey of the Sun as the soul's sojourn through time and the experiences of the zodiac archetypes. If we view the fire of the Sun as an agent of transformation, we can take a brief alchemical look at the the twelve signs.

The first sign Aries embodies the initiating force that emerges out of the collective nature of the twelfth sign Pisces. Aries is irresistible force, and represents the principles of resurrection and individualization, the symbolic point of all beginnings, and the onset of the circle of the seasons. The second sign Taurus embodies the principle of pure substance. Taurus is the matrix that absorbs the impact of the intense energy projected outward by Aries. Energy is action. Matter is reaction. In alchemical symbolism, the matter of Taurus is precipitated from the waters of Pisces, the twelfth sign, by the fire of Aries. The third sign Gemini embodies the principle of motion that is the result of the irresistible force of Aries impinging on the immovable object, Taurus. Spinning motion on an axis is the result. Gemini's expression is to adjust and adapt in an ever-widening collection of data and search for meaning.

The fourth sign Cancer adds the powerful quality of emotion to the mental nature of Gemini. Cancer acts like the womb, and is the universal mother principle, providing the vessel from which all forms are born. The fifth sign Leo brings about the process of individuation through the fire and focus of the individual will. Virgo is the sixth sign and brings the idea of differentiated matter into forms that can become highly specialized. At this phase of the Zodiac, plans can be carried out in detail.

Libra is the seventh sign and embodies balance, and the principle of equilibrium, which results from the interaction of Leo and Virgo, a marriage of spirit and matter. The eighth sign, Scorpio represents the idea of dynamic power. This potent energy of desire can be used in construction or destruction, death or resurrection, and is characterized by great intensity. This is a path of regeneration of the desire nature.

Sagittarius is the ninth sign and embodies the idea of illumination that results from balanced power between Libra and Scorpio. Sagittarius energy is philosophical in nature, seeking wisdom and an understanding of first principles. In the tenth sign Capricorn, matter can now be organized into perfect forms. Capricorn's energy is governing and conserving, focused on achievement, integrity, recognition and responsibility.

Aquarius is the eleventh sign where the unfolding sequence of the zodiac now expresses in group consciousness. At this stage it is possible to be unified by a common ideal. Aquarius looks for truth in all things and desires to unite with others on a universal level. The twelfth sign Pisces can be seen as the universal solvent that both dissolves the boundaries of separation created by all the preceding signs, and creates the fluid environment in which the seeds of a new cycle can germinate. In Pisces the sorrows and joys of others are keenly felt, and this is the sign where compassion is born.

Many spiritual traditions have taught that the fire of the Sun can be used for transmutation. If we are open to the spiritual truth that is not apparent in our science, we can be transformed at a deep level, harnessing the power of the Sun, burning away the imperfections in our personalities, and radiating our own unique light into the word.

Atlantis Rising #35 August 2002

PART II

THE MOON

6. MOON SIGNS: CONSTANCY AND CHANGE

"Swear not by the moon, the inconstant moon, that monthly changes in her circled orb, lest thy love prove likewise variable."

Juliet, *Romeo and Juliet*, William Shakespeare

Moonlight - Shackleton circa 1921 (SnappyGoat.com)

Can monthly lunar motions reveal insights about our inner selves? The ebb and flow of the oceans are part of the ever-changing constants of life, and the Moon's gravitational pull on Earth's waters is the biggest influence on tides. It's often been said that since our bodies are at least seventy percent water (estimates vary), then the Moon must have some effect on the watery aspect of our nature, creating some version of shifting tides within us.

In alchemical symbolism fire represents projective masculine energy while the element of water is seen as feminine and receptive. Likewise water symbolizes our emotions and like the ocean can change its nature from calm and nurturing to violent and destructive. Water also represents subconsciousness and the part of our psyche that exists below the level of waking consciousness.

Since astronauts have walked on the Moon, and returned home with moon rocks, scientists have been able to study the Moon's origins first hand. In the past multiple theories competed to explain how the Moon came to be circling Earth. As a result of analyzing the geology of the Moon, and using high-tech computer-generated images, scientists now believe that 4.6 billion years ago there were two planets circling the Sun where the Earth and Moon are now.

In this scenario, a Mars-sized planet, traveling in a tight orbit with Earth, collided with us, stirring up and jettisoning a great deal of planetary matter. After cooling and coalescing our Moon formed and settled into orbit around Earth. So rather than planet and moon, we are two planets, poetically termed Terra and Luna by astronomers, moving in a circular *pas de deus* around the Sun. No wonder our bond with the Moon is so strong; she is more sister than satellite.

Astrological interpretation has long understood this intimate and symbiotic relationship. Astrologically, the Moon represents our instincts, memories, the past, our habitual behaviors, and our inheritance. The Moon is seen symbolically as our lost psyche, separated from our waking consciousness as we journey through time. The Moon reflects our instincts and our evolving personality. The hidden side conceals our habitual selves and unconscious patterns that need to be healed or reclaimed. The cycles and phases of the Moon's reflected light offer periodic illumination into our individual and collective nature. Just as space travel has given us a glimpse of the Moon's hidden side, the relationship between Earth and Moon is a journey of ever-changing, but ever-increasing, light and consciousness.

As Earth goes around the Sun each year this journey creates the illusion that the Sun is moving through the sky. Using the seasons of the year as signposts, the Sun appears to travel through each of the twelve signs of the Zodiac. These are divisions of space based on the solar year, not to be confused with the constellations which gave them their names thousands of years ago. So as Earth moves in a year, changing signs, the dance of the Moon follows, highlighting a different kind of energy in turn. Each planet in the Solar System likewise occupies a Zodiac sign from our viewing perspective on Earth. There is intensity or focus of the energy of whichever sign they occupy.

Although Juliet's remark about the inconstant Moon may seem true on the surface, the changing patterns of the Moon are remarkably consistent over time. The Moon has two cycles each month. It takes about 27.5 days to complete the Sidereal period where the Moon moves through the complete Zodiac. What is termed the Synodic cycle of about 29 days is the time from New Moon to New Moon. The second period is longer because the Earth is also moving around the Sun, and the Moon has to catch up. There is a third and longer lunar cycle, similar to the solstices of the Sun, which takes 18.6 years to complete, in which the Moon slowly moves from its extreme northern position to its most southern position in the sky.

In contrast to the Sun's annual journey, the Moon passes through all twelve signs each month, creating a microcosm of the Sun's apparent motion. As the Moon orbits the Earth each month her shape and place in the sky changes. This is a result of the relationship between the Sun and Moon from our perspective. If we could see this motion from above it would resemble an oscillating sine wave pattern that has its trough at the New Moon and crests at the Full Moon.

Each phase of the monthly lunar cycle is characterized by an angular relationship. At the New Moon the Sun and Moon seem to be in the same place in the sky and are in conjunction, or in the same Zodiac sign. At the quarter moon they are separated by ninety degrees or in square relationship, which places the energies at odds. At the Full Moon they are on opposite sides of the sky from our perspective with Earth in the Middle, creating 180 degrees of separation, and highlighting issues of polarity.

All the planets in the solar system orbit the Sun on the ecliptic although Pluto's orbit is more elliptical and erratic. This circular plane of space is the apparent path of the Sun and gets its name because this is where eclipses occur. Whether by random chance or divine design the Sun is nearly four hundred times the size of the Moon but is almost that many times as far from Earth, so from our vantage point the Sun and Moon appear to be the same size. The Earth and Moon are also tilted on their axes, so eclipses happen when the horizontal alignment of Sun, Moon, and Earth is exact enough to cast a shadow on the Moon or block the Sun's light, providing breathtaking sky-watching events.

Because the Zodiac is defined in four "elements" of fire, earth, air, and water and three "qualities" of cardinal, fixed and mutable as planets move through the signs their expression is enhanced or diminished based on the relative combinations. The Moon's nature is symbolically described as watery and receptive so as she moves through fire or air signs her nature is colored differently. Likewise as she transits water signs, or those of more receptive nature, she feels more at home and expresses more easily. Everyone is born with the Moon occupying one of the twelve Zodiac signs. Knowing this placement can shed light on unconscious motives and automatic behaviors.

Moon in Aries - Ardent, passionate, putting the force of feeling into everything with an emotional intensity that can be difficult to contain. There can be a risk of emotional domination and a "my needs first" attitude that can't see the emotional needs of others.

Moon in Taurus - Taurus Moon seems to attract physical abundance. Sometimes there is so much "stuff" that possessions become a burden. The receptivity of the Moon combines with the element of earth in a fertile combination, but the inner motive is always security.

Moon in Gemini - Here the airy nature of Gemini creates a restless search for truth and knowledge. The mind is in constant motion, seeking a safe place to rest. But even when at rest physically the mind still races.

Moon in Cancer - The Moon is said to rule Cancer as the energy is most similar, so the feelings are hypersensitive with strong ties to home and tradition. The image of the crab with the hard shell to protect a soft center, scurrying sideways to avoid a threat is an appropriate image.

Moon in Leo - Engenders a noble spirit with a great deal of pride. Often desires to be the power behind the throne, needing to wield influence for change. The lion's need to be ruler is focused on the domain of feelings that are powerful and protective.

Moon in Virgo - Proper and conservative with a desire to serve others. Analytical and potentially too fussy about details. Virgo's innate quest for perfection becomes personal so there is frequently a deep sense of inferiority and fear of imperfection that must be healed.

Moon in Libra - Gentle and sweet on the surface, masking an inner strength. Wants desperately to be liked and can desire peace at any price, which of course is not peace at all. The will is directed to maintain the illusion of harmony while suppressed emotions can eventually be stormy.

Moon in Scorpio - Brooding and often impatient. This is the classic case of still waters run deep. Tends to hold onto hurt feelings whether real or imagined. Needs to learn to forgive and forget and direct powerful emotional currents into constructive channels such as healing.

Moon in Sagittarius - Outgoing with a generous spirit, restless and constantly wants to be on the move. There is a tendency to overdo because of a buoyant internal optimism that believes anything is possible and then runs out of gas on the metaphorical highway.

Moon in Capricorn - Feelings crystallize as a result of past hurts or erect shields in fear of potential hurts. The individual needs to feel very safe to be vulnerable. The influence of parents is strong for either good or ill and will leave a lasting mark on the psyche.

Moon in Aquarius - Original thinkers and often progressive in outlook. The feeling nature in not engaged here and there is an emotional detachment that can border on coldness. Get out of the "head" and perceive the feelings of others and cultivate a sympathetic outlook.

Moon in Pisces - Romantic, visionary, dreamy and sensitive. Can feel almost cursed with a sort of "divine discontent" that nothing in earthly life will remove. Sympathetic and compassionate to others. Often carries the emotional weight of the world.

The Moon can be seen as a lens or a magic mirror, continually reflecting sunlight through the colored panes of the Zodiac signs, creating a spiritual Kaleidoscope. If we learn to move in tune with these changing patterns we can sense the resonance of Creation, turning, shifting, changing form, but always seeking a balance of light and dark.

Atlantis Rising #57 April 2006

7. MOON PHASE ASTROLOGY

"Marco could not have known about the mystical effect of a full moon on cats and books left on their own in the library. Not until he saw the lines breathe, the words unveiled."

Rahma Krambo,
Guardian Cats and the Lost Books of Alexandria

Cat and Full Moon Halloween Night Sky (SnappyGoat.com 972603)

The Moon is about one quarter the size of the Earth, and is believed to be four billion years old. Our Moon is the fifth largest satellite in the solar system and causes our planetary tides, which are due to the gravitational interaction between the Moon and Earth. The Moon revolves around the Earth in an elliptical orbit, lasting 27.32 days. The Moon also rotates on its own axis in the same amount of time, forming a synchronous rotation with the Earth. Therefore, the same side of the Moon is always visible from Earth.

Contrary to whimsical nursery rhymes, the Moon is not made of green cheese, but instead has a thick outer crust of solid rock, and a central core of solid metal, with a very small inner core of molten metal. The cratered surface of the Moon is covered with a layer of fine dust. The Moon has no atmosphere, and temperature extremes range from +100°C to -200°C, depending where the Sun's rays fall on the lunar surface.

Moons in our solar system can be small objects that were captured by their parent planets, or big objects that rival planets in size. Jupiter has sixty-three moons at last count, and Jupiter's largest moons, Io, Europa, Ganymede, and Callisto, discovered by Galileo in 1610, are like a mini solar system. Saturn has sixty-one known moons, including the mysterious Titan, which possesses a hazy, nitrogen-rich atmosphere, thicker than Earth's atmosphere. Most of the large moons in the Solar System were created as proto-planetary disks, dusty disks that surrounded the planets during their formation. The moons condensed in much the same way the planets did, coalescing out of the solar nebula.

Since astronauts have returned home with Moon rocks, scientists have been able to study the Moon's origins and geology first hand. They now believe our Moon formed in a different manner than other moons. Using high-tech computer-generated images, scientists believe that 4.6 billion years ago there were two planets circling the Sun where the Earth and Moon are now. In this scenario, a Mars-sized planet, traveling in a tight orbit with Earth, collided with us, stirring up and jettisoning a great deal of planetary matter. After cooling and coalescing our Moon formed and settled into orbit around Earth.

The Moon rises and sets every day, appearing on the horizon just like the Sun. The time of moonrise depends on the phase of the Moon. She rises about 30 to 70 minutes later each day, so the Moon is visible during the day as often as at night. Therefore, in a symbolic sense, part of our night time subconscious awareness is available to us during the day. A lunar eclipse occurs during a full Moon, when the Earth's shadow falls on the Moon. Lunar eclipses occur, on average, about every six months. A total eclipse of the Moon occurs when the entire Moon enters the Earth's umbra, the darkest part of Earth's shadow. A partial eclipse happens when only part of the Moon enters Earth's shadow.

The term lunacy derives from *Luna*, the Roman Moon goddess. In eighteenth-century England, a murderer could plead "lunacy," and get a lighter sentence, if the crime was committed during the full Moon. Psychologist Arnold Lieber, and his colleagues at the University of Miami, Florida, collected data on homicides in Dade County over a period of fifteen years — 1,887 murders in all. When they matched the incidence of homicides with the phases of the Moon, they were surprised to find that the two rose and fell together like a tide for the entire fifteen year period. As the full or the new Moon approached, the murder rate rose sharply and distinctly declined during the first and last quarters of the Moon. They repeated the experiment using homicide data from Cuyahoga County in Cleveland, Ohio, and the statistical pattern repeated.

An earlier report by the American Institute of Medical Climatology to the Philadelphia Police Department entitled, "The Effect of the Full Moon on Human Behavior," found similar results. That report showed that the full Moon marks a monthly peak in various kinds of psychotically oriented crimes such as murder, arson, dangerous driving, and kleptomania. Dr. Lieber speculated that since the human body is composed of almost 80% water, some kind of "biological tide" may affect human emotions. For persons already on psychologically shaky ground, such a biological tide might push them over the edge. Like legends of werewolves, potent archetypal material may come to the surface of consciousness from the shadow, or "dark side," during the light of a full moon. For some, facing these psychological demons could result in irrational behavior.

At night we face away from the Sun, looking instead at the Moon and stars in a dark sky. Symbolically, the Moon is seen as the agency that reflects different kinds of archetypal light into "earthly" consciousness. Astrologically, the Moon represents our instincts, memories, the past, our habitual behaviors and our inheritance. The Moon reveals and conditions our evolving personality. This hidden side of our nature conceals our habitual selves and unconscious patterns that need to be healed or reclaimed. As science may now be explaining, the Moon is seen symbolically as our lost psyche, separated from our waking consciousness.

In Indian, or *Vedic* Astrology, the Moon is revered as a god named *Chandra* and is the most important planet in the horoscope. This masculine deity rules women and mothers, and signifies feminine qualities. Eastern astrologers also pay attention to the Moon's Nodes, named Rahu and Ketu, as indicative of major soul lessons. The nodes are the two points in the Moon's monthly orbit when it crosses the ecliptic, the Sun's apparent path. In China these points of intersection are called The Dragon's Head and Tail.

As the Moon circles the Earth, the shape of the Moon appears to change because different amounts of the illuminated part of the Moon are facing us. The shape varies through eight phases, ranging from a new Moon, when the Moon is between the Sun and the Earth, to a full Moon, when the Earth is between the Sun and the Moon. The cyclical relationship of the Moon to the Sun produces what is called the lunation cycle--the Moon's phases. The Moon increases in light, fullness, and distance from the Sun as she waxes from conjunction to opposition, and the process reverses during the second half of the cycle as she grows dark again.

Like a mini-year, the waxing and waning cycle of Moon is a microcosm of the seasons. The darkness of the new Moon is compared to the long nights at Winter Solstice, and the full Moon is akin to Summer Solstice and the longest day. The eight lunar phases are also symbolically linked with the stages in the planting cycle, beginning with the potential represented by the seed as new Moon, and the culmination of the fruit and the subsequent "death," and return to seed, as the closing of the lunar phases.

Like the apparent annual journey of the Sun, the Moon's monthly path is also a circle of 360 degrees, from the zero point of the Moon-Sun conjunction. The degrees of separation, noted below, delineate the shifting from one phase to the next. The phases of the Moon's reflected light are thought to offer periodic illumination into our individual and collective nature.

1. **New Moon** - 0-45 degrees. Winter Solstice -- new beginnings, instinctual awareness, emergence, projection and rebirth. At the New Moon, the Moon and Sun are conjunct and in the same sign. Symbolically, this may represent an emphasis on subjective and emotional stimulation. There is an innate curiosity; this phase represents the beginning of the planting cycle, when the seed sends forth new shoots while still in darkness.

2. **Crescent Moon** - 45-90 degrees. Imbolc, or Candlemas, Feb 2-- - Expansion, initiative, challenge, struggle and opportunity. The Moon is growing in light and is halfway between New and First Quarter Moon. Astrologically, the individual may be driven by the momentum of past lives and have a knee-jerk reaction to problems. There is an act first, think later mechanism. The Crescent phase may provide an impulse to change old ways. In the planting cycle, the sap begins to run through branches again as the plant prepares for a new cycle of growth.

3. **First Quarter Moon** - 90-135 degrees -- Compared to Spring Equinox. Key words are growth, expression, and action. The Moon is waxing and can be either square or trine to the Sun. Individuals at this lunar phase usually have a strong will. This calls for forceful activity, building an energetic scaffold to hold the structure of new thought. This phase is often called crisis in action, and the lesson involves seeing the consequences of our choices. This represents the time in the planting cycle when the organism puts out leaves and branches; it's a time of rapid growth.

4. **Gibbous Moon** - 135 - 180 degrees. Analogous to Beltane, May 1st - half way between the Vernal Equinox and the Summer Solstice. Key words are analysis, perfection, expansion, and development. The waxing Moon is halfway between First Quarter and Full Moon. Those born during this phase are often motivated by intense devotion or zeal and must learn to trust and become more receptive. In the planting cycle, the bud begins to form, holding the promise of the flower.

5. **Full Moon** - 180-225 degrees. Summer Solstice - Clarity, illumination, and fulfillment. The Moon and Sun are in opposition with the Earth between. This is the time of maximum light in the cycle of the seasons, and is the point in the lunar cycle where conscious creation is possible. Here, what is felt emotionally can also be "seen." It's a time to pause to understand how creation takes place. This corresponds to the time when the flower emerges.

6. **Disseminating Moon**- 270-315 degrees. August 2-- Lammas, Harvest Festival - Sharing, teaching, distributing, adjusting, and reaping. In this phase, the Moon is waning, halfway between Full and

Last Quarter Moon. Individuals born at a Disseminating Moon can be driven to spread their strong ideas with the fire of a crusader, so a synthesis of beliefs is required. In the planting cycle this corresponds to the first appearance of the plant's fruit, midway between the Summer Solstice and the Fall Equinox.

7. **Last Quarter Moon** - 270 - 360 degrees. Fall Equinox - decline, decrease, cleanse, revise, and reorient. In this phase, the Moon is waning and square or trine to the Sun. This point is described as a crisis in consciousness as developing principles must be turned into concrete systems or outcomes. We have to learn and accept what isn't working. The last quarter represents the harvest and the time when the plant dies back, while what is left of the fruit prepares its seeds for planting.

8. **Balsamic Moon** - 315 - 360 Samhain, Halloween, October 31st, midway between Fall Equinox and Winter Solstice, when the veil between worlds is thin. Key words are letting go, transition, separation, synthesis, and release. The lessons of the cycle must be distilled and turned into "solution." The Moon is waning and halfway between Last Quarter and New Moon. In the final state of the planting cycle the plant dies away and life energy becomes concentrated in the seed being prepared for the next cycle.

Just as space travel has given us a glimpse of the side of the Moon's we don't see, the relationship between Earth and Moon is a journey of ever-changing, but ever-increasing, light and consciousness. Everything is always in motion and in relationship to everything else. If we are wise, we learn to seize the unique nature of the moment and flow gracefully into what the future offers.

Atlantis Rising #83 August 2010

8. THE WHITE GODDESS: SHOULDN'T THE MOON HAVE A NAME?

"It's never too late to become who you might have been."

Mary Ann Evans, Victorian era novelist, poet, translator—known by her pen name George Eliot

Clipeus Selene Terme - Photograph from a Roman Tomb Relief -
public domain

There are 166 known moons in our Solar System and our Moon is the
fifth largest. Mercury and Venus are the only planets without satellites,
likely due to their proximity to the Sun's gravity. If moons orbiting
dwarf planets, Trans-Neptunian Objects, Trojan moons, and asteroids
are included, the number rises to 336. Another 150 small objects have
been observed inside Saturn's rings, and Saturn's moon Rhea is
thought to have a moon of its own. The number of moons and
moonlets continues to increase as technology improves our ability to
detect them.

Some moons are large enough that they may be reclassified as dwarf
planets at some point (although that would require changing the
definition). Some have volcanoes and others are thought to have sub-
surface oceans. At least four moons have active tectonic plates, and a
few have atmospheres containing oxygen; Jupiter's Moon Io is the
most volcanically active. Jupiter's Europa, among others, is thought to
be capable of supporting life. Ganymede, another moon of Jupiter, is
the largest in the Solar System, larger than Mercury and Pluto, and

three times larger than our Moon. If Ganymede broke free of Jupiter's gravity to orbit the Sun it would be classified as a planet.

Our Moon passes through the whole zodiac each month, creating a microcosm of the Sun's apparent annual motion, and the Moon's shape and place in the sky also changes as she circles the Earth. The phases are a result of the relationship between the Sun and Moon from our perspective and how much of the Sun's light is reflected based on the Moon's position. If we could see this motion from above it would resemble an oscillating sine wave with its trough at the New Moon and crest at the Full Moon.

The Moon's changing patterns are remarkably consistent over time. The Moon takes 27.5 days to complete the Sidereal period where the Moon moves through the complete Zodiac. The Synodic cycle of 29 days is the time from New Moon to New Moon. The second period is longer because the Earth is also moving around the Sun, and the Moon has to catch up. A third cycle, similar to the solstices of the Sun, takes 18.6 years, in which the Moon slowly moves from its extreme northern position to its most southern position and appears to "stand still," or rise and set in the same place for three years at either end of the cycle.

As the Moon travels around the Earth in a counter-clockwise orbit, it also completes one full rotation on its axis, also moving in a counter-clockwise direction. Since the Moon's period of rotation exactly matches its orbit around Earth, we always see the same face. At the New Moon, when we cannot see the Moon at all, her hidden side is fully illuminated by the Sun. The Sun is nearly four hundred times the size of the Moon but is almost that many times as far from Earth, so from our vantage point the Sun and Moon appear to be the same size. Therefore the "luminaries" seem to be of similar significance. The Earth and Moon are also tilted on their axes, so eclipses happen when the horizontal alignment of Sun, Moon and Earth is exact enough to cast a shadow on the Moon, or block the Sun's light, providing breathtaking sky-watching events.

The Moon's gravitational pull on Earth's oceans is the biggest influence on tides. Estimates vary, but it's said that our bodies are seventy percent water, so the Moon must have some effect on this fluid aspect of our nature, perhaps triggering our emotions and creating shifting inner tides. In alchemical symbolism fire represents projective masculine energy while the element of water is seen as feminine and receptive. Water symbolizes our emotions, and like the ocean, our feelings can fluctuate from calm and nurturing to violent and destructive.

Astrologically, the Moon represents our instincts, habitual behaviors, legacies, emotions, mothers, and our intimate selves. The Moon is seen as our hidden psyche, separated from our waking consciousness as we journey through time. She carries memories of the past and brings these influences to bear on the present. The Moon shapes our evolving personality, holding unconscious patterns that need to be healed or reclaimed. The Moon's cycles and phases of reflected light offer periodic illumination into our individual and collective nature. Just as space travel has given us a glimpse of the Moon's hidden face, the relationship between Earth and Moon is a journey of ever-changing, but ever-repeating, light and darkness.

The Moon is Queen of the Night and her nocturnal creatures but the Moon generates no light of its own. The alchemical element is silver, like the quality of moonlight. The Moon can be seen as a lens, a concave mirror that both reflects and contains, reflecting sunlight through the colored panes of the Zodiac signs. This creates a constantly changing but ever-repeating symbolic Kaleidoscope--nested cycles of light in the day, month, year and perhaps the ages. In a seemingly contradictory way, the Moon signifies both fullness and fragmentation, wholeness and pieces, that continually separate and rejoin. If we learn to move in tune with these changing patterns we can sense the resonance of Creation, turning, shifting, changing form, but always seeking a balance of light and dark.

In myth Moon goddesses are often linked to the phases of the Moon, which are seen to symbolize the stages of a woman's life. The names have a beautiful sound—Maiden, Mother and Elder, or Crone. The three stages of a woman's life are linked to the waxing crescent, the full moon, and the waning crescent, forming a trinity. In this view, pregnancy, breastfeeding, and other female reproductive processes, are ways that women may embody the Goddess, making the physical body sacred. Wiccans and other neopagans worship this Triple Goddess, and this three-part symbol is also seen as the crown of the High Priestess in Tarot.

Robert Graves, author of *The White Goddess*, proposed the existence of a European deity, the "White Goddess of Birth, Love and Death," inspired and represented by the phases of the Moon, who lies behind the faces of the diverse goddesses of various European and pagan mythologies. Graves argued for early worship of a single ancient goddess under many names, an idea that gained popularity in the feminist theology of the seventies.

The Illustrated Key to the Tarot: The Veil of Divination by L. W. De Laurence

The Maiden phase represents new beginnings, birth, and enthusiasm, represented by the Waxing Crescent Moon. The Mother represents ripeness, fertility, sexuality, fulfillment, stability and child rearing and is represented by the Full Moon. The Crone, or Elder, represents wisdom, repose, death, and endings and is represented by the Waning Crescent Moon. Helen Berger writes that "according to believers, this echoing of women's life stages allowed women to identify with deity in a way that had not been possible since the advent of patriarchal religions." This Triple Goddess theme is echoed in other mythological systems such as the three Arabian goddesses Al Uzza, Al Lat and Al Menat, the Three Fates, and the three Norns of Norse mythology. A similar trinity of Celtic moon goddesses includes Elaine, Arianrhod and Andraste.

Most cultures have their own names for the Moon; many are deities and some use different names for the Moon's phases. Because the monthly cycle of the Moon is seen to have an implicit relationship with women's cycles, Moon goddesses seem to be the most well known. However, many cultures see the Moon as a god and the Sun as a goddess. In English we simply call her the Moon, with nothing to distinguish her nature or close relationship with Earth. This seems a shame since she is our closet planetary kin.

Artemis was a moon goddess and one of the most widely revered deities of the Ancient Greeks. Many scholars believe her origins preceded the Greeks. The origin of her name is uncertain although scholars suggest it is related to *arte*, meaning "great, excellent and holy." She is identified with the great goddess worshipped at Ephesus whose temple was one of the seven wonders of the ancient world. Her Roman equivalent was Diana. Artemis was a maiden goddess, and although she protected women in childbirth, she was never a mother. She was one of the twelve Olympians and was often depicted as a huntress, carrying a bow and arrows with a crescent Moon above her forehead. Deer and cypress trees were sacred to her. The Arcadians of the Greek mainland considered her to be the daughter of the Titan Demeter.

In classical times Artemis was equated with Selene, the Greek goddess of the Moon. Selene was the daughter of the Titans Hyperion and Theia, sister of the sun god Helios, and of Eos, goddess of dawn. Her name means "bright" or "shining." Selene rose from the ocean each night and drove her moon chariot across the heavens pulled by two winged white steeds.

Both Selene and Artemis were also associated with Hecate, whose Roman equivalent was Trivia, goddess of crossroads—all three were regarded as lunar goddesses. Artemis was the maiden and related to the Waxing Moon. Selene was the mother and the Full Moon, and Hecate was the Crone whose symbol was the Waning Crescent Moon. Hecate was associated with the underworld and endings. Selene was the Mother, for she had many daughters with the mortal shepherd prince Endymion, who was her great love.

Other goddesses were associated with the moon, but the old Greek poets represented only Selene as the moon incarnate, its personification and physical embodiment. Her Roman equivalent Luna had the same attributes. As Luna, she had temples in Rome on the

Aventine and Palatine hills. Selene's lunar sphere was represented as either a crown set upon her head or as the fold of a raised, shining cloak. She was also a teacher of magicians, linking her to Isis. In the earlier Age of Taurus, the Bull, she was said to drive a team of oxen, rather than horses, and her lunar crescent was likened to the horns of a bull, similar to the crowns of Isis and Hathor in Egypt.

Most of our planetary names were inherited from Greco-Roman mythology, although Earth derives its name from an Anglo-Saxon root that means "ground." A name has power, and in ancient Egypt Isis was the queen of magic, especially a form of magic called *hekau*. This secret knowledge concealed the nature of sound and vibration and the ability to speak words of power that were understood to be vibratory formulae. One Egyptian story tells how Isis obtained the secret name of Ra the sun god to use in her search for her husband Osiris. A special goddess named Renenet was said to give each child their *ren*, their name of power, after they were born. A similar system called Gematria exists in Qabalah and also has a Latin version. Sounds are vibration and names held great import and were carefully chosen in many ancient cultures.

Myths and goddesses from many cultures were available for inspiration, but after this exploration it seems right and consistent to choose a goddess from Greco-Roman mythology. Since in our astrology the Moon rules the sign of Cancer, and is related to the mother and the home, it seemed that a mother goddess would be most appropriate. If we call the Moon Luna, that would be in line with the Roman names of the other planets. But the immediate link to the words "lunacy" and "lunatic" seemed too close and unfortunate, although her name is the origin of those words. Therefore I departed from convention and chose to call the Moon Selene. She was the daughter of powerful Titans, and I can recognize her companion goddesses Artemis and Hekate as the Moon waxes and wanes each month. Selene was the fruitful mother honored at the full moon. That the Greeks saw Selene as the actual embodiment of the Moon is also very compelling.

Selene has a beautiful sound, and although not familiar to most people, it brings a name and a goddess who has been essentially hidden for 2,000 years into our awareness. Selene means bright or shining, and it seems fitting that we recognize her light and call upon her mysterious radiance and periodic darkness to gain courage to face our shadows when we feel them tugging on our inner tides.

Atlantis Rising #106 June 2014

9. THE LUNAR MANSIONS OF VEDIC ASTROLOGY

"What is night for all beings is the time of awakening for the self-controlled; and the time of awakening for all beings is night for the introspective sage."

The Bhagavad-gita

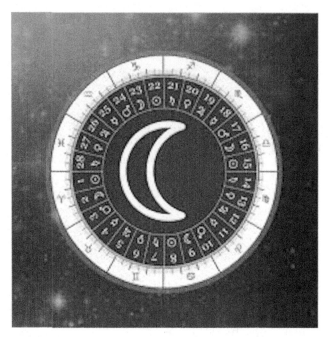

Illustrations of Lunar Mansions (www.Astro-Seek.com)

The Hindu Vedas are the sacred literature of India and form the tradition of what is known as Hinduism. The Bhagavad-gita is considered to be the essence of Vedic knowledge and is one of the most important Upanishads in Vedic literature. The Vedas are attributed to several divinely inspired poets, or Rhsis. Scholars believe they were written about three thousand years ago although their mythical origin stretches back into prehistoric antiquity. The Rhsis, or seers, were men and women who were believed to distill spiritual truths, recording and transmitting them for posterity.

The Vedic hymns reflect a great wonder and awe at the majesty of nature. Even today the culture of India is largely agricultural and therefore still consciously linked to the sky and the changes that cyclically occur there.

Four separate Vedas were passed down by oral tradition through generations of families of Brahmin priests. The oldest is the Rig Veda, *Rgveda*, the Veda of hymns. The *Yajurveda*, the Veda of prayers, and the

Samaveda, the Veda of chants, are largely variations of the Rig Veda. The *Atharvaveda* was the last of the four to be recorded and displays a detailed interest in the celestial motions of the heavenly bodies. At the time this Veda was written the system of the *naksatras*, or Lunar Mansions, had already developed in India.

The Vedic *naksatras* are twenty-seven groups of stars through which the Moon journeys each month. The original sequence of mansions began with the Pleiades, called *Krttika*, but has since shifted to the stars of Aries. This may mark a point in time when these stars rose at spring equinox. The Pleiades are also one of the most recognizable groups of stars close to the ecliptic.

The Lunar Mansions, or *naksatras*, of Vedic (Hindu) Astrology are part of a legacy of knowledge that predates the incorporation of the Greek zodiac into Indian Astrology and are believed to be very ancient. The Lunar Mansions were known and used in the west until about a century ago. Although this component of Astrology fell out of use, the study of Vedic Astrology, including the *naksatras*, is experiencing a resurgence among western astrologers.

Like the Egyptian Thoth, Chandra, the Moon in India, is perceived as a male god. He is depicted clothed in white, holding two water lilies, which open at night, and is drawn across the sky in a chariot pulled by ten white horses. The origins of the name Chandra mean shining or bright but also stem from a root which means "to measure." The regular movement of the Moon has been linked to measurement from ancient times.

The Lunar Mansions are envisioned as dwelling places, each possessing individual character. Each mansion is ruled by a god, and the mansion's quality corresponds with the nature of the deity. We might imagine stars residing in stellar palaces, which are in turn ruled over by a god. As each month passes the Lunar Mansions imbue each day with a quality. People can choose their endeavors based on whether they will be helped or hindered by the quality of the day. The Moon's presence in a particular mansion endows a person born on that day with certain qualities. This is a distinct influence from the interpretation of the Moon in a sign of the Tropical zodiac.

The Lunar Mansions contain stars that are close to the ecliptic where the Moon moves. In her book *The Circle of Stars*, Valerie Roebuck states that "other stars were important, some of them being thought of as forms of the Vedic Rsis (sages). The bright star Canopus (alpha Carina) was identified with the sage Agastya, who is believed to have taken Vedic teachings to South India. His star rises only in the more southerly parts of the subcontinent. The seven brightest stars of the Great Bear were called the Seven Rsis, after a prestigious group of Seers."

China also uses a similar system known as the twenty-eight *Sieu*, meaning "night inns." This system began with the star we call Spica, alpha Virgo. The Chinese called this star Kio, the Horn. Valerie Roebuck believes this may point to a time when Spica marked the autumn equinox.

Arabic astrology also uses twenty-eight *manazil*, meaning "stations" or "houses." The Arabic system, like the earlier Vedic, begins with Al Thurayya, the Pleiades. During the Renaissance, after the Dark Ages in Europe, astrologers absorbed the Arab system of lunar stations into Western Astrology. In *The Art of Memory* Frances Yates relates how Giordano Bruno, the noted philosopher of the 16th century, created a sophisticated mnemonic system based on images of the lunar mansions, planets, houses and decans designed to enable an adept to order and recall all knowledge.

An exploration of myth, and the stellar lore of ancient cultures, reveals issues of viewing perspective of the sky based on variables of latitude, climate, and the ability to see the horizon. How the sky was watched depended on the point of view of the observer. Chinese astrologers, for example, use the celestial equator (extension of Earth's equator into space), and chart the motions of stars around the pole. Indian astrology uses the ecliptic (Sun's apparent path in the sky) like astrologers in the west. Likewise Vedic and western systems both use the same zodiac, inherited from the Greeks, which is divided into twelve equal signs. The difference is the starting point of the cycle.

Since the time of Ptolemy most western Astrologers use what is termed the Tropical Zodiac, which places the beginning point of the cycle, zero degrees of Aries, at the vernal point (spring equinox) where the Sun appears to cross the equator on its annual northward trek. Indian astrology utilizes the Sidereal Zodiac, which places zero Aries at a certain place among the backdrop of stars relative to the backward march of precession. Neither system uses the actual constellations, which are of unequal size.

From the Vedic perspective the stars remain fixed, but the equinox points slip backward at the rate of fifty minutes of arc per year due to precession. As a result, the planets, rising sign, and house cusps have to be adjusted. This adjustment factor is known as *ayanamsa*, a Sanskrit word that does not really translate to an English equivalent. There is disagreement among Indian astrologers as to the amount of the adjustment, but the correction requires subtracting around 24 degrees of arc.

Perhaps the *naksatras* fell out of favor in the West because of arithmetic. The Lunar Mansions are based on the movements in the cycle of the Moon and denote the slice of sky through which the Moon moves in one night. The Moon's lunation cycle, or Synodic motion, takes slightly more than 29.5 days to move from New Moon to New Moon. The sidereal month (the Moon's return to the same position relative to the stars) takes 27.3 days. Therefore the Mansions have to divide the ecliptic by either twenty-seven or twenty-eight, and either way the divisions will not be round numbers.

The Lunar Mansions are also distinct from the Moon's phases since the new and full Moons occur in different Mansions each month. As the Earth moves around the Sun the Moon's relative place in the sky also changes. Arab, Chinese, and Renaissance astrologers used twenty-eight mansions since this conveniently worked with a system of seven planets and four-week months. This did not solve the problem of dividing the 360 degree circle of the ecliptic by any multiple of seven.

The Indian system generally uses twenty-seven mansions since this more closely corresponds to the actual sidereal movement of the Moon (return to the same place in the stars). Likewise this fits with a nine planet group, including Rahu and Ketu, the Moon's nodes, which over time have achieved nearly planetary status in interpretation in Vedic astrology.

Following are three examples from the twenty-seven Lunar Mansions and their influences.

Third Mansion -- Krttika, the Cutters. This mansion is comprised of the six brightest stars in the Pleiades and is depicted as a sharp-edged weapon, or a flame. The Moon in Krttika is said to make the person bright, full of energy, enjoying sensual pleasure and likely to be famous.

Sixth Mansion -- Ardra, the Moist One. Pictured as a tear drop this mansion corresponds with Betelgeuse, the alpha star of Orion. The energy of this mansion is said to make one proud, ungrateful, and tending toward violence. This is a warrior star and as such is likely to bring tears.

Eighth Mansion -- Pusya, Nourishment. This mansion is marked by three stars in the constellation of Cancer. Perceived as a beneficent mansion Pusya confers luck, peace, and wisdom. Those born with the Moon in this mansion are said to walk in dharma, or right relationship to all things.

Both systems work because they seem to function on different principles and vastly different cultural orientations. The Lunar Mansions are based on influences that come from the stars themselves and which are likely to be far older. The quality of the *naksatras* is imbued with the archetypal force of gods from the Indian pantheon that correlate with the stellar influences. The Tropical system is an interpretation based on time and relative position in a repetitive cycle of manifestation that begins with spring and moves through the seasons. The common denominator in any archetypal system is a skilled and intuitive interpreter of the symbols. In the final analysis it's the talent of the astrologer, regardless of system, that makes the difference.

Atlantis Rising #34 June 2002

10.ONCE IN A BLUE MOON

"We can thank our lucky stars when once in a blue moon we find rare and kindred souls along the pathways of our lives."

Laurel Burch, artist

"Blue Moon" in daytime (SnappyGoat.com 1457229)

The accepted definition of a "blue Moon" is a second full Moon in a calendar month. This assertion is backed by such diverse and impressive authorities as *Sky & Telescope Magazine* and the Trivial Pursuit Game. But this technical-sounding description is something of a red herring, pardoning the mixed metaphor, and tracing the origin of the expression becomes an object lesson in the mechanism of folklore and idiom.

The root of the problem lies in the modern calendar. Before clocks and calendars the motions of the Sun, Moon and stars gave us divisions of time. A day is one rotation of Earth, sunrise to sunrise. The passage of the Earth around the Sun gives us the year; the Sun's apparent path in the sky. The idea, and Anglo-Saxon word for month, came from the movements of the Moon. But these familiar cycles move at different rates relative to each other.

The Moon's motion is complex because the Sun, Earth, and planets all tug on the lunar body. The Moon rotates on its axis every 27.3 days, the same time it takes to circle Earth. This is called the Sidereal period as the Moon returns to the same place relative to the stars. This dual motion is why the same side of the Moon is always turned toward Earth. However, the far side is not always dark since the Moon's rotation exposes the whole surface to sunlight.

The Synodic month (29.5 days) is the time between successive New Moons. This period is longer because while the Moon is orbiting Earth, we have traveled about thirty degrees of arc in our annual trek around the Sun, and the Moon has to catch up.

Numerous cultures throughout millennia have wrestled with this problem. Indigenous cultures give names to the Moons, relative to the solstices and equinoxes, describing what occurs at the time of year. The most familiar of these is the Harvest Moon, which is the full Moon closest to Autumn Equinox. Similarly, in Astrology there is usually one New Moon and one Full Moon in each of the twelve zodiac signs as the Moon circles Earth, which in turn orbits the Sun. We've adopted some of the names of the Moon, like Harvest Moon or Hunter Moon, but we've forced them into the calendar months.

Dividing the 365.25 days of the year by the 29.53+ days of the lunar cycle yields about 12.37 New or Full Moons. There's no easy way to make these important cycles move in synch, and there is no inherent reason why our modern year begins on the first of January. It makes more sense to begin either at Winter Solstice when light returns, or Spring Equinox when the new cycle of growth begins. Today we use the Gregorian calendar with twelve fixed months of differing lengths, so as the cycles change, the shorter lunar cycle (29.5 days) can fall twice in a calendar month, resulting in what's now called a Blue Moon.

In a tumble down the rabbit hole with Alice in Wonderland, the evolution of the idea of a blue Moon is a bit surreal. According to the *Oxford English Dictionary*, the first reference to a blue Moon appeared in the year 1528 in a poem titled "Rede Me and Be Not Wroth."

> "If they say the moon is belewe (blue),
> We must believe that it is true."

One linguistic interpretation suggests that the word "belewe" originally implied betrayal, suggesting that the early use of the term had to do with deception. For the most part however, modern researchers assume the expression meant that a blue Moon was an absurd idea. But to further confuse the issue, sometimes the Moon looks blue. If a substantial amount of sulfuric dust fills the air, resulting from a volcanic eruption or forest fire, the Moon takes on a bluish hue. This literal blue-tinted Moon is rare.

Jumping ahead in our story 300 years to the 1800s, the next reference quoted is from a *Maine Farmer's Almanac*. Here a blue Moon is defined as the third full Moon in a season that has four full Moons. This definition stems from ecclesiastical rules for determining the dates of Easter and Lent. Easter Sunday is observed on the first Sunday, following the first full Moon after Spring Equinox, which can fall in March or April. Lent begins forty-six days before Easter Sunday and must contain the last full Moon of winter, called the Lenten Moon in Church parlance. According to the almanac, when there are four full Moons in the winter season, the Lenten Moon (third one) became a "blue Moon."

In a March 1999 article in *Sky & Telescope* magazine, Philip Hisock, noted folklore expert and archivist at the Memorial University of Newfoundland Folklore and Language Archive, traced the origin of the term "blue Moon." He concluded that two full Moons in a month was not the original definition. The May 1999 issue of the magazine featured a red-faced follow-up article, revealing that *Sky & Telescope* had actually, and inadvertently, created the current meaning back in 1943 through a misinterpretation of the Maine Farmer's Almanac.

"Star Date," a popular radio show hosted by Deborah Byrd in the 1970's, further spread the idea by repeating the "wrong" answer to a 1943 "star quiz" from *Sky & Telescope,* which included the question about two full Moons in a calendar month. The quiz gave the answer as "blue Moon." A later article in 1946 in the same magazine repeated the misinterpretation, and the definition gained ground. Then adding momentum, the 1986 Genius II edition of Trivial Pursuit included the blue Moon question, also with the answer as two full Moons in a calendar month. Trivial Pursuit cited their source as a children's "Fact and Records" book published in 1985.

Therefore, the now-accepted definition for a blue Moon is two full Moons in a calendar month, but this description has nothing whatsoever to do with astronomical phenomena or the color of the Moon. The authors of the May 1999 *Sky & Telescope* article admitted, "With two decades of popular usage behind it, the second-full-Moon-in-a-month (mis)interpretation is like a genie that can't be forced back into its bottle."

The making of a blue Moon increases our understanding of the mechanism of folklore and the process that creates a cultural idiom. An idiom is defined by Webster as "A phrase established by usage whose meaning is not deducible from the individual words." Somehow, an idea takes hold in the collective psyche and becomes a common cultural conception of reality without regard for technical truth. The blue Moon chronicle is filled with Medieval charm, human frailty, and a generous dose of whimsy, and blue Moons are now part and parcel of our lexicon. Science and folklore have jointly created a new definition.

Colloquially, "once in a blue moon," means rare, and actually happens about every thirty-three months. We experienced a blue Moon of this kind on July 31, 2004. (The next "blue Moons" will be June 30, 2007 and December 31, 2009). Perhaps July's blue Moon came and went without much fanfare because it has no intrinsic or symbolic significance. It's an arbitrary, if agreed-upon term. Unlike the amusing chronicle of blue Moons, another fascinating story is unfolding that is filled with symbolism and significance and concerns the Moon's origins and the relationship between Earth and Moon.

Since astronauts have walked on the Moon, returning home with moon rocks, scientists have been able to study the Moon's origins first hand. Prior to that multiple theories competed to explain how the Moon came to be circling Earth. One knotty problem is the Moon is too big to be a "moon." Analysis of the geology of the Moon, coupled with high-tech, computer-generated images, is resulting in a fascinating thesis.

Scientists now believe that 4.6 billion years ago there were two planets circling the Sun where the Earth and Moon are now.

In this scenario, a Mars-sized planet, traveling in a tight orbit with Earth, collided with us, stirring up and jettisoning a great deal of planetary matter. After a lot of cooling and coalescing our Moon formed and settled into orbit around Earth. So rather than planet and moon, we are two planets, poetically termed Terra and Luna by astronomers, moving in a circular *pas de deus* around the Sun.

Cutting edge astronomical theory is supported by astrological symbolism. Astrological interpretation has long understood this intimate and symbiotic relationship. Astrologically, the Moon represents our instincts, memories, the past, our habitual behaviors and our inheritance. The Moon is seen symbolically as our lost psyche, separated from our waking consciousness as we journey through time. The Moon reflects our instincts and our evolving personality. The hidden side conceals our habitual selves and unconscious patterns which need to be healed or reclaimed. The cycles and phases of the Moon's reflected light offer periodic illumination into our individual and collective nature. Just as space travel has given us a glimpse of the Moon's hidden side, the relationship between Earth and Moon is a journey of ever-changing, but ever-increasing, light and consciousness.

Astronomy is science, based on observation and measurement. Astrology is an interpretative discipline that applies meaning and correspondences to what has been observed over thousands of years. Not so long ago they were the same.

I believe we've lost a great deal as a result of the extreme polarization of these two disciplines. When we separate meaning from measurement, and cleave two halves of the same pursuit, we tear apart the mind and heart. Clocks and calendars are useful devices, but they make it easy to loose touch with the real rhythms we're biologically and spiritually tuned to. Artificial light disconnects us from the night, sweeping lunatics and werewolves under the carpet, and denying our instinctual response to these deep impulses.

Gratefully, there is a tremendous resurgence in backyard astronomy, and sales of small telescopes is sharply on the rise. Likewise there's an enormous interest in astrology, and this subject tops the charts of "new age" book sales. In both cases I believe it's because we long to feel connected and crave purpose and meaning. It's a lovely and synchronous irony that the idea of blue Moons unwittingly made partners of science and folklore. As the eye of science peers further into the history and workings of the Universe, it's my belief and heart-felt desire, that the two ends of the star-gazing spectrum will in time be reunited in a circle.

Atlantis Rising #47 August 2004

PART III
THE PLANETS

11. MERCURY, MESSENGER OF THE GODS

"**W**ords are of course the most powerful drugs used by mankind."

Rudyard Kipling

NASA/JPL

Mercury — image credit NASA/JPL

Mercury lives at the Sun's front door and as a result has the smallest orbit of the planets, only eighty-eight days, two to three times faster than Venus or Earth. But in contrast to Mercury's speedy orbit the planet rotates very slowly on its axis, making only one rotation in fifty-nine Earth days, leaving one side of the planet in darkness for weeks at a time. Mercury's orbit is also quite eccentric causing changes in speed. If we could watch the Sun's apparent motion from the surface of Mercury the erratic motion would appear very strange.

Mercury spends most of the time invisible to us except for periods when the small planet appears before dawn or after sunset. Because of its small size, and the overwhelming brilliance of the Sun, Mercury is difficult to see unless the viewer knows what to look for. Mercury is so close to the Sun that the planet never rises or sets very far from the solar orb and appears in the skies in all its positions about three times a year.

Mercury is the Roman name of the Greek god Hermes, who in turn came from the earlier Egyptian Thoth. The same archetype of wisdom, measure, and language harkens back to the Babylonian god, Nabu, who with his wife Tashmetum, was credited in their epoch with the invention of writing.

Mercury has dominion over communication and was depicted with wings on his feet and a zany winged helmet, symbolizing speed of thought and ceaseless mental activity. The root of the word Mercury survives in "commerce" and "merchant," both of which involve exchange of goods and information. As such he is an appropriate mercurial icon for FTD floral delivery.

The root of the word Hermes in Greek comes from "herm" which means stone, indicating a linguistic connection to the magical Philosopher's Stone of Medieval alchemy. In their quest for immortality Chinese alchemists consumed Mercury and knew that it was the only substance that could dissolve gold. Hermes was the guardian of boundaries and thresholds and in ancient times stone sentinels were placed at doorways and portals. Stone piles called hermations were erected at crossroads and borders to invoke his protection. Traveling merchants, heralds, and pilgrims added to the piles to invoke protection from the god of highways during their journeys and placed more stones as tokens of gratitude on their return.

In keeping with his role of protector of passages Mercury was the only Olympian who could make the journey between the heights of Mount Olympus, the fabled abode of the gods, and the depths of Hades. Mercury made this dangerous journey between paradigms by virtue of his Caduceus, a gift from his brother Apollo, the sun god. In Mercury's role as psychopomp, or guide of souls in the nether realms, he also conducted souls to Hades.

The Caduceus wand is depicted as two entwined serpents around a central staff or pillar. The top of the Caduceus has a sphere with wings and this portion of the Caduceus can still be seen over doorways, or portals to other realms, in Egyptian temples. Like the later idea of a hermation the winged sphere was both a symbol of protection and a warning of transition into a different state. One aspect of the path of Mercury is grasping the meaning of the spiritual template the Caduceus represents.

Every culture has an image of a World Tree as part of their cosmology. Indigenous cultures have shamans who travel up and down the World Tree or Tree of Life by virtue of magical knowledge and skill, navigating the portal between ordinary reality and the confusing and potentially dangerous realm of non-ordinary reality. The Norse god Odin also went up and down the Tree of Life.

Caduceus (SnappyGoat.com)

Indigenous cultures believe ability to navigate in both worlds with grace and skill is a sign of mastery and also often believe that their greatest teachers and healers come from the ranks of those who have sunk to the depths and emerged. These are the individuals who can relate to the struggles of others with compassion and insight.

The planet Mercury represents the mind and functions as a conduit between spirit and matter, heaven and earth, and soul and personality in the same way the mythical messenger of the gods traveled between Mount Olympus and Hades. In human beings it is the intellect that has the potential to mediate between the pairs of opposites. There is no intrinsic label of good or evil placed on the extremes of these polarities. How thought and choice shape the raw material of consciousness determines the outcome. A toddler playing with clay produces a different result than a mature Michelangelo.

In this vein Mercury has two distinct natures. One aspect is the mischievous trickster archetype, the shape shifter, an androgynous and precocious youth without experience or a sense of responsibility. Mercury is patron of games of chance and synchronous events. He is the god of thieves, clever, cunning and devious. Mercury's quicksilver energy, the metal assigned to the planet in alchemy, has a "now you see it, now you don't" effect. If you blink you miss it and the proverbial pick pocket has time to snatch your wallet. Here we see the curious exploration of the child without regard for labels of good and evil. Acting on its own this energy is without conscience or morality as we think of it. Mind is devoid of heart; producing a cold intellect without compassion.

In an astrological horoscope the placement of Mercury reveals the particular channel or vehicle through which the faculty of will can express itself. In the physical body Mercury is the nervous system and shows how the individual is engaged and affected by external stimuli that act on the sensory apparatus of the nervous system. If Mercury is weak and challenged by aspect it's akin to a having a broken leg. It is more difficult to move and make the body do the will's bidding. It's not impossible but life lessons will include shaping ingenious ways to adapt to the challenges.

Astronomically changes in the relative positions of Earth and the other planets are called planetary phenomena that affect when other planets are visible to us. The angle between the Sun and a planet as viewed from Earth is called the planet's elongation. When a planet is east of the Sun that is its eastern elongation and the planet will be visible in the evening sky after sunset. We call those "evening stars." Conversely, when a planet has a western elongation it will rise during the night before the Sun and will appear as a "morning star" at dawn. We are accustomed to think of Venus in these terms because she is the most brilliant object in the sky next to the Moon.

As we monitor the motion of a planet in the sky over time it usually seems to move easterly against the background of stars. In fact the word planet comes from a Greek word which meant wanderer. Periodically when one of the inner planets passes Earth, or when Earth passes one of the outer planets, that planet (Mercury in this case), will seem to stop its eastward motion and appear to move west or backward. This apparent change of direction is called retrograde motion, and although it is only an illusion the effect feels real. It is like sitting in a parked car when the one next to you moves. Your body thinks you're moving in reverse and automatic physiological responses kick in.

Mercury is the emissary of the Sun, sometimes going before as herald and other times following respectfully behind. Mercury has three periods of retrograde each year, occasionally four, lasting on average twenty days each. Most people say it feels longer. All sorts of symptoms have been linked to Mercury's retrograde motion. Mercury retrograde seems to engage the vexing quality of the trickster aspect of the archetype, opening the door to what can feel like Poltergeist influences.

When Mercury is retrograde everything to do with communication and travel can be compromised. Travel by trains, planes, boats, and cars can have schedule delays and quirky things like flight numbers being changed at the last minute, gates reassigned, and traffic snarls while you drive to the airport. Cell phones may malfunction or major telephone trunk lines could be accidentally sliced by well meaning construction crews.

In the case of the written word correspondence and mail can go awry. Stamps fall off envelopes or packages blow out of the UPS truck. The registered letter may mysteriously languish behind a cabinet at the Post Office. Messages may get misplaced or not be received. You wonder if you really spoke aloud or only thought you did. Where contracts are concerned it becomes vital to read and reread the fine print. With verbal communication great care must be taken with choice of words—crystal clarity is paramount. When in doubt, put it in writing and don't take a chance with a verbal agreement. Follow up and don't leave any detail to chance. In short, Mercury retrograde has the potential to cause prematurely gray hair.

Having painted this dark picture of Mercury's retrograde motion, there is naturally an upside to this influence. When the Messenger of the gods travels backward it's as if the tape is rewound and things that were dropped along the way can be recovered. Because retrograde motion seems to put things in reverse, things that were lost or fell victim to the shenanigans of an earlier retrograde period may suddenly reverse themselves and move forward. The lost letter may arrive months later. The article that disappeared may suddenly reappear in the back of the closet or behind the washing machine. The contract you thought fell through is revived and signed. As if by magic, now turns out to be the right time to put the house on the market.

As a subset of Mercury's role as guardian of portals retrograde motion seems to melt the veil to the dream world. Many of my clients have reported deeper and more significant dreams during this influence. Mental blocks clear and innovative ideas emerge. Likewise unspoken feelings and long-held silences can be addressed while Mercury seems to move backward. It's a good time to clear up communications that need to be aired, releasing painful past emotions. It can be a powerful time to speak the truth, addressing old wounds or troublesome secrets.

 Mercury's astrological and alchemical symbol is a combination of the circle, cross, and crescent. The half circle, or partial reflection, is above the circle of spirit, showing limitation of eternal expression, but both are above the cross of materiality. Contained within this symbol is the path of learning the right use of will and the creative, or destructive, power of the word. Mercury is thought by some astrologers to find its greatest potential for expression in the fixed air sign of Aquarius, domain of the higher mind, where the intellect is set free to connect with the higher faculty of intuition.

Mature right action and compassion ultimately come through the positive synergy of all the planets. Whether Mercury moves forward or backward it is our challenge and opportunity to use our minds in the most constructive way to bring about this positive synergy.

Atlantis Rising #58 June 2006

12. VENUS: THE MYSTERIOUS MAGIC OF THE MORNING STAR

"As we let our light shine we unconsciously give others permission to do the same. As we are liberated from our own fear, our presence automatically liberates others."

Marianne Williamson, *A Return to Love*

The Birth of Venus - Sandro Botticelli 1484 (public domain)

Venus is the second planet from the Sun and the brightest object in the sky after the Sun and Moon. Dense yellow clouds of sulfuric acid obscure the view of the surface. Before radar penetrated this thick shield intense speculation of the reality of Venus reached into the realm of extreme science fiction. Astronomers believe Venus may have once been covered in oceans like Earth, but perhaps due to proximity to the Sun, or because of the dense atmosphere, the oceans evaporated and left a very inhospitable place.

Venus orbits the Sun in 224.7 days, but only rotates once on its axis every 243 Earth days, so one "day" on Venus is longer than its year. Venus also has the unique status in our Solar System of rotating clockwise on its axis. The rest of the planets, except Uranus which actually spins on its side, rotate and orbit the Sun in a counterclockwise or eastward direction. Likewise, the orbit and rotation of Venus are synchronized in such a manner that Venus always presents the same face to us when Earth and Venus are closest.

As the third brightest object in the sky Venus has been watched and revered since antiquity. More than three thousand years ago, on a stone in Babylon, images were carved of the Sun, Moon and Venus. Venus was known as the star of Ishtar, who has mythically come down to us through the ages as Astarte, Innana, Aphrodite, Venus and others from different cultures. Galileo observed the phases of Venus through his telescope, changing from crescent to full phase like the Moon, thereby supporting Copernicus in his view that the Sun is at the center of our solar system.

The Dresden Codex, one of the few remaining Mayan texts, reveals that the Maya tracked the morning star rising of Venus and shows the planet was at the heart of Mayan calendars and cosmology. The Greeks called the morning star Phosphoros, "Bringer of Light," or Eosphoros, "Bringer of Dawn." The evening star was Hesperos.

In later myth Venus was the Roman goddess of spring growth and the ordered nature of the seasons. Her name derives from *venustus*, which means "graceful." Julius Caesar claimed to be her descendant and dedicated a temple to her in gratitude for his war victories. Her deeper nature is related to a state of grace, the more subtle meaning of her relationship to the earlier Greek Charis, goddess of grace.

In the myth of Aphrodite, Venus's Greek predecessor, after she was "foam born," the meaning of her name, from the severed phallus of her father Cronus, she challenged the status quo on Mount Olympus. All the gods desired her and much melodrama resulted. It is also intriguing, since Venus alone rotates toward the west, that in myths around the world goddesses reside in western gardens.

In Astrology Venus represents the principle of attraction and the energy of desire. In a horoscope Venus reveals how "attractive" we are, or how likely we are to magnetically draw things to us. This can be through physical beauty or what may appear on the surface to be luck, which in truth, is more related to the idea of grace mentioned earlier.

Therefore relationships, and whatever draws things and people together, are her domain. Ironically, the planet of relationship has no satellite of her own. Beauty, art, music, color, harmony in form, order and proportion are all her attributes. It is the sense of harmony and order that relates her to the principle of balance and justice. When strong in a horoscope she gives a keen aesthetic sense. Venus is thought to give us our social sensitivity and to influence the nature of our values, what's most important to us, and what we desire.

Because she embodies the principle of beauty Venus also gives a love of adornments and the wish to possess lovely things. She is said to rule the harmonies of number and the vibrations that give rise to musical expression. Venus influences the affections and creates a desire for sensual gratification. Venus is said to be the goddess of love so she also embodies the feminine ideal as well as the ideal of harmonious relationship. This hints at the deeper significance of her mythical and enduring but conflicted relationship with Mars, the god of war.

The Babylonian star of Ishtar was depicted with eight-points, revealing that the Babylonians were aware of the planet's eight-year cycle. We know this from Omen Texts in the British Museum dating to the first Babylonian dynasty (1,900 BCE), which tracked the appearance and disappearance of Ishtar's star.

The Venus Rose formed by Orbital Resonance

Eight is significant because it take takes eight years for Venus to complete one full pattern of five appearances as morning and five as evening star, forming an 8:5 ratio. Each rising as morning star occurs every 584 days. These cycles are completed in eight years, less fifty-six hours. This ratio traces an invisible but potent geometry in the sky, forming a five-pointed figure which has been called a rose, a star or pentagram. As Venus and Earth meet in a synodic cycle (synod means "meeting"), one point of the star is formed. Imagine looking down on the solar system as the motion of Venus relative to Earth draws a five-petaled flower in the sky. Around the world and through time the rose has been linked to the goddess, representing both desire and love. This geometry is due to something astronomers call orbital resonance between Earth and Venus. Earth orbits the Sun eight times for Venus's thirteen cycles around the Sun. This resonance, combined with the phenomenon of retrograde, an apparent backward motion, create the geometric pattern. Venus also turns on her axis exactly twelve times during this time, always presenting the same face to us when Earth and Venus are closest.

A Venus cycle begins at an inferior conjunction with the Sun, when Venus is between Earth and Sun, nearest to us and invisible, and in the middle of the planet's retrograde period. Retrograde motion is an apparent backward motion caused by different planetary rates of speed. Since it takes eight years to complete one fivefold pattern, this creates an 8/5 ratio. 8/5 equals 1.6, which is a close approximation of the Golden ratio of Phi. This ratio is said to be pleasing in art and architecture and was especially prized during the Renaissance. In music these numbers relate as 5/8, which is called a sixth, and relates to the harmonious tuning of strings.

The Phi ratio can be seen in the well-known series of numbers noticed by Leonardo Fibonacci of Pisa, Italy. The spiral formed by this series of numbers is logarithmic and appears in nature in everything from whirling galaxies and hurricanes to sea shells and sunflowers, so it should really come as no surprise that this ratio appears in the orbital resonance of Venus and Earth.

Because the exact alignment is off only 56 hours, the pentagram shape of the Venus Rose moves slowly backward in the sky. As the star pattern precesses through the zodiac signs, which are related to the seasons, different spots in the zodiac are impacted. The pentagram ticks through the whole zodiac in 1,215 years. In our time the zodiac signs (not the constellations), impacted by this fivefold pattern are: Aries, Gemini, Leo, Scorpio and Capricorn. Although this is advanced

astrological work, it is possible to overlay a template of this star
pattern on a horoscope and reflect on how Venus may be subtly
awakening someone to the deep stirring of emotional unfoldment.

Venus is between the Earth and Sun and, like us, is tilted on her axis, a
whopping 178 degrees compared to our 23 plus. Periodically, every 120
years or so, the Sun, Earth, and Venus align horizontally. This creates
what astronomers called a Transit of Venus, not to be confused with
the ordinary motion of the planets in the sky. Astronomically, a Venus
Transit is similar to the Moon eclipsing the Sun, but because Venus is
so close the planet looks like a small black dot passing against a fiery
background. (See Chapter 14). Rather than blocking the Sun's light like
the Moon does during a Solar Eclipse, we witness the passage of Venus
as the planet moves across the face of the Sun. Since Venus is the only
goddess among the planets it may be that her appearance on the
surface of the Sun serves to temporarily heighten the influence of the
divine feminine.

Venus Transits are rare events, unlike Lunar and Solar eclipses that
occur roughly every six months. But like those eclipses Venus transits
also occur in pairs eight years apart. In 1,215 years, the amount of time
required for the Venus Rose to circle through the zodiac, Venus will
transit across the face of the Sun twenty times, or ten pairs eight years
apart. On June 8, 2004 Venus passed across the surface of the Sun, and
the second in this series will occur in June of 2012. As we approach the
closing of an important cycle related to the Sun and the Galaxy in 2012,
a Venus Transit could be seen to contribute the energy of love to the
passage.

If we only look at Venus as a harsh rock-strewn planet, shrouded in
toxic clouds of sulfuric acid, we risk missing something grander. The
same could be said for life. For me the larger significance, available to
us all, is that Creation is encoded with exquisite mathematical
proportions and harmonies. Resonance is not random but rather
expresses the intrinsic quality of existence. As Plato said, "God ever
geometrizes."

In earlier times myths were the way people transmitted their most sacred truths. How we experience Venus through her cycles, myths and astrological interpretation may have to do with the innate harmony of the spheres and the Dance of the Rose we do with her as a planet and in our personal and global relationships.

I am always awed by the subtle and profound manner in which truth is communicated to us, and I believe that the Divine is revealed as we cultivate an attitude of stillness and reflection, paying attention to the nature of Nature. As we recognize the beauty of the orbital resonance existing between Earth and our sister Venus, we can reflect upon the deeper meaning of number and vibration that occupied the minds of the ancients. The Venus Rose is an exquisite example of what has been called the Music of the Spheres. Whether we choose to dance to this music is up to us.

Atlantis Rising #69 April 2008

13. ATHENA OR APHRODITE: DECODING THE DUAL NATURE OF VENUS

"When archeologists discover the missing arms of Venus de Milo, they will find she was wearing boxing gloves."

John Barrymore

Venus surface (SnappyGoat.com 11022)

The planet Venus, named for the Roman goddess of love and beauty, is second from the Sun and has an orbit of 224.7 Earth days. After the Moon, Venus is the brightest natural object in the night sky. Venus also has phases like the Moon. When visible, Venus reaches its maximum brightness shortly before sunrise, or shortly after sunset, and has been called morning star or evening star by many cultures. Venus rises before the Sun for about nine months and then disappears, reappearing at sunset for about nine months. The whole cycle takes 584 days.

Babylonian cuneiform texts describe observations of Venus thought to be nearly 4,000 years old. The Babylonians named the planet Ishtar; the Sumerians called her Inanna, the personification of womanhood, and goddess of love. She also had a dual role as a goddess of war, presiding over both birth and death. The ancient Egyptians calling the morning star *Tioumoutiri* and the evening star as *Ouaiti*. The ancient Greeks called the morning star *Phosphoros*, "bringer of light," and the evening star was *Hesperos*, "star of the evening." By about 325 BCE the Greeks had named the planet Aphrodite, after their goddess of love, who is similar to the Phoenician Astarte. In Iranian mythology, especially Persian, the planet corresponds to the goddess Anahita.

The Mayan calendar system is based in part on Venus. The Maya were aware of the planet's synodic period and could compute it to within a hundredth part of a day. They called the morning star "awakener" and the evening star "false sun." War was declared when Venus rose as morning star, but her appearance as evening star signaled the stoking of strong desires.

The Maasai people of Kenya call the planet *Kileken* and have an oral tradition called *The Orphan Boy*. The aboriginal Yolngu people of Northern Australia gather after sunset to wait for the rising of Venus, which they call *Barnumbirr*. As she approaches before dawn, she draws a rope of light attached to the Earth, and along this rope, with the aid of a richly decorated "Morning Star Pole," the people communicate with departed loved ones. In Indian Vedic astrology, Venus is known as *Shukra* in Sanskrit, meaning "clear, pure, or bright," and is thought to affect wealth, pleasure, and reproduction. Modern Chinese, Japanese and Korean cultures refer to Venus as the "metal star" based on the five elements of their systems.

Scholars of Neolithic and Bronze Age art and culture have realized that earlier peoples were more aligned with the stages of fertility represented by agricultural cycles. Time was experienced as circular and growing cycles of earth were honored. They worshiped a Great Goddess who was perceived to have three aspects: Maiden, Mother, and Crone, representing the stages of a woman's life. The maiden goddesses related to fertility and agriculture and symbolically corresponded to the new and waxing crescent moon. Mother goddesses were guardians of birth, children, home and hearth and related to the full moon. Crone, or elder, goddesses were aligned with the waning crescent moon and were keepers of wisdom and rites related to death. Many goddesses emerged from this ancient trinity.

Marija Gimbutas, professor of anthropology and author of *Language of the Goddess*, discovered an alphabet carved in bone and stone that told the story of this vastly ancient deity. The symbolic themes of this goddess are birds, serpents, and spirals. Gimbutas also identified a Lady of the Beasts, a bear goddess, and a snake goddess. She coined the term Bird Goddess in relation to Neolithic Europe. A few later examples are Aphrodite's dove, Hera's peacock, Athena's owl, and the priestesses of Artemis who were beekeepers, another winged creature. In the Hindu pantheon Saraswati had a sacred swan.

Scholars of myth have noticed that the tenor of the stories changed about 4,000 years ago when aggressive nomadic herders, who worshipped vengeful sky gods, conquered peaceful agricultural settlements. The shift in Greek myths included an increasing glorification of war and a deteriorating value of agriculture and cyclical time. Goddesses were gradually diminished through marriage to gods, becoming a god's daughter, or being turned into a demon. In the monotheistic religions, a solitary and authoritarian male god replaced once-powerful goddesses.

In astrological terms planets are said to "rule" certain signs. However, since there aren't twelve planets, Venus and Mercury rule two signs each. Venus is said to rule Taurus and Libra, and Mercury is said to rule Gemini and Virgo. In the current astrological model, the planet Venus is the archetype of love and beauty, having dominion over romance and relationships as well as the arts.

Taurus, the Bull, is the second sign of the zodiac and represents the fertile earth. Rites of spring and newborn animals, including the calves that have been spawned by bulls, are everywhere evident. Taurus is the sign of sprouting new growth and seasonal flowering. It is a feminine sign and should probably be called Taurus, the Cow. Taurus energy is sensual, and life is structured for maximum comfort and pleasure.

Libra, the Scales, is the seventh zodiac sign. Libra's nature is like the symbol, weighing, balancing, and taking the measure of everything. Libra weighs issues and concerns and is related to the principle of justice. Because balance also relates to harmony, the sign of Libra is thought to relate to balance in relationships, negotiating contracts, and to the principles of beauty and proportion in art.

Is it possible for one planet to have two mythic identities since it shares rulership with two signs and each is seen to have a different nature? Since Venus manifests as morning star and evening star, it seems plausible. As the signs that relate to desire and fertility, and justice and wisdom, it seems appropriate to distinguish the archetypes of goddesses that align with them. Looking through the eyes of ancient myths, I believe that the aspect of Venus that relates to Taurus is Aphrodite, the Evening Star, and the nature that belongs with Libra is Athena, the Morning Star, goddess of wisdom and strategy.

Aphrodite, Taurus, and the Evening Star - Aphrodite is the Greek goddess of love, beauty, pleasure and procreation. She was Venus to the Romans, and the ancient Greeks identified her with the Egyptian goddess Hathor. Doves, which are lovebirds, were sacred to her. According to Hesiod's *Theogony* she was born when Cronus (Saturn), castrated his father Uranus. He threw the genitals into the sea, and Aphrodite rose from the churned up sea "foam," *aphros*. The Furies and the nymphs of the Ash tree emerged from drops of his blood. Hesiod states that the genitals "were carried over the sea a long time, and white foam arose from the immortal flesh; within it a girl grew." Aphrodite floated ashore on a scallop shell.

She is consistently portrayed as having had no childhood and born as a nubile, infinitely desirable adult, hinting at earlier origins that were literally transported across the sea. Because her beauty fanned the flames of desire, the gods feared rivalry would disrupt the fragile peace of Mount Olympus, so Zeus married her to Hephaestus. Because of his ugliness and deformity the blacksmith god was not seen as a threat. Although she was one of the few gods in the Greek Pantheon to be married, she had many lovers. She slept with gods, such as Ares (Mars), and men, and many beings were said to be children of

Aphrodite. This was expected of ancient fertility goddesses whose role was to abundantly populate Earth.

Aphrodite/Venus aligns perfectly with Taurus, the sign of fertility. Her sensual desire nature also compares with the amorous meaning given to the evening star in numerous cultures. The ruler of Taurus should be a beautiful and youthful goddess of fertility and pleasure who awakens our passions. If we think of Taurus as feminine, like the Earth awaiting the seeds of spring, we can better appreciate the goddess who is her ruler.

Athena, Libra and Morning Star - Although later Greek myths say Athena was Zeus's daughter, born as a fully armored adult war goddess, earlier myths say she was the principle of wisdom that created the Cosmos. Athena is the goddess of wisdom, law and justice, just warfare, mathematics, strategy, the arts, crafts, and skill. Minerva is her Roman counterpart. Metalwork of weapons also fell under her patronage and she is similar to the Egyptian goddess Neith. Athena used diplomacy and declared war only as a last resort. She then led battles with the disciplined, strategic side of war, in contrast to her brother Ares (Mars), the patron of violence, bloodlust, and slaughter.

The Athenians founded the Parthenon on the Acropolis in her honor. Athena's veneration as patron of Athens seems to have existed from the earliest times and was so persistent that archaic myths were recast to adapt to cultural changes. The connection between serpents and Athena was explicit in ancient Greece, and serpents are universal symbols of wisdom. As stern guardian of the Acropolis, the Goddess was accompanied by a great snake that encircled her shield. Herodotus reported that in Athens "they have a great snake that guards the Acropolis and to which each month offerings of honey cake are made, and graciously received. By the time of the Persian invasion, the snake refused the offering. When the priestess announced this, the Athenians deserted the city because they believed the Goddess herself had deserted the Acropolis."

Archaic Athena was not a Greek goddess; her name does not have a Greek etymology. She is an echo of an ancient goddess, perhaps a bird goddess from ancient Crete, where women had considerable power. Athena's name, which means "Lady of Athens," has survived in Linear B tablets from the Minoan period. In poetry from Homer onward, Athena's most common epithet is *glaukopis*, usually translated "bright-eyed," or "with gleaming eyes. " *Glaux*, "owl," is from the same root, presumably because of its own distinctive eyes. Another symbol of wisdom, an owl was her constant companion.

Libra is a cardinal air sign, "masculine" in polarity and mental in nature. Although Libra is often characterized by a love of beauty and a desire for harmony, as the opposite sign to Aries it takes "warfare," strategy, and conflict resolution into the realm of relationships, legalities, and contract negotiations. Courtrooms become battlegrounds. Many famous generals have been Libras, displaying keen strategic minds. Lawyers and judges who balance the scales of justice don't back away from a good fight. Athena's wisdom, strategy and keen eyes are a good match for Libra. She can guide us through the sometimes painful path of relationships that have entered the stage of commitment.

Should astrological interpretation follow ancient mythic tradition and allow for a dynamic where one planet can express a different and distinct energy depending on the sign to which it relates? We can learn a great deal by decoding the symbolism in ancient myths. It may also be possible that a theorized, but yet-to-be identified planet, perhaps a Brown Dwarf companion to our Sun, called Tyche by some scientists, may eventually be confirmed and become the ruler of Libra.

Atlantis Rising #104 February 2014

14. JUNE 2012: VENUS KISSES THE SUN—A ONCE IN A LIFETIME EXPERIENCE

"Willingly would I burn to death like Phaeton, were this the price for reaching the Sun and learning its shape, its size, and its distance."

Eudoxus

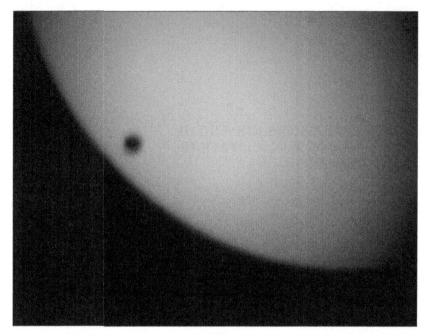

June 2012 Venus transit of Sun (the photo was taken by author through a telescope set for the event)

On June 5, 2012, Venus will "kiss" the Sun. From Earth we will see the distant planet as a small black disk gliding slowly across the fiery surface of the Sun. Astronomically, when two objects in the sky come together from our viewing perspective, it is called a conjunction. The term transit is used when the nearer object in the sky appears considerably smaller than the more distant object. When the nearer object appears larger, and completely hides the more distant object, it is called an occultation. The Venus transit will be best viewed from the Pacific Ocean. North America will be able to see the start of the transit the evening of June 5, while South Asia, the Middle East, and most of Europe will catch the end of it. The transit will not be visible in most of South America or western Africa. The duration of such transits are usually measured in hours; the transit of 2004 lasted six hours.

Historically, this alignment of Venus and the Sun is how the size of our Solar System was measured. Edmund Halley was the first to realize that transits of Venus could be used to measure the Sun's distance, establishing the absolute scale of the solar system from Kepler's third law, published in 1619, which captures the relationship between the distance of planets from the Sun and their orbital periods. Halley's method proved impractical since timing the desired accuracy is impossible due to the unpredictable effects of viewing through atmospheric diffraction. However, the 1761 and 1769 expeditions to observe the transits of Venus gave astronomers their first good value for the Sun's distance from Earth, now called an Astronomical Unit—approximately 93 million miles and 150 million kilometers.

Venus Transits are rare events, unlike lunar and solar eclipses, which occur roughly every six months. But like eclipses, Venus transits typically occur in pairs, in this case, eight years apart. Eight is significant because it take takes eight years for Venus to complete one full pattern of five appearances as morning and five as evening star, forming an 8:5 ratio. Each rising as morning star occurs every 584 days. These cycles are completed in eight years, less about 9.5 hours. Each of these "meetings" of Venus and Earth creates one of the five points of a pentagram or star. Each period of 584 days marks one point of the star, and it takes eight years to complete the figure. This is called the Venus Rose or Venus Star. In 1,215 years, the amount of time required for the Venus Rose to circle through the entire zodiac, Venus will transit across the face of the Sun twenty times, or ten pairs eight years apart.

A Venus cycle begins at an inferior conjunction with the Sun, when Venus is between Earth and Sun, nearest to us but invisible in the Sun's halo, and in the middle of the planet's retrograde period. Because the exact alignment is off only 9.6 hours, the pentagram shape of the Venus Rose moves slowly backward in the sky. The five-pointed star pattern precesses through the whole zodiac in 1,215 years. This pentagonal geometry is due to the orbital ratio between Earth and Venus. Earth orbits the Sun eight times for Venus's thirteen cycles around the Sun. This resonance, combined with the phenomenon of retrograde, an apparent backward motion caused by different orbit sizes and speeds, creates the geometric pattern. Venus also turns on her axis exactly twelve times during this time, creating a synchronized pattern with Earth's orbit that results in the same face of

Venus always being presented to us when Earth and Venus are closest.

Venus is the second planet from the Sun and the brightest object in the sky after the Sun and Moon. Dense yellow clouds of sulfuric acid obscure the view of the surface. Before radar penetrated this thick shield, intense speculation about the reality of Venus reached into the realm of extreme science fiction. Astronomers believe Venus may have once been covered in oceans like Earth, but perhaps due to proximity to the Sun, or because of the dense atmosphere, the oceans evaporated and left a very inhospitable place.

As the third brightest object in the sky Venus has been watched and revered since antiquity. More than three thousand years ago, on a stone in Babylon, images were carved of the Sun, Moon, and Venus. The so-called Babylonian star of Ishtar was depicted with eight-points, suggesting that the Babylonians were aware of the planet's eight-year cycle. Omen Texts in the British Museum, dating to the first Babylonian dynasty (1,900 BCE), tracked the appearance and disappearance of Ishtar's star. Venus has mythically come down to us through the ages as Astarte, Innana, Aphrodite, Venus and others from different cultures.

Galileo observed the phases of Venus through his telescope, changing from crescent to full like the Moon, thereby supporting Copernicus's view that the Sun is at the center of our solar system. The Dresden Codex, one of the few remaining Mayan texts, reveals that the Maya tracked the rising of Venus as morning star and shows the planet was at the heart of Mayan calendars and cosmology--although there is no mention of the transit. The Maya called Venus Noh Ek, "the Great Star," or Xux Ek, "the Wasp Star." The Greeks called the morning star Phosphoros, "Bringer of Light," or Eosphoros, "Bringer of Dawn." The evening star was Hesperos.

Venus orbits the Sun in 224.7 days, but only rotates once on its axis every 243 Earth days, so one "day" on Venus is longer than its year. Venus also has a unique status in our solar system of rotating clockwise on its axis. The rest of the planets, except Uranus, which actually spins on its side, rotate and orbit the Sun in a counterclockwise or eastward direction.

In Roman myth Venus was the goddess of spring growth and the ordered nature of the seasons. Her name derives from *venustus*, which means "graceful." Julius Caesar claimed to be her descendant and dedicated a temple to her in gratitude for his war victories. Her deeper nature is related to a state of grace, the more subtle meaning of her relationship to the earlier Greek Charis, goddess of grace.

In Astrology Venus represents the principle of attraction and the energy of desire. In a horoscope Venus reveals how "attractive" we are, or how likely we are to magnetically draw things to us. This can be through physical beauty or what may appear on the surface to be luck, which in truth, is more related to the idea of grace. Therefore relationships, and whatever draws things and people together, are her domain. Ironically, the planet of relationship has no satellite. Beauty, art, music, color, harmony in form, order and proportion are all her attributes. It is the sense of harmony and order that relates her to the principle of balance and justice. When strong in a horoscope she gives a keen aesthetic sense. Venus is thought to give us our social sensitivity and to influence the nature of our values, what's most important to us, and what we desire.

Because she embodies the principle of beauty, Venus also gives a love of adornments and the wish to possess lovely things. She is said to rule the harmonies of number and the vibrations that give rise to musical expression. Venus influences the affections and creates a desire for sensual gratification. Venus is said to be the goddess of love so she also embodies the feminine ideal as well as the ideal of harmonious relationship. Since Venus is the only goddess among the planets, it may be that her appearance on the surface of the Sun serves to temporarily heighten the influence of the divine feminine.

Venus is the brightest object in the sky next to the Moon. That's because she is relatively close to us and has thick clouds that are highly reflective and act like mirrors for sunlight. The percentage of sunlight reflected from a body is called the body's *albedo*. Venus has an albedo of about 75% compared to Mercury, which does not reflect much light. The Moon's *albedo* is only 12%.

Several powerful influences converge in June 2012 at the time of the Venus transit. As we see Venus move across the solar surface on June 5/6, the planet is conjunct the Sun at 16 degrees of Gemini in the Tropical Zodiac. This is called an inferior conjunction, when Venus is between the Earth and Sun, rather than on the backside of the Sun relative to Earth. Venus conjunct the Sun is seen to be a very positive combination, and Venus will be visible during this rare transit. This might be interpreted as intensifying the influence, setting fire to our passions. This conjunction also forms one point of the Venus star or rose, and in this case we can actually see Venus.

One day before the transit, there will be a Full Moon lunar eclipse at 14 Sagittarius. That means the Moon in Sagittarius will oppose Venus and the Sun in Gemini, so the light of the Full Moon will reflect the combined radiation of Venus and the Sun. The strong solar-venusian energy will be beaming at the Moon. At the very least, our eyes will be drawn toward heaven.

During the transit, instead of seeing Venus appear like a brilliant star, shining from reflected light, she will be visible in the daytime as a black circle on the face of the Sun. Instead of blocking the Sun's light like the Moon does during a Solar Eclipse, we witness the passage of Venus as the planet moves across the face of the Sun. This is a once-in-a-lifetime sight. Although the lunar eclipse is partial, the influence of the Full Moon right before the Venus transit can be seen to build the energy of the transit like a drum roll.

Two hours before the culmination of the Full Moon, Neptune turns retrograde at 3 degrees of Pisces, its own sign. This could serve to deepen the emotional impact of these powerful influences. In addition, Jupiter will be at 28 degrees of Taurus, which is the Celestial Longitude of the Pleiades star cluster. The Pleiades is close to the ecliptic, and like Venus, has been watched and revered by every culture throughout time. The cluster is almost always seen as feminine. The Pleiades are often seen to connect with sorrow, or dealing with loss. Perhaps this connection to the timing of the Venus transit might represent what needs to be released in our lives, or finally putting to rest an old grief.

The Moon enters Capricorn after the Full Moon and will move into a conjunction with Pluto at 9 Capricorn, expressing a powerful energy than can transform structures. If we can let go of what we have been clinging to, there will be room to build a new world.

Astrologically we might wonder if the energy and significance of Venus is consumed by the Sun. Or conversely, does it signify that her significance of beauty, love, harmony and overwhelming passion are strengthened and fueled by the Sun's fire? It's fascinating that as cycles and synchronicities occur, that a Venus Transit occurs six months in advance of an important cycle related to the Sun and the Galaxy in December of 2012. This could be seen to contribute a powerful infusion of feminine energy, perhaps even love, to the passage. This powerful energy of love is something the world desperately needs.

Atlantis Rising #93 April 2012

15. MARS: GOD OR WAR, OR BRAVE HERO OF THE SKY

"War must be while we defend our lives against a destroyer who would devour all; but I do not love the bright sword for its sharpness, nor the arrow for its swiftness, nor the warrior for his glory. I love only what they defend."

J.R.R. Tolkien, *The Two Towers*

Mars (SnappyGoat.com 884709)

Mars, the red planet, is fourth in order from the Sun and second closest to Earth after Venus. Mars made its closest approach to Earth in nearly 60,000 years on August 27, 2003, bringing its telescopic presence into sharp focus. Mars orbits the Sun in 687 Earth days, but one rotation on its axis is 24 hours and 37 minutes, remarkably close to one Earth day. Mars has approximately half the radius of Earth and only one-tenth the mass, but its surface area is only slightly less than the total area of Earth's dry land. The gravity on Mars is roughly one-third of Earth's.

Mars boasts the tallest mountain and volcano in the Solar System named Olympus Mons, which is three times taller than Mount Everest. The Valles Marineris, the greatest gorge on any planet in the Solar System, was caused when Martian volcanoes erupted, leaving a huge valley. Mars tilts on its axis 25.2°, which is close to Earth's tilt of 23.45°. Therefore, Mars has seasons, and like Earth, the southern and northern hemispheres have summer and winter at opposite times. The red-orange appearance of the Martian surface is caused by iron oxide, and

Mars's sky is red due to the iron-rich dust blown upward during storms.

Mars has two irregularly shaped moons, which are probably captured asteroids. They are not large enough to become spherical, and their synchronous orbits result in the same side always facing their parent planet. They were discovered by Aspah Hall in 1877 and were named Phobos, "fear" and Deimos, "panic." In myth they were the twin children of Ares, the Greek predecessor of the Roman Mars, and Aphrodite (Venus). They were the constant battlefield companions of their father, along with his sister Eris "discord," and her son "strife." The war goddess Enyo, Bellona in Latin, also accompanied this dire group into battle.

Mars's dramatic role in fiction has been inspired by its red color and by early scientific speculations that surface conditions might be capable of supporting life. The best known science fiction story is *The War of the Worlds*, by H. G. Wells, where Martians seek to escape their dying planet by invading Earth. A radio version of *The War of the Worlds* was presented as a live broadcast in October, 1938, and many listeners thought it was reality. Other stories include Ray Bradbury's *The Martian Chronicles*, in which human explorers accidentally destroyed a Martian civilization, Edgar Rice Burroughs' *Barsoom* series, and a number of Robert A. Heinlein stories. Jonathan Swift made reference to the moons of Mars in *Gulliver's Travels*, about 150 years before their actual discovery, giving fairly accurate descriptions of their orbits.

The so called Face on Mars, thought to be pure fancy by some, and tangible evidence of earlier habitation by others, stirred up a red dust of controversy beginning in 1976. Thirty years later the search for life on Mars received a boost when NASA announced that newer photographs taken by the Mars Global Surveyor revealed bright deposits seen in two gullies on Mars that suggested water carried sediment through them sometime during the past seven years. In May 2008 NASA photographed and collected ice near the Martian North Pole. Liquid water is considered necessary for life.

Mythology

Mars is named for the Roman god of war, and he has a long list of epithets ranging from lightning to agriculture, which linked him with other "foreign" gods. His name was likely derived from the earlier Etruscan god Maris. The month of March is named for Mars, and his sacred day was Tuesday: Martis in Latin, Martes in Spanish, and Mardi in French, the origin of *Mardigras*. Mars, portrayed in full armor, wearing a crested helmet and carrying a shield, was a familiar Roman omen, a symbol for war and aggression.

In ancient times the archetype of Mars was a sacrificial god of spring, born of a celestial virgin without the aid of a sky god. In Babylon the month of atonement for this yearly sacrifice was Marcheshvan. The Roman poet Ovid wrote that Hera conceived Ares (Mars), without Zeus by virtue of a special flower, probably a lily, a gift from the goddess Flora.

In Greek mythology Ares was unpopular; even his parents disliked him. His sister, Athene, called him "a thing of rage, made of evil, a two-faced liar." Unlike Athene, a cool-headed and clever strategist, Ares lost his temper easily and rushed into battle. But the Romans who came after held Mars in high esteem. He was the most prominent of the military gods worshipped by the Roman legions. Mars was also the tutelary god of the city of Rome. As he was regarded as the legendary father of Rome's founder, Romulus, Romans believed they were descendants of Mars.

Diverse cultures have seen Mars as fiery and usually warlike. He is the red blood of battle while ancient goddesses ruled over the red blood of birth. In Babylonian myth Mars was called Nergal and was the god of war, the scorching noonday sun, plagues, epidemics, and disasters. When the Greeks equated the Babylonian Nergal with their god of war Ares, they named the planet *Areos Aster*, "star of Ares." Then, following the identification of Ares and Mars, it was translated into Latin as Stella Martis, or "star of Mars," or simply Mars. The Greeks also called the planet Pyroeis meaning "fiery."

Mars was Heru-khuti, in Egypt, and the planet was known as" Horus the Red." It's believed the name of Cairo originated from Al Qahira, an ancient Arabic name for Mars. His Persian name was Pahlavanu Siphr, and in Norse myth he was Tiu. His Scandinavian name was Tyr and in Olde English, Tiw. The Hindus called Mars Kartikeya. In Vedic astrology Mars is called Angaraka in Sanskrit, after the celibate god of war, who "possesses the signs of Aries and Scorpio, and teaches the occult sciences." The Hebrews named the planet Ma'adim "one who blushes." Mars is known as Al Mirrikh in Arabic, and Merih in Turkish. In Urdu and Persian it is known as Merikh. The Chinese, Japanese, Korean and Vietnamese cultures call Mars the fire star.

Mars is energy in action, and he embodies the principles of projection, heat, and activation. Symbolically Mars thrusts himself into the world, and when this happens constructively, there is vigor and positive expression of energy. When Mars expresses in a less than constructive way there is aggression and even violence. Mars 1.8 year orbit causes the red planet to spend about two months in each zodiac sign as he circles the Sun.

The older symbol for Mars showed the circle of spirit with the cross of matter directly above, an exact reversal of the symbol of Venus which is a circle above a cross. Earth, poised between these two planets in the solar system, is symbolized by a cross inside a circle. Earthly incarnation is consciousness embodied in matter. Ultimately, our lessons are about choice, will and discernment.

Mar's symbol is now the circle with an arrow projecting outward to the right, acting to pierce through whatever barrier seems to block the way and being ready to do battle if necessary. Some envision this as a shield and spear. This is also the biological symbol for a male and the alchemical symbol for iron, connected to Mars. While Venus holds a mirror and represents the principle of attraction, Mars wields a sword and embodies the idea of separation and cleaving apart. Venus magnetically draws things to her while Mars sets out to capture and conquer.

Mars is the energy of initiation, aggression, willfulness and combativeness and reveals how we go after what we want. Mars in a horoscope shows how we focus energy and turn our desires into action for accomplishment. If Venus is our sister planet then Mars is our brother. Earth's path is between Venus and Mars, pulled inward on the one hand, longing to merge and return to the source, and outward on the other, forging a quest to conquer the physical world.

As the energy of Mars is channeled into a horoscope this archetype drives certain qualities and behaviors. He embodies directed power. If Mars is strong in a horoscope he engenders the ability to risk and gives us the courage to move forward with our ideals. Exertion, and the force of will, is required to make our way in the world. Mars is a potential leader but needs to learn tact, diplomacy, and cooperation. Mars energy can be pioneering, blazing a new trail and leading the way. His action is initiating and incisive, forceful and inclined to be impulsive and quick acting, boldly rushing in where angels fear to tread.

The nature of Mars has been seen in a similar light around the world. It's speculation or intuition on my part, but I believe the planetary archetypes took on their nature at the beginnings of the Solar System. Current theory about star and planet formation holds that our Solar System began as a nebula that began to spin as the result of gravity from other sources in the galaxy and its own mass. Eventually enough heat built up at the center, creating fusion, and our Sun caught fire. The planets coalesced and moved into orbits around our star.

In a Quantum sense our Solar System can be seen as a unit of which we are a part, and the character of the planets might be seen like frequencies, or colors in the spectrum of visible light—as above, so below. In Hindu teaching our spiritual anatomy includes chakras, "wheels" in Sanskrit. In alchemy the chakras are called "interior stars" and are correlated with the planets.

We all have the capacity for war or peace, cowardice or heroism, and we are ultimately defined by our choices. In The Lord of the Rings by J.R.R. Tolkien, the author quoted at the beginning of this article, the hero who is destined to become king is reluctant and feels unworthy to claim his destiny. His quest is to claim and reforge the ancestral sword on behalf of Middle Earth. We might ask ourselves, when does a war lord become a valiant hero? What defines the actions of a Gengis Khan, a King Arthur, or a Queen Boadica, who launched the most fierce rebellion against the Romans?

The archetypal story of the hero's journey is found in cultures around the world. If this tale encodes our own spiritual quest, then Mars is the energy that drives us into the unknown and gives us the courage to face the inherent tests, trials, and dragons we encounter along the path. Mars teaches the nature of heroism and the consequences of wielding power. Without conscious choice and focused will we remain only observers, never setting foot on the Path or reaching our goal. The archetype of Mars takes us out of our narrow concerns and teaches us what we would be willing to die for.

Atlantis Rising #72 October 2008

16. THE MARS EFFECT: ASTROLOGY AND STATISTICAL SIGNIFICANCE

"The universe is fantastic; don't you realize that?"

Michel Gauquelin, *Planetary Heredity*

Maars with Cupid by Guercino (SnappyGoat.com 1649)

Mars was named for the Roman god of war, and he has a long list of associations ranging from lightning to agriculture, which linked him with other ancient gods. His name was likely derived from the earlier Etruscan god Maris. In ancient times the archetype of Mars was a sacrificial god of spring, born of a celestial virgin without the aid of a sky god. In Babylon the month of atonement for this yearly sacrifice was Marcheshvan.

In Greek mythology Ares was unpopular; even his parents disliked him. His sister, Athena, called him "a thing of rage, made of evil, a two-faced liar." Unlike Athena, who was a cool-headed and clever strategist, Ares lost his temper easily and rushed head first into battle. However, the conquering Romans held Mars in high esteem, and he was the most prominent of the military gods worshipped by the Roman legions. Mars, portrayed in full armor, wearing a crested helmet and carrying a shield, was a familiar Roman omen, a symbol of war and aggression—linked to his red color. Mars was also the tutelary god of Rome. Since he was regarded as the legendary father of Rome's founder, Romulus, the Romans believed they were descendants of Mars.

The symbol for Mars is a circle with an arrow projecting outward to the right, acting to pierce through whatever barrier seems to block the way, and being ready to do battle if necessary. Some envision this symbol as a shield and spear. This is also the biological symbol for a male, and the alchemical symbol for iron, the metal alchemically connected to Mars. While Venus holds a mirror and represents the principle of attraction, Mars wields a sword and embodies the idea of separation and cleaving apart. Venus magnetically draws things to her while Mars sets out to capture and conquer.

In astrological symbolism Mars is energy in action, embodying the principles of projection, heat, activation, and muscular tone. Symbolically Mars thrusts himself into the world, and when this happens constructively there is vigor and positive expression of energy. Mars can be connected to the qualities of valor and courage. When Mars expresses in a less than constructive way there is aggression and even violence. An example would have been the Roman gladiators.

Mars is the energy of initiation, willfulness, and combativeness, and he reveals how we go after what we want. Mars in a horoscope shows how we focus energy and turn our desires into action and accomplishment. Earth's orbital path is between Venus and Mars, pulled inward on the one hand, longing to merge and return to the source, and outward on the other, forging a quest to conquer the physical world.

As the energy of Mars is channeled through a horoscope this archetypal energy drives certain qualities and behaviors. If Mars is strong in a horoscope, he engenders the ability to risk and gives us the courage to move forward with our ideals through directed power. Exertion, and the applied force of will through conscious choice, are required to make our way in the world. Mars is a potential leader but needs to learn tact, diplomacy, and cooperation. Mars energy can be pioneering, blazing a new trail and leading the way. His action is initiating and incisive, forceful and inclined to be impulsive and quick acting, boldly rushing in where angels fear to tread.

In the modern period what has come to be called the "Mars Effect" is a statistical correlation been athletic prowess, and the position of the planet Mars relative to the time of birth, that was based on four decades of research by Michel Gauquelin and his wife Francoise, who was his research partner. Gauquelin held degrees in psychology and statistics from the University of Paris (Sorbonne). He conducted his research at the Psychophysiological Laboratory at Strasbourg University in France where he studied the relationship between cosmic and biological phenomena. The term "Mars Effect" was coined by researchers who later investigated the evidence compiled by the Gauquelins.

By age seven Michel Gauquelin knew all the Sun Signs and was called Nostradamus at school for his unusual ability to construct astrological charts. He said of himself that at age twenty he was fascinated by all things astrological. In his own words, "In *The Influence of the Stars* I published numerous works regarding my discovery of a series of highly significant statistical correlations between planetary positions and the birth times of eminently successful people. One of the strongest correlations I observed was that sports champions tend to be born when the planet Mars is either rising or culminating in the sky, much more often than it does for ordinary people." Since success in sports is easier to quantify it is this aspect of the Gauquelins' work that gained the most notoriety.

The strength of his own research came as a surprise to Gauquelin since he actually began by attempting to disprove astrological influence. By 1969 he had lost his earlier enthusiasm for astrology and had become doubtful. He remarked at that juncture, "The signs in the sky that presided over our births have no power whatever to decide our fates or to affect our hereditary characteristics."

At first his work caused him to reject the conventions of natal astrology as it is practiced in the modern world, especially the West. He focused on "highly significant statistical correlations between planetary positions and the birth times of eminently successful people." In spite of his own skepticism, the research data led Gauquelin to observe a strong correlation between "athletic eminence" and the position of Mars relative to the horizon and the mid-heaven based on time of birth. Gauquelin divided the plane of the ecliptic, the Sun's apparent path, into twelve sectors that astrologers call houses, identifying two "key" sectors to be of statistical significance. These sectors are two of the "angles" in a horoscope--the eastern horizon and the zenith.

His research was not limited to Mars. His research also correlated eminence in fields that are seen to be compatible with traditional planetary rulers of five planets: Moon, Venus, Mars, Jupiter, and Saturn. In an article titled *The Gauquelin Controversy,* author John Anthony West (*The Case For Astrology*) reported "A study of a group of 576 birth charts revealed a correlation of Mars and Saturn with physicians at a chance level in the millions to one."

Another study of 508 birth charts, with similar statistical results, showed correlations with professions and astrologically connected planets: artists and musicians with Venus, politicians and executives with Jupiter, writers with the Moon, military officers with Mars, and scientists with Saturn. These effects did not seem to be present for "ordinary" people but rather for those who rose to prominence in their fields. These results were upsetting to skeptics and confusing to astrologers, particularly the connection of writers with the Moon.

Gauquelin's work was accepted by the notable psychologist and statistician Hans Eysenck and others, but later attempts to validate the data and replicate the effects produced uneven results. These varied results sometimes stemmed from disagreements over methodology of sample selection and analysis of the data set. Replication was problematic. For astrologers the accuracy of information and ability to interpret the data depends having the exact time and place of birth. Likewise, the criterion of "eminence" has to be determined and defined. Gauquelin was also accused of bias in his samples, for example, he eliminated female athletes. His work has remained controversial.

Although his research was ultimately verified in subsequent tests, there was too much prejudice to allow general acceptance. Some critics tried to explain away the Mars effect by suggesting that the champions who were studied were chosen in advance based on being born in a key sector of Mars and rejecting those who were not from the sample. Other skeptics actually accused parents of reporting wrong birth times to justify results. Sadly, at the end, Gauquelin was so distraught that he ordered all of his numerous files destroyed and committed suicide at the age of sixty. His wife Francois continued the research for another decade on her own.

Although Gauquelin's work remains the best known, recognized, and comprehensive statistical study of astrological significance, a relationship between athletic prowess and astrology has also been demonstrated by the Magi Society, an international association of astrologers. Magi Astrology is a system of astrology originated by the Magi Society and was introduced through its three books published from 1995-1999. The Magi astrological system is fundamentally based on planetary geometry, or aspects, the angular relationships between planets.

According to extensive research by the Magi society, all great athletes, without exception, have identifiable athletic signatures with specific planetary alignments in their natal charts. In a manner similar to Gauquelin's of observing "eminence," the Magi Society conducted research on every single contemporary professional baseball, basketball, football, and North American hockey player. Every all-time-great player for any era was added to the list, and the best tennis or golf players throughout history were included. The Magi research is said to be one of the largest and most comprehensive astrological studies ever attempted.

Kevin McCorry, a Magi Astrologer in Colorado (www.makeagreatchoice.com) says, "There are planetary aspects with precise athletic symbols that illuminate the specific type of skills an athlete possesses. Some sports require tremendous stamina. Most sports require speed and agility as well as superior coordination. All sports require the ability to rehabilitate quickly from injuries."

Magi astrology has observed a hierarchy of sports aspects and divided them into the following three categories: Ultimate Sports Champion Aspects; Super Sports Champion Aspects; and Sports Champion Aspects. Each of these is demonstrated by geometric planetary relationships that correlate with the level of "stardom." A professional athlete requires a combination of multiple Super Aspects and multiple Sports Aspects. Those who possess Ultimate and Super Sports Aspects as a part of the equation tend to be the superstar players.

This work is immensely gratifying for those of us who live with prejudice and criticism about astrology. However, the deeper and more mysterious question is not that astrology works but how and why. What mystical mechanism drives the process and arranges the timing? What quality of soul, Karma, or destiny facilitates the moment of birth, or critical planetary geometry, that holds the unique potential for a sports champion, an artistic genius, or a famous surgeon? We still have to make the tough choices in life.

The ancient symbol for Mars showed the circle of spirit with the cross of matter directly above, an exact reversal of the symbol of Venus, which is a circle above a cross. Earth, poised between these two planets in the solar system, is symbolized by a cross inside a circle. Earthly incarnation is consciousness embodied in matter. Ultimately, our lessons are about choice, will, and discernment. The astrology we are born with does not determine our destiny, but it does provide the vehicle to help get us there.

The archetypal story of the hero's journey is found in cultures around the world. If this tale encodes our own spiritual quest, then Mars is the energy that drives us into the unknown and gives us the courage to face the inherent tests, trials, and dragons. Mars teaches us the nature of heroism and the consequences of wielding power. Without conscious choice and focused will we remain only observers, never setting foot on the Path or reaching our goal.

Atlantis Rising #119 August 2016

17. THE SKY GOD'S QUEST FOR FIRE: JUPITER IN SAGITTARIUS, NOV 2019-DEC 2019

"Character cannot be developed in ease and quiet. Only through experience of trial and suffering can the soul be strengthened, ambition inspired, and success achieved."

Helen Keller

Jupiter with Earth (SnappyGoat.com 11617)

Officially the Solar System now has, in decreasing order of size: four gas giant planets; Jupiter, Saturn, Neptune, and Uranus; four rocky planets, Earth, Venus, Mars, and Mercury; five officially recognized dwarf planets, Eris, Pluto, Haumea, Makemake, and Ceres; and an enormous number of asteroids. Pluto was once the ninth planet but was demoted to a dwarf planet, a Plutoid, because of numerous objects in his neighborhood that could also become dwarf planets. Astronomers estimate that there may be 200 dwarf planets in the Kuiper Belt, the icy ring at the outer edge of the Solar System where Pluto lives, and more than 10,000 in the region beyond.

In January of 2016, Konstantin Batygin and Michael Brown, at the California Institute of Technology, announced calculation-based evidence of a massive planet in our Solar System--they dubbed the object "Planet Nine" (sorry Pluto). Batygin and Brown postulated the planet's existence through mathematical modeling and computer simulations, but the newest member of the Solar System has not yet been directly observed.

While scientists were searching for Planet Nine in 2017, they discovered twelve new moons orbiting Jupiter, bringing the total to 79, the most known planetary moons, and increasing the official population of identified objects in the Solar System. Astronomers announced the discovery in July of 2018. Earlier, in March 2017, Jupiter was in the perfect location to be observed using the Blanco telescope at the Cerro Tololo Inter-American Observatory in Chile, which has the Dark Energy Camera and can survey the sky for faint objects. Astronomer Scott Sheppard, of the Carnegie Institution for Science, and his team were using the telescope to search the edge of the Solar System for evidence of Planet Nine and realized they could observe Jupiter at the same time.

Jupiter's satellites orbit at three different distances. Closest to their parent planet are Jupiter's largest Galilean moons--Io, Europa, Ganymede, and Callisto. They are among the largest objects in the Solar System besides the Sun and eight planets. Ganymede is actually larger than Mercury, is only slightly smaller than Mars, and would be a planet if it orbited the Sun instead of Jupiter. Farther out are the prograde moons, orbiting in the same direction as Jupiter orbits the Sun. Much farther out is a massive group of small satellites whose orbits move in the opposite, or retrograde, direction. These small objects orbit Jupiter in three clusters.

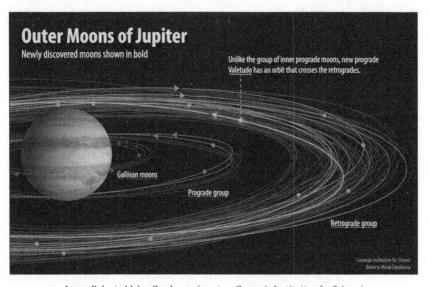

Image Roberto Molar-Candanosa (courtesy Carnegie Institution for Science)

In addition, Jupiter has 4,800 "Trojan asteroids," locked by orbital dynamics in what are called Lagrange points, where the gravity of the Sun and Jupiter are equal. With dozens of moons and thousands of other satellites, Jupiter is an enormous energetic collective that certainly must be much stronger in impact than just the planet.

Two of the newly-discovered moons are closer to Jupiter and move within the prograde group, while nine of the new moons are part of the distant retrograde group and have orbits of about two years. The twelfth moon is an anomaly and has a totally unique orbit from other Jovian moons. This moon has been nicknamed Valetudeo after the Roman goddess of health and hygiene--a great-granddaughter of Jupiter. Valetudo has a prograde orbit, but is very distant and at a different inclination, which means it actually crosses the plane of the other retrograde moons and moves in the opposite direction. Scott Sheppard likened it to a car driving the wrong way on a freeway. Scientists speculate that Valetudo is a remnant of a much larger prograde moon that collided with another object some time in the past.

Next to the Sun (and maybe Planet Nine) Jupiter is the largest object in the Solar System and has the most objects attached to its gravity. Jupiter's myths encoded this idea of largesse and abundance thousands of years before we could see his moons. How did ancient mythology so accurately describe Jupiter's characteristics without the aid of telescopes? There is still so much we don't know about the influences of unseen energies. Perhaps there are modes of perception and understanding that operate in a realm beyond technology.

The Roman Jupiter was the earlier Greek Zeus and Egyptian Min-Amon. King of the gods, Zeus was considered the god of light and therefore wisdom. As king of heaven Zeus/Jupiter ruled supreme over the Olympian gods, wielding his thunderbolts. According to myth, the infant Jupiter was raised on the milk of a goat whose horns continually overflowed with food and drink. This is the origin of the cornucopia, the horn of plenty, and mythically encodes Jupiter's expansion and abundance and the idea of magical unending supply. This aligns with the presence of numerous moons and asteroids that are part of his family.

Symbolically, Jupiter wants more and bigger of everything. As ruler of wide-ranging Sagittarius, Jupiter wants to look through a telescope, exploring far and wide, expanding his vast knowledge, and eventually gaining wisdom through diverse experiences. Jupiter deals with the realm of super-consciousness and acts to expand, and hopefully enlighten, the area he visits. Jupiter's positive qualities include a jovial expansiveness, a sporting approach to life, and an unquenchable optimism. His influence is generally seen as fortunate, benevolent, and generous. However, exaggerated or used unwisely, these same characteristics can become extremist in viewpoint, disregarding of resources, and trusting too much to luck, which leads to misfortune. Because Jupiter always wants to take the larger view, there is a risk of dismissing details as insignificant.

Sagittarius, the Archer, is depicted as a centaur. This mythical creature is half horse and half human, and in the case of the ninth zodiac sign, the centaur has a bow and arrow. How he is armed forms a critical component of his symbolism. The arrow implies the need for direction, and in order to hit the mark, the archer must take careful aim. The risk with exuberant Sagittarius energy is the potential for his arrows to take random flight and cause unintended harm. The centaur's bow is meant to be aimed toward heaven and symbolizes the noble goal of liberation from his purely instinctual lower nature. He represents a phase of human experience that propels us to rise through our earthly sojourns and consciously choose targets to realize our potential on the higher planes.

Animal instinctual power, human will that is activated through arms and eyes, as well as the focused energy of the bow, if aimed properly, combine to send the arrow to the heart of its intended target. The symbolism implies an evolution of consciousness that builds on earlier levels of awareness to create a more potent vehicle of expression. Sagittarius represents the quest for wisdom that is gained through experience. Astrological tradition holds that those born in this sign spend the first half of their lives focused outwardly, trying to gather as many diverse experiences as possible. In the second half of life the exploration turns inward with the potential to find meaning. The key word for Sagittarius is perception. At an unconscious stage of awareness perception is highly relative and is usually based on pride and prejudice. As we evolve, spiritual perception develops through the faculty of enlightened intuition.

Since Jupiter is said to rule Sagittarius, the mythical sky god is in his own domain when he transits this sign. He is therefore at his most regal and perhaps most ostentatious. Jupiter in Sagittarius is big, bold, and brash. When Jupiter transits Sagittarius the Archer is filled with confidence that his arrows will hit the mark. Careful analysis of the correct target should accompany the light speed arrows that fly from his bow. Without foresight it's ready, fire, and then aim. Jupiter in Sagittarius can also be "father knows best," combining the archetypes of teacher and preacher--just because he thinks he's right doesn't mean he always is.

Sagittarius is said to rule all the ways that we expand our horizons-- long journeys, higher education, and foreign lands. Jupiter in Sagittarius loves to explore and speculate, but like an untamed stallion, this energy can be difficult to rein in—after all, the centaurs were a rowdy bunch. Procrastination can be problematic, even with the best of intentions, the power of this positive energetic combination can be dissipated.

This transit can provide a much-needed sense of optimism and a widened philosophical view. Jupiter in Sagittarius engenders a love of freedom, an urge toward philanthropy, a heightened concern for the welfare of others, and a willingness to share blessings. Resources can be scattered, but they won't be hoarded, as there is a tendency toward generosity that borders on extravagance. There's an inherent belief that supply is endless and the tendency toward growth and expansion never seems to end. The risk is a rose-colored-glasses effect that perceives things as better than they are, basking in the imaginary glow of artificial light, and not dealing with matters at hand.

Sagittarius is the sign of the quest, an unending search for meaning. Jupiter in Sagittarius at its highest expression can be the quest for the fire of aspiration and inspiration. I believe Jupiter's expansive search for truth can aid the evolution of consciousness that is currently taking place and shed the light of a higher ideal on what otherwise feels like a no-win standoff. There is potential to enhance intuitive faculties or mystical tendencies.

It's interesting that during Jupiter's transit through his own sign, Saturn and Neptune are also transiting their own signs of Capricorn and Pisces, which should amplify all of those planetary energies as they are "at home." In a sense, this amplifies the energies of these gas giants to express their true natures. Jupiter in Sagittarius is free to expand and explore, Saturn in Capricorn structures our reality and disciplines our intentions, and Neptune in Pisces can lift us to a higher and more rarified realm, perhaps aiding the passage from the Age of Pisces. We live at the cusp of an age, a time when the previous dispensation must give way to a new infusion of archetypal energy. It's always a time of crisis and upheaval. Pisces must give way to Aquarius, which will be characterized by a search for freedom and the impulse to cast off authority.

Technological advances are also part of the incoming Aquarian Age energies. As technology allows us to perceive more of the Solar System, the Milky Way, and the deep space beyond, we realize the vastness and complexity of the Universe of which we are but a tiny part. Science widens our vision and increases our knowledge but does not necessarily deepen wisdom and understanding. For that we must add meaning to measurement. Knowledge alone will not lead to illumination or engender a loving heart. At this stage of our development on our small planet we have a long way to go to express the qualities of love and light.

But we can set our sites on the highest we can envision and hope that humanity will ultimately outgrow its arrogance and hubris and reach the potential encoded in the divine plan. In the meantime, we must work in earnest with the spark that has the potential to one day become an eternal flame.

Atlantis Rising #132 October 2018

18. SATURN: CELESTIAL RINGMASTER OR COSMIC PRINCIPLE OF ORDER?

"Once the Chess game is over the king and the pawn go back in the same box."

Italian proverb

Saturn - (Snappygoat.com 67671)

Saturn is the sixth planet from the Sun and the second largest in the Solar System, after Jupiter. Along with Jupiter, Uranus, and Neptune, Saturn is classified as a gas giant. Much of what we know about Saturn came from the Voyager explorations in 1980-81. Saturn's day is 10 hours, 39 minutes, and the planet is visibly flattened at the poles as a result of this fast rotation on its axis. The atmosphere is composed primarily of hydrogen, with small amounts of helium and methane, and Saturn is the only planet in our Solar System that is less dense than water. Saturn's hazy yellow color is marked by broad bands in the atmosphere which are similar to but fainter than those found on Jupiter.

Saturn's prominent rings provide one of the most beautiful objects in the solar system to gaze at through a telescope. Space probes indicate that the main rings are composed of large numbers of narrow ringlets which are mostly ice particles with a smaller amount of rocky debris and dust. One theory for the ring's origin is that they are shattered remnants of larger moons impacted by comets and small meteors.

Sixty-one known moons orbit Saturn, not counting hundreds of "moonlets" within the rings. (82 in 2020) Fifty-three of Saturn's moons have been named. This diverse group includes rough, cratered surfaces and porous moons that are coated in ice particles. Titan is Saturn's largest moon, and the Solar System's second largest, after Jupiter's Ganymede. Titan is the most Earth-like world discovered so far, and is of great interest to scientists because it has a substantial, active atmosphere and complex, Earth-like processes that shape its surface.

With its thick planet-like atmosphere, more dense than Mercury, Earth or Mars, and organic-rich chemistry, Titan resembles a frozen version of Earth, several billion years ago, before life began sending oxygen into the atmosphere. Titan's air is predominantly nitrogen with other hydrocarbon elements, which gives Titan its orange hue. These hydrocarbon rich elements are the building blocks for amino acids necessary for the formation of life. Titan is therefore a possible host for microbial extraterrestrial life, or a prebiotic environment rich in complex organic chemistry. Titan is the only object, other than Earth, known to have stable bodies of surface liquid. Researchers have suggested a possible underground liquid ocean might serve as a biotic environment.

Titan's naturally-produced photochemical smog obscured its surface prior to the arrival of the Cassini spacecraft. On January 14, 2005, the European-built Huygens probe achieved humankind's first landing on a body in the Outer Solar System when it parachuted through Titan's murky skies. Cassini revealed that Titan's surface is shaped by rivers and lakes of liquid ethane and methane, the main component of natural gas, which forms clouds and occasionally rains from the sky as water does on Earth. Intense winds carve vast regions of dark, hydrocarbon-rich dunes that circle the moon's equator and low latitudes. Volcanism may occur, but liquid water erupts instead of molten lava. Although Titan is classified as a moon, it is larger than Mercury. In fact, if Titan orbited the Sun, rather than Saturn, it would be considered a planet and have a marked role in astrology.

Not only is Saturn famous for its spectacular rings and intriguing Earth-like moon, but another enigmatic geometric feature of the planet puzzles scientists. First glimpsed by Voyager in 1979, Saturn has a unique hexagon-shaped cloud which circles the north pole. Nothing like this phenomenon has been observed anywhere else in the Solar System, and scientists are stumped by its presence. In October 2006, the Cassini craft found that it is still there, further astounding scientists.

The hexagon is similar to Earth's polar vortex which has winds blowing in a circular motion around the pole. Saturn's hexagonal vortex could contain four Earths. The hexagon's origin is a matter of intense speculation. Most astronomers believe it is some sort of standing-wave pattern in the atmosphere, but the hexagon might also be an unusual sort of aurora. Polygon shapes have been replicated in spinning buckets of fluid in a laboratory.

Saturn's intriguing hexagon
(PIA20513 - Wikimedia Commons
public domain)

The hexagonal feature does not shift in longitude like the other clouds in the visible atmosphere. It's intriguing that such a geometric enigma, along with the most dramatic planetary rings, should appear on the planet which astrologically symbolizes the principle of form and structure. Pythagorus is quoted as saying, "God geometrizes," and one wonders what message from Nature might be contained in this conundrum.

Saturn is an old Italian god who is identified with the earlier Greek Cronus, Chief of the Titans, who is one of the great figures of myth. He is also equated with the Babylonian Ninurta and the Hindu Shani. One tradition portrays Cronus as a selfish and autocratic ruler, intending to maintain his reign at any cost. Cronus swallowed his own children so that none of them would supplant him. His wife Rhea, herself a very ancient pre-Hellenic goddess from Crete, foiled this attempt by giving him a swaddled stone instead of his last-born child Zeus (Jupiter.) Subsequently, Jupiter tricked Cronus into coughing up the rest of his siblings and went on to become King of Heaven.

In Orphic cosmology however, which traces its roots to Egypt, Cronus was seen as a beneficent king, ruling over both heaven and earth. In this guise Cronus ruled during a halcyon golden age in antiquity. Cronus is also sometimes identified with Chronus, who is not depicted as a personified being, but rather as Time itself, which of course does swallow all of its children in due course.

Astrologically, Saturn's influence is the embodiment of form, and the dramatic rings that surround the physical planet represent the idea of limitation. The ringed planet gives form to our life experiences and therefore provides our lessons. In Qabalah, Saturn corresponds to the Sephirah Binah on the Tree of Life. Binah is the Great Mother, matrix of form and template of the manifested universe, whose limitation and form-giving power is a fundamental principle of creation. Saturn represents the force of gravity and embodies concrete reality, which gives form to energy. Saturn represents how we have structured our reality through our thoughts, and in a quantum sense Saturn represents the way we perceive reality as our individual and collective conscious has created and structured it.

Saturn is sometimes pictured as the Grim Reaper, wielding a scythe, and cutting a wide swath in human affairs. Saturn's symbol bears a likeness to the god's sickle. In this role he delivers his trials as a stern but wise task master. The reaper is only "grim" if we have sowed metaphorical seeds of destruction. Saturn is often viewed in a dim light, but it is our veiled and incomplete understanding of the nature of how consciousness partakes in the creation of reality that is the problem with his reputation.

Saturn acts to eliminate the results of our wrong choices, and this process often feels like loss. Saturn actually works to bring us closer to our heart's desire by showing us the consequences of prior choices that led in the opposite direction. Astrologically, Saturn is seen as lord of time, and when he connects to points in our horoscopes we feel his heavy hand. The influence of Saturn by sign serves to limit or control circumstances in our lives and can also indicate how we will be limited, controlled, frustrated or delayed by what seems to be the cruel hand of fate, according to the sign Saturn transits.

In a paradoxical manner, Saturn seems to act as an external teacher, manifesting tests in our lives through people and events. In actuality, it is our own inner consciousness, seeking balance, and striving toward fulfillment, that brings about these "tests." This is not really an external process, although it seems to be outer events that provide the class room. With benefit of hindsight, most of us give credit for our most profound lessons to our toughest teachers. We look back in gratitude to those who expected the most from us, or held our feet to the proverbial fire. Saturn is at heart a wise teacher even if he seems to be a stern taskmaster. When we are truly wise we understand that Saturn plays the role of tough-love teacher, and if we accept his lessons gracefully we are invariably strengthened in character.

Because we live in a three-dimensional world Saturn is perhaps the most important transiting influence to understand. Saturn demonstrates how we have structured our personal and collective universe. If Saturn represents the principle of order, structure and form, what is his relationship to the opposite principle of chaos in the Universe? In Greek myth Chaos was the original matrix, or womb, out of which everything emerged, similar to the Babylonian Tiamat.

In mathematics, chaos theory describes the behavior of certain systems whose states evolve over time. Such systems become unpredictable over time, and as a result of this initial sensitivity, the behavior of chaotic systems appears to be random. In popular terms, this is called the Butterfly Effect and describes a sensitivity to initial conditions, which is described in chaos theory. This idea gave rise to the notion of a butterfly flapping its wings in one area of the world, causing a tornado, or some such weather event, in another remote area of the globe.

The term "chaos theory" comes from the fact that the systems the theory describes are apparently disordered, but chaos theory is really about finding the underlying order that exists in apparently random data. The first true experimenter in chaos was a meteorologist, named Edward Lorenz. In 1960 he was working on the problem of weather prediction. He programed a computer with a set of twelve nonlinear equations to model the weather. It didn't predict the weather itself, but did theoretically predict what the weather might be.

Nonlinear problems are of interest to physicists and mathematicians because most physical systems are inherently nonlinear in nature. Nonlinear equations are difficult to solve and give rise to interesting phenomena such as chaos. The weather is famously nonlinear, where simple changes in one part of the system produce complex effects throughout. Many of the shapes that describe nonlinear systems are fractals, a set of shapes that are self-similar on smaller and smaller scales with no limit to the size of the scale. Fractals were discovered by Benoit Mandelbrot at IBM.

Astrology has ever been about finding order and seeing patterns in heaven reflected in earthly life. I believe the lesson to be learned from a deeper understanding of Saturn, and the order concealed in apparently random events, is learning to understand what the "initial conditions" are in our lives. When we start a ball rolling through choice, and an act of will, the gravity of those initial conditions will sooner or later produce an effect that is related to the cause. Life itself might be described as a nonlinear equation, and part of the evolution of conscious involves perceiving and directing the initial conditions that influence the direction we're heading.

Atlantis Rising #77 August 2009

19. HOROSCOPES OF DESTINY: CONSIDERING THE POWERFUL ASTROLOGY OF 9/11

"No trumpets sound when the important decisions of our life are made. Destiny is revealed silently."

Agnes de Mille

Nemesis - Alfred Rethel 1837; The Hermitage, public domain

History chronicles defining moments, suspensions in time. These moments become "freeze frames," and subsequent history is forever after changed relative to these events. September 11, 2001 was such a defining moment, and astrologers feverishly analyzed horoscopes of America, New York, the Pentagon, Afghanistan, and Osama bin Laden. Themes that emerged included ideological collisions, retribution and justice, Karma, and the distribution of wealth.

The United States birth is acknowledged as July 4, 1776. The time of birth, denoted by the signing of the Declaration of Independence, is disputed. The chart most Astrologers use was cast at 2:17 AM Local Time. This horoscope has accrued great legend and mystery, relating to a clandestine meeting of Freemasons in the early morning hours of July 4, 1776.

In the introduction to *The Book of World Horoscopes* Nicholas Campion stated that the British Astrologer "Ebenezer Sibly was a Freemason and in the 1780s was a member of the Lodges first in Portsmouth and then in Bristol, two cities intimate with trading connections with the USA." Sibly worked within the established mainstream tradition of Medieval astrology of the time, adapted from Masha Allah and Abu Ma'shar. (Ma'shar is credited with writing the *Centiloquium*, conventionally attributed to Claudius Ptolemy).

This tradition was established by the great mundane (world events) astrologers of the Islamic world. The approach focuses on locating the horoscope that signifies the event under consideration rather than setting a horoscope for the exact time at which an historical event took place. This is a divinatory paradigm where time is organic rather than linear; today we might say quantum.

In 1776 there were no Americans, only a troublesome group of subjects of the British Crown. Sibly's chart for the birth of America was cast in 1787 while the revolutionary events of July 4, 1776 were still central to contemporary politics. He placed the time at 5:10 PM Local Time. I believe the chart cast for the early morning hours (Gemini rising) represents the ideal to which America is called, and the horoscope calculated for late afternoon (Sagittarius rising) indicates the work required to achieve the ideal.

In the skies above America on September 11, 2001 a celestial drama unfolded. Saturn and Pluto were on opposite sides of the sky. The polarization of these two planets provides the dominant influence in world affairs from August of 2001 until May of 2003. We have not heard the last of this. An opposition between Pluto and Saturn is a standoff between raw power and the vested interests of the current established order. Who has the power, and who controls the infrastructure? In world politics these energies are playing out in overt and covert struggles over energy (oil) and the distribution of wealth.

Saturn is the force that concentrates. Saturn's lessons are duty, integrity, responsibility, order and form, and this planet's experience tests how we interpret the structures and forms in our lives. Saturn's arena is Karma, the outworking of the principles of cause and effect. Saturn executes the reward or punishment that has been set in motion by choices. In this sense the outworking of Saturn's effects are predestined.

The psychological attributes of Pluto are hidden power, death and rebirth, metamorphosis, annihilation and resurrection. Symbolically Pluto's tests deal with power, who has it, and how it is wielded. Pluto's action is like a volcano—pressure builds beneath the surface in a fiery furnace, and when a critical mass is reached, a violent explosion results.

I believe the events of September 11, 2001 were of such a magnitude as to merit a new horoscope. This chart can be analyzed and monitored as time marches forward. On the morning of the attacks, the Sun was in the sign of Virgo, making a ninety degree angle to the Pluto and Saturn opposition, "squaring off" with these planets, and further igniting the polarized energies.

At 8:46 AM EDT Mercury, Messenger of the Gods (said to rule Virgo), was rising in the east, just above the horizon, at fourteen degrees of Libra. A message was certainly sent in a dramatic way. Mercury had barely entered the area of the horoscope that symbolizes what is hidden or denied (twelfth house). Fourteen degrees of Libra was the exact degree of Saturn, planet of Karma, in July of 1776. Saturn is said to achieve its highest form of expression in Libra where the energy that takes form in matter operates through the sign of justice, harmony and beauty. America was born with this potential.

On September 11, 2001 Saturn occupied fourteen degrees of Gemini, making a harmonious trine to the original placement. This will help us transcend the shattering energy of the Saturn-Pluto opposition, making it possible to bring good out of "evil." When linked to Mercury by transit on September 11, a Karmic collision of major proportions was triggered. Time will tell how we respond.

In a nation's chart the Moon reflects her people. On September 11 the Moon occupied the same degree of celestial longitude (28 degrees of Gemini) as two powerful stars: Polaris, the Pole Star and Betelgeuse, the alpha star of Orion. These energies amplify the possibility of transforming a devastating attack into a transcendent healing. In the context of this chart, a new vision will only come from the grass roots. Leaders with a vested interest in the status quo will not be inspired to change direction. There is also potential for seeking truth, higher wisdom, and taking the moral high ground. Jupiter in Cancer rides high on the Midheaven in close proximity to the Moon. This gives us the potential to be wise where our homeland is concerned.

From the standpoint of Deep Sky Astrology, when a cosmic connection is made to a Black Hole in a horoscope, a portal opens into another dimension, presenting an opportunity for a new way of being. I have worked with these archetypes in my own deep sky astrological research and have found Black Hole energies to be equivalent to the transforming nature of a Near Death Experience. At the moment of impact at the World Trade Center, the planet Mercury, rising above the eastern horizon (at fourteen degrees of Libra), connected with a powerful Black Hole.

From the standpoint of physics Black Holes represent the ultimate triumph of gravity. As the accumulated force of gravity draws everything including light beyond the event horizon into the heart of the Black Hole, a death of light occurs accompanied by a scream of X-rays. This X-ray signature is how Astrophysicists detect Black Holes.

Astrologer Alex Miller-Mignone researched known or suspected Black Holes and analyzed their influence in the horoscopes of individuals and nations. He linked their natures with powerful figures from world-wide myth and associated archetypes with the way these potent energies engaged charts. After years of correlation he gave certain Black Holes archetypal names and published his results in 1995. Years ago Mignone named this Black Hole Nemesis.

According to Robert Graves (*The White Goddess*), the original meaning of the Greek word Nemesis was "due enactment." Elizabeth Hamilton

(*Mythology*), explains it as "divine retribution." Nemesis is sometimes portrayed as a goddess and at other times as an abstract principle. She is alternately seen as sister to the three Fates, or an over-arching goddess, combining all three. In either case her essence causes downfall, or creates something that cannot be conquered—a kind of Achilles Heel.

Philosophically, the Goddess Nemesis acts as a moral equilibrium, a cosmic balancing function, so that mortals won't anger the gods through wrong doing or make them jealous with too much success. From the Greek perspective, rising above the human condition made humans vulnerable to reprisal from the gods because a balance or order was upset. Too much success needed adjusting as much as an evil deed as the scales of Libra swung out of balance.

Nemesis is similar in nature to the Hindu concept of Karma and the Egyptian goddess Sekhmet, the avenging eye of Ra. In the positive sense Nemesis also resembles the Egyptian goddess Ma'at, divine principle of truth and justice. The Norns of Norse myth served a similar function. Spinners of the threads of human destiny, the Norns were three wise mistresses of fate who judged gods and humans and guarded the Well of Urdr, the Spring of Fate, which bubbled below the World Tree, Yggdrasil.

As Zechariah Zitchin pointed out in *The Cosmic Code*, Fate and Destiny, although interchangeable in English, are not the same concept. Fate is fickle and can be influenced, but destiny is predetermined and cannot be avoided. Echoing this philosophical theme are the Hindu Yugas, or ages. Spanning vast periods of time from humanity's perspective, these ages were named after an ancient Indian game of chance, suggesting at one level that fate, or human existence, can be perceived as a cosmic crap shoot.

A scholar and expert on Osama bin Laden was interviewed on CNN during the early days following the September attacks. He remarked that someone advised him two decades earlier to watch bin Laden because he had a destiny and would make a mark on the world. He has been a shadowy figure, operating behind the scenes. Bin Laden received security training from the CIA. The Afghan jihad was backed with American dollars, and had the support of Saudi Arabia and Pakistan. Bin Laden fought under the approval of the US and Saudi governments for a decade to evict the Soviets from Muslim territory. Then, he turned his attention toward us.

His birth date is uncertain. There are three dates from different sources including Interpol, the CIA, and FBI. The chart I find most compelling is March 10, 1957. Bin Laden's Saturn at birth (fourteen degrees of Sagittarius) aligns with the current Saturn-Pluto opposition. A Pisces Sun casts bin Laden in the role of sacrificial lamb for his brand of fundamentalist Islam. Many in the West see him as Satan, but his followers see him as saint and savior.

The authors of *Hamlet's Mill* demonstrated how myths conveyed that the changing of the ages were seen as times of crisis and turbulent change. We are poised at such a juncture. Many environmental scientists believe our approach to energy has nearly destroyed the planet, bringing us to the brink of extinction. The events of September have the potential to become a catalyst for global awareness.

When the ancients examined an event they asked, "Was the event destined, and therefore unalterable and unavoidable, or was it instead a combination of chance and luck?" Did we as a nation set forces in motion for which we are now paying the price? In the big picture, what is the role of Osama bin Laden as Nemesis and Karmic equalizer? What must we change? I believe we must ask these hard questions.

As the next eighteen months unfold astrologers will look for more triggers as Saturn and Pluto dance in and out of opposition. The combined energies of these planets will continue to shatter structures, laws, and established order that no longer serve so that a higher order can be rebuilt. This operates in individual psyches and in the fate of nations. We cling to an unconscious status quo at our peril.

Atlantis Rising #31 December 2001

20.SATURN-PLUTO CONJUNCTION —JANUARY 2020

"We are living in what the Greeks called *kairos*--the right moment for a 'metamorphosis of the gods,' of the fundamental principles and symbols."

Dr. Carl G. Jung

Persephone & Hades Tableau- author Diderot (Wikimedia Commons; public domain)

Saturn and Pluto will form an exact conjunction in a single intense pass on January 12, 2020. The two planets conjoin roughly every 33-38 years as Pluto's eccentric orbit causes the timing to shift by zodiac sign. (Saturn and Pluto were opposed on 9-11-2001). The conjunction will contain five planets at 22 degrees of Capricorn that includes the Sun, Ceres, and Mercury. It's a powerful lineup as the planet of structure combines with the energy of hidden influences and is fueled by the force of the Sun. This rare concentration could trigger a redistribution of power globally and nationally. Corrupt structures may be revealed, and we may see deconstruction and reconstruction based on tests of integrity and unraveling moral fiber. The conjunction will also offer a preview of the Pluto return in America's horoscope in 2022.

Earlier interpretations of Saturn/Pluto conjunctions have focused on the dark side and chronicled violent upheavals. (As the conjunction was exact a global pandemic of Covid-19 was unfolding around the globe). These energies cannot be denied as this planetary combination can bring things to a dramatic end. But there is potential for an expanded view of this energetic combination based on a re-examination of their myths.

Before telescopes only five planets were visible to the naked eye. The Greeks called them *asteres planetai* "wandering stars" as they appeared to be bright lights that moved against the background of "fixed stars." They named these moving stars after their gods, and the Romans followed the Greeks. The fastest moving planet was named Mercury, after the swift-footed Messenger of the gods. Venus was bright and beautiful, so she was named after the goddess of love and beauty. Mars looked red in the sky, so it seemed apt to name that planet after the god of war, and Jupiter was king of the Olympian gods.

Saturnus was an old Roman agricultural god who ruled in a past golden age. Under Saturn's rule, humans enjoyed the spontaneous bounty of the earth without labor in the "Golden Age" described by Hesiod and Ovid. The Romans equated Saturnus with the Greek Cronus, although their natures were quite different in some ways. Saturnus taught the Romans agriculture, and his annual winter solstice festival called Saturnalia bore hallmarks of our Christmas and New Year celebrations. We do not know why the Greeks named the planet we call Saturn after the elder Titan god Cronus rather than another one of the Olympians. We can suppose the Greeks acknowledged the idea of time, since this planet was the slowest moving of those visible, and therefore signified the slower motion of old age.

Astronomy has retained the Roman planetary names, and astrology still uses the archetypes of Greco-Roman gods, complete with their flaws and foibles. With increasingly powerful telescopes we can now see the planets and peer deep into space. Our ability to experience the influence of planetary energies has also grown, and modern changes in society should be taken into account. Therefore, I believe it is time for a "metamorphosis of the gods" and a re-examination of symbolic identities. The Saturn-Pluto conjunction offers just such an opportunity.

Since 2006 Pluto has been designated as a dwarf planet. Pluto's moon Charon is half the size of Pluto, and is tidally locked, so the two are considered a dynamic binary dwarf planet. The other known moons of Pluto are Nix and Hydra, Kerberos, located between the orbits of Nix and Hydra, and Styx. All of Pluto's moons were named for mythological figures associated with the underworld, a naming convention begun by 11-year-old Venetia Burney in 1930.

The underworld idea took root. Astrologically Pluto governs the symbolic underworld--what has not yet been redeemed in our psyches. This includes hidden and dormant conditions that need to be brought to conscious awareness, purged, and transformed into new sources of power. Pluto is the urge to regenerate and transform. Pluto rules those who work under the surface such as miners, psychologists, nuclear physicists, and undertakers. Certainly the darker side of Pluto can't be ignored as the idea of plutocracy, an elite class whose power derives from wealth, stems from Pluto's misuse. Gold is the source of wealth and the origin of greed--it is a well known axiom that power corrupts.

The standard interpretation of Pluto can be expanded and deepened if we look at earlier myths, as Pluto was not always the god of the underworld. Pluto is cognate with the Greek *Plutos,* which means "riches." He was the Greek god of wealth, giver of gold, silver, and other subterranean substances. Because these gifts were mined, Plutus became recognized as the god of the physical underworld, which in turn became the spiritual underworld, and therefore death. In Greece, this earlier god was sometimes called Hades, which was also the Underworld itself.

According to Hesiod, Plutus was born in Crete and was the son of the goddess Demeter and the Cretan Iasion. Sometimes he was the child of Pluto (Hades) and Persephone, where in the theology of the Eleusinian

Mysteries, he was regarded as the "Divine Child." In art he usually appears as a child with a cornucopia and is shown with Demeter and Persephone.

Demeter and her daughter Persephone were the central figures of the Eleusinian Mysteries, a religious tradition that predated the Olympian pantheon, and lasted for 1,800 years. Similar rites occurred in agricultural societies of the Near East, Egypt, and Minoan Crete. The mysteries were secret initiatory rites that represented the symbolic abduction of Persephone by Pluto-Hades in three phases: descent (loss), search, and ascent. The marriage of Pluto and Persephone was at the heart of this religion, and the main theme was the ascent, or return, of Persephone and annual reunion with her mother. This cycle is parallel to the archetype of the heroic journey described by Joseph Campbell.

Within the Olympian pantheon, Pluto-Hades was permanently confined to the Underworld. It was Persephone, the feminine aspect, his wife and queen, who made the annual depth journey and return to the surface of Earth. Each year Persephone descended into shadows and dark places, the realm of death and buried secrets. Symbolically, she is soul and psyche, representing the psychological work of the shadow. She always returned to the surface, bringing light and warmth, while Pluto remained below as king of the Underworld and all it contained—gold and old bones.

In the case of Saturn, the astrological influence is the embodiment of form, and the dramatic rings surrounding the planet represent the idea of limitation. Saturn is the cohesive force that binds. The ringed planet gives form to our life experiences and also provides our lessons. Saturn constructs, deconstructs, and reconstructs—no form is permanent. When we deal with Saturn we deal with authority, both our own capacity to wield authority, and our ability to be led by and learn from others.

Saturn's influence by transit brings a reckoning, facing payment of what has come due. If we squander our resources we become bankrupt, but if we are prudent our assets can grow. This is not a cruel or vindictive figure wielding a scythe, but rather a principle of equilibrium, seeking balance. This law is a self-correcting mechanism that brings an end to structures whose life cycle is ending and are beginning to decay.

An alternative mythic identity for the ringed planet could be Demeter. Like the other visible planets, she was one of the twelve Olympians, goddess of the harvest who presided over grains, agriculture, cycles of the year, and the fertility of Earth. More importantly, she was the goddess who presided over sacred law and the repeating cycle of life and death. One of her titles was *Thesmophoros*, "Law Bringer," an apt name for the planet said to be exalted in Libra. Sacred law, like karma, is not punishment but the direct consequence of choice and action; we reap what we sow.

There is precedent for Saturn being a feminine planet, even among the Greeks. In an early text by Hellenistic astrologer Dorotheus of Sidon, *Carmen Astrologicum*, he states "the feminine planets are Saturn, Venus, and the Moon, and the masculine planets are the Sun, Jupiter, and Mars." Mercury was seen as both. This brings more balance to the planetary gender polarities. Isabelle Hickey, author of *Astrology: A Cosmic Science*, describes Saturn as both the Dweller on the Threshold and the Angel of the Presence, the testing and teaching agency by which we learn and master our life lessons. She describes Saturn as a feminine archetype and penned a poem about her, saying "freedom is only found through Saturn's discipline."

In Qabalah, Saturn corresponds to the Sephirah (sphere) Binah on the Tree of Life. Binah is the Great Mother, matrix of form, and the template of the manifested universe, whose limitation and form-giving power are the womb of creation. The word matter stems from the same root as matrix and mother.

How might we recast the conjunction of Saturn and Pluto if we include the Eleusinian mysteries and alternate myths in the interpretative mix? If Pluto has an aspect of giving gifts mined from the deep parts of our psyches, how might we view his energy in a different light? And, if Pluto is seen not as the vile abductor of an innocent virgin, but rather as acting in concert with his wife Persephone, it's possible to better understand the nature of cyclic loss and symbolic resurrection.

If we consider Saturn as Demeter, something profound can be understood in the mythic encoding of the cycle of the year. Death does not triumph but is rather a change of state, offering a time of rest and renewal. A wise teacher once said, "All pain is caused by holding on." Willingly letting go, we can gracefully surrender the forms that need to die, trusting the process of rebirth and reformation.

Perspective is what matters. After the harvest we do not weep for the death of the wheat. Instead, we celebrate the abundance of crops and move with the cycle of the year until spring returns and it's time to plant again. Likewise, if we have been good stewards of our symbolic fields, we can rejoice. If we have made poor choices we can learn from our mistakes and move on. If we embrace this wisdom we can face what has outgrown its time and be courageous enough to stop clinging to the past. Our openness will make room for new life, and we can make a fundamental course correction.

However we choose to cast the characters in this morality play, the Saturn-Pluto conjunction offers a powerful time of reckoning. We must face the truth of structures of power that have become corrupt, and we can expect some chaos. Collectively we must clear the fields and winnow the wheat, making way for new structures for the next cycle. We should take care at the dawn of a new age what seeds we plant for the future.

**This would have been in *Atlantis Rising* #136, but the issue never went to print.

21.URANUS AND NEPTUNE: DECONSTRUCTION AND DISSOLUTION

" S pace, the final frontier . . ."

Star Trek, Gene Roddenberry

*Uranus - NASA/JPL image and Neptune - taken by Voyager
Spacecraft*

Before telescopes, the night sky was thought to consist of two similar components: fixed stars, which remained motionless in relation to each other, and wandering stars, which appeared to shift their positions relative to the fixed stars. The earliest astronomers counted five planets--the moving "stars," which were visible to the unaided eye. The term planet, *asteres planetai* in Greek, was broadened to include the Sun and the Moon, particularly in the Middle Ages. These were called "lights," and brought the total to seven. The planets that required telescopes have revealed themselves to us over the last three centuries: Uranus in the 18th, Neptune in the 19th, and Pluto in the 20th. The 21st century is taking us "where no one has gone before," reprising *Star Trek* again, into the outer reaches of our Solar System.

Uranus - 18th century -- Uranus was discovered in March of 1781 by British astronomer Sir William Herschel. Uranus is inclined so far on its axis that it rotates on its side. Uranus orbits the Sun in 84 years, so a person may live long enough for Uranus to return to the place it occupied at birth. The revolution of the American Colonies from England took place around this time, and a few years later in 1789, the French revolution occurred. In art and literature, the discovery of Uranus coincided with the Romantic movement, which emphasized individuality and freedom of expression.

Uranus rules the sign of Aquarius and is linked to potential genius, individuality, unorthodox and unconventional ideas. Uranus is related to scientific discoveries, electricity, inventions, as well as the beginning of the industrial revolution. Socially conscious Uranus is said to govern groups that are dedicated to humanitarian ideals and progress. Uranus, which seems to act in sudden and unexpected ways, rules freedom, independence, equality, and originality.

One critically important function of Uranian energy is to shatter forms, crystallized by Saturn, which have outgrown their purpose or time. The principle of form is not negative, in fact it allows the manifest universe to exist, but it is limiting and temporary. What shows up in our lives that looks like sudden, unexpected events without apparent cause, may in fact be earlier choices that are no longer perceived at the conscious level. We get these de-constructions harshly or gently, depending on our state of consciousness.

Neptune - 19th century -- Neptune was discovered in September of 1846. Neptune takes 165 years to orbit the Sun, spending approximately 14 years (13.75) in each zodiac sign. Therefore, someone might live to see Neptune oppose the place it occupied at birth. Neptune's appearance was linked in time to the rise of nationalist movements throughout Europe and coincided with the utopian ideals of Communism. Marx and Engels first published *The Communist Manifesto* in 1848. In art, the impressionist movement began.

Neptune's magic and mystery is connected to the illusory areas of film and mass media. Neptune is associated with idealism and compassion and connects us to faith and belief, and therefore with religion, spirituality, and mysticism. The misty planet of illusions also rules drugs, hypersensitivity, fantasy and imagination, psychic phenomena and altered mental states. Neptune's sighting coincided with the discovery of anesthetics and hypnotism. Neptune is linked to hospitals, prisons, mental institutions, and monasteries, where people withdraw from society.

The solidity of form is an illusion. Scientifically we know this, but the illusion is very compelling. Saturn is the Great Teacher, and his energy binds light so that forms seem to exist. This furthers the illusion by creating the sense that creation exists apart from us. Neptune is the ruler of Pisces, and is called the Dissolver. In this case Saturn's forms are melted away, dissolved rather than deconstructed, and the process is more subtle.

20th & 21st Centuries -- Pluto was discovered in February 1930, and then there was a long silence. Since 1992, coinciding with a conjunction between Uranus and Neptune, more than a thousand objects have been identified beyond the orbit of Neptune. Called Trans Neptunian

Objects, the list of TNOs just keeps growing. Pluto is no longer considered a planet, but is now a member of a growing body of newly identified members of our enlarging solar system. It's daunting to imagine what our Solar System will encompass by the 22nd century.

Symbolically, the outer planets teach us about energies that are larger than ourselves, and because of the length of their orbits, they influence generations and groups more than individuals. Uranus and Neptune facilitate the breaking up of old patterns and hopefully inspire the creation of new ones at a higher level. Since 1993 Uranus and Neptune have been combining their energies in several ways.

Conjunction - Roughly every 172 years, they come together in a sign, combining their influence according to the nature of the sign. In 1993 they formed a conjunction in Capricorn. The one prior was in 1820. The next conjunction in 2165 will be in Aquarius. We might describe these periodic connections as idealism for social change inspired and infused with spiritual inspiration. Rapidly advancing technology has given us the global Internet and cell phone proliferation, connecting people instantaneously in real-time around the world through mass communication, affecting mass consciousness. I can e-mail someone on the other side of the planet and have the message instantly translated into Chinese, for example. Not so long ago that was science fiction on *Star Trek*.

Mutual Reception - When Uranus passed through Aquarius and into Pisces in 2004 the two planets came into a Mutual Reception, which will last until 2011. In Astrology, Mutual Reception occurs when any two planets are in the signs ruled by the other. At present Uranus is in Pisces and Neptune is in Aquarius. Uranus can be electrifying and Neptune can be sedating, but it's like living in someone else's home. The Fishes normally swim in the ocean of collective consciousness, while the Water Bearer dwells in the lofty heights of the higher mind. When they trade places they link above and below in a dramatic reversal.

The challenges from this energy exchange come as Pisces in Aquarius is like a fish-out-of-water, and the higher mental states of Aquarius can become drowned by Pisces emotions. Pisces is forced to breathe Aquarian air, and Aquarius gets a cold shower. This initial phase is a wakeup call for all of us. Then, as the planets adapt to a new element, reflection and synthesis can occur. There can be a true humanitarian view of the collective and a chance to see the big picture in a clear light without emotional drama. A sudden awakening of transcendental awareness is possible, but a realization of the true nature of reality is called for. Self-centered ego, which can engender rigid fundamentalism, must be surrendered on behalf of a realization of oneness.

Semi-sextile - The third combination is a semi-sextile aspect of thirty degrees, 1/12th of a circle, which happens when planets are in adjacent signs. This aspect bridges different polarities, elements and qualities, and in this case, also blends the energies of the Piscean and Aquarian Ages. Aquarius and Pisces are always related to each other mathematically by thirty degrees of separation. Now, their ruling planets, in each other's signs, are also thirty degrees apart.

Until 2011, essentially for the remainder of Uranus's transit through Pisces, Uranus and Neptune will form a semi-sextile aspect, ranging from 23-28 degrees of Pisces and Aquarius. The semi-sextile is seen as a teaching aspect, presenting a karmic lesson that is created by low-level tension between sharply contrasting energies. There is a subtle friction that underlies ordinary conscious awareness. When we are open to the tension, rather than resisting it, a profound lesson can be learned. Our task is to open to the hidden lessons that Uranus and Neptune have to teach in each other's signs.

Aquarian Age - Finally, we are poised at the changing of an age, and some scholars believe it is also the end of one complete cycle of the ages, which further strengthens the Uranian and Piscean influences as they are the rulers of these ages. Uranus is the planetary influence of the incoming Aquarian age, while Neptune is the ruler of the sign of Pisces, the outgoing age. After 2,000 years human consciousness is reaching out of the Piscean energy and into the Aquarian.

The Age of Pisces held a dispensation of hierarchy and patriarchy, and as the Age of Aquarius dawns, we are witnessing a reawakening of feminine energies. Ancient cultures coded their most sacred truths in myth, and in these archetypes the oceans were always the domain of a goddess. Mythically, Neptune had to marry the goddess Amphrite, the literal embodiment of the ocean, before he could become lord of the sea. Today our oceans are in danger, so regaining this balance of masculine and feminine is critical. Likewise, as Uranus, the sky god, remembers that Gaia, the Earth, was both his mother and his mate, a greening of the Earth is taking place. Around the world there is an unprecedented and spontaneous uprising of hundreds of thousands of grassroots movements for social justice and environmental change. New words like "bioneer" and "green-collar economy" have been added to our lexicon.

At the cusp of the New Age, we feel the impact of the shift, a blend of the outgoing energies and the incoming dispensation, along with a sense of temporal acceleration. With Uranus and Neptune in each other's signs, and these signs representing the changing of an age, we are receiving an intense and heightened preview of coming attractions. But there is a power struggle as the old ways weaken but battle to remain in form. The new and unfamiliar energies flex their unfolding muscles and make their presence felt, triggering a consciousness revolution. The aeonian changing of the guard challenges our fundamental world view and offers a choice about how we see reality.

At issue, I believe, is humanity's dawning recognition on a wide scale of how we participate in Being/Existence. Liberation of consciousness and synthesis of variant energies is possible. We are not simply created beings apart from, and at the whim of, a distant and temperamental Creator. Rather, in a Quantum sense, we partake of an immense Reality in which we participate. As consciousness moves into the realm of the Aquarian Age our awareness moves more into the domain of causes and interconnections.

We are waking up, rudely or gracefully, losing a sense of separation and difference in favor of awareness of our shared experience and common destiny. We can become awake in the dream of manifestation and learn to take responsibility for what we bring to the collective. We can choose to be conscious co-creators, claiming how our thoughts and states of consciousness affect the collective. In this way we learn, like Goethe's *Sorcerer's Apprentice*, popularized by Disney, stark lessons of responsibility. Reality is a shared dream, and this stranger-than-fiction condition is resolved when we recognize and accept the role of individual choice.

Atlantis Rising #75 April 2009

22. URANUS-PLUTO SQUARE: THE UNFOLDING ASTROLOGY OF EVOLUTION AND REVOLUTION

"R uin is the road to transformation. "

Elizabeth Gilbert, *Eat, Pray, Love*

Arab Spring 2010 (NPR.org)

Astrologer Dane Rudyar has called Uranus, Neptune, and Pluto
"Ambassadors of the Galaxy," as they inhabit the outer part of the
Solar System. Large astrological cycles, and aspects between these
ambassadors, are thought to influence the evolution of consciousness.
Rudyar died in 1985,so he didn't live to see Pluto's change of status or
other dwarf planetary entities emerging from the remote and frigid
darkness of our Sun's domain.

A cycle of aspects between two planets begins when they form a
conjunction. Called synodic cycles, from the Greek word that means
"meeting," these cycles create an unfolding angular sequence between
planets like the phases of the Moon, or partners in a dance who move
together and then apart. The orbits of Uranus and Pluto are 83.75 years
and 245.33 respectively, and their full synodic cycle takes an average of
128 years due to their retrograde motions.

The current synodic cycle between Uranus and Pluto began in 1962
with a conjunction in Virgo, uniting revolutionary Uranian energy
with the Plutonian potential for deep transformation in the sign of the

working collective. The conjunction peaked during 1965-1966 while opposed to Saturn in Pisces. The decade of the sixties saw the Civil Rights Act, the Viet Nam war, Flower Power and the resulting peace movement, and the first Moon landing. This period also saw the genesis of the personal computer, a term first used in the New York Times in 1962. Seen in a larger context the decade of the sixties was a stage in a much longer evolutionary process.

Five decades later in 2010, Uranus entered Aries and will transit through the sign of the Ram until 2018. We have reached the next critical stage in the synodic cycle where Uranus, the faster moving planet, has advanced 90 degrees ahead of Pluto. The focus of this pattern is radical change and momentum toward higher awareness. The mechanism is a systemic reconstruction before a higher level re-patterning can occur.

These planets will move in and out of an exact square seven times from 2012 – 2015 as the two planets shift in their retrograde motions. This 90-degree angle is arguably the most significant and challenging planetary influence of our time, and we should expect to see continued upheaval and extremes. The first two exact squares occurred in June and September of 2012. The third happened on May 20, 2013. The centerpiece square, the fourth of seven, will form on November 1, 2013, and make a T-Square formation with the Moon in Libra. Two days later there will be a Solar Eclipse, further ramping up the volatile energy of the Uranus-Pluto square. Shocking secrets may emerge from the shadow. In April of 2014 number five in the series will occur and form a powerhouse Grand Cross with Mars and Jupiter. This kind of tension sets the stage for dramatic events. The last two in the series will occur December 15, 2014 and March 17, 2015; we'll continue to monitor developments as they unfold.

As this pattern of squares repeats, we are witnessing political unrest, revolutionary energy, extremes and catastrophes. As Uranus advanced to within a few degrees of its first square to Pluto, revolutionary movements spread throughout the world, and record-breaking storms battered the country. The Arab Spring is a media term for the wave of revolutionary demonstrations, protests, riots, and civil wars in the Arab world that began in December of 2010. The protests have shared techniques of civil resistance in sustained campaigns involving strikes, demonstrations, marches, and rallies, as well as the effective use of social media to organize, communicate, and raise awareness in the face of state attempts at repression and Internet censorship.

Rulers have been deposed in Tunisia, twice in Egypt, Libya, and Yemen. Civil uprisings have erupted in Bahrain and Syria, now a war, and there have been major protests in Algeria, Iraq, Jordan Kuwait, Morocco and Sudan with minor protests in other locations. There were border clashes in Israel in 2011 and protests in Iranian Khuzestan by the Arab minority. Weapons and Tuareg fighters returning from the civil war in Libya stoked a simmering conflict in Mali that is considered "fallout" from the Arab Spring. Sectarian clashes in Lebanon have been labeled as spillover violence from Syria.

Pluto entered Capricorn in 2008, which coincided with the dramatic breakdown (Pluto) of global financial structures (Capricorn). Pluto's prior transit through Capricorn, 1762 through 1778, witnessed the American Revolution and the Declaration of Independence. The high side of Pluto's energy is transformation, which at its best offers a complete metamorphosis like a caterpillar becoming a butterfly, or a phoenix rising from the ashes of its former self. Astrologer Rick Levine has aptly described Pluto as "a tsunami moving at the speed of a glacier."

Pluto will remain in Capricorn until 2024, and toward the end of the transit, will pass over the natal placement of the US Pluto at 27 degrees of Capricorn. This is called a Pluto return and happens once in 245 years. Pluto will come within a degree of an exact conjunction in April of 2021, and then turn retrograde. In 2022 there will be three exact "hits" to the US chart. If the intractable divisiveness in American politics continues or worsens, perhaps this will prepare the ground for another American revolution.

The most positive outcomes of these combined energies are constructive evolution, empowered awakening, and enlightened freedom. Pluto's powers of transformation in the sign of structure are combining with the potentially shattering, awakening and revolutionary force of Uranus. We are living through a major generational upheaval, and we are challenged to examine old structures and patterns that need to be deconstructed. Resistance to this energy builds to a pressure point that can bring an explosive and volcanic release when planetary triggers form.

The last series of squares between Uranus and Pluto was eighty years ago, between 1932 and 1934, with five exact hits. Uranus was also in Aries at that time, and Pluto was in the cardinal sign of Cancer, opposite to Capricorn. Early in the 1930's we witnessed the Great Depression, political and social upheaval, and the rise of dictators and extremism. Stock markets crashed and unemployment rose sharply. (In the wake of the January 2020 we are witnessing similar events). Adolf Hitler cemented his power in January 1933 when he became Chancellor of Germany. Soon afterward the Reichstag fire led to a decree that eliminated many German civil liberties.

What's radically different now is technology. Since the mid-1990s, the Internet has revolutionized culture and commerce, including the advent of electronic mail, instant messaging, Voice over Internet Protocol (VoIP) phone calls, two-way interactive video calls, and the World Wide Web with its discussion forums, blogs, social networking, and online shopping. Facebook and cellular phones have dramatically changed the game as witnessed in Egypt's revolution and the Occupy Wall Street Movement. Mobilizing and spreading the word are now nearly instantaneous worldwide.

Aquarius energy belongs to the group, and it is a new paradigm of approaching problem solving where power is shared and distributed. Governance and leadership are being redefined. Examples of Aquarian mechanisms (for better or worse depending on one's view), are Wikileaks and Anonymous. WikiLeaks began in late 2006 as a disclosure portal, initially using the Wikipedia model. Volunteers wrote restricted, or legally threatened, material that had been submitted by whistleblowers. It was Julian Assange, an Australian

Internet activist and journalist, and the *de facto* editor-in-chief of WikiLeaks, who had the idea of creating what software engineer Ben Laurie called an "open-source, democratic intelligence agency."

Spy agencies and hackers can also use the same technology that has the ability to transmit information easily. Anonymous, a group of so-called "hactivists," operating behind the scenes through technology, have hacked into high security, and often high profile, databases and Internet sites. Anonymous has come to be recognized by Guy Fawkes masks. The mask is a stylized depiction of the best-known member of the Gunpowder Plot, an attempt to blow up the House of Lords in London and overthrow the monarchy in 1605. The mask portrays a stylized a white face with an over-sized smile and red cheeks, a wide moustache upturned at both ends, and a thin vertical pointed beard, designed by illustrator David Lloyd.

The icon came to represent broader protests after it was used as a major plot element in *V for Vendetta*, published in 1982, and then in the 2005 film adaptation. After appearing in Internet forums, the mask became a symbol for the Occupy Movements and then for Anonymous. According to *Time* in 2011, the protesters' adoption of the mask led to it becoming the top-selling mask on Amazon.com, selling hundreds of thousands a year. This electronic proliferation of a symbol is very Aquarian, the sign ruled by Uranus.

Bradley Manning, now Chelsea, was a soldier who served in Iraq. He released the largest set of restricted documents ever leaked to the public. Denver Nicks, one of Manning's biographers, writes "the leaked material, particularly the diplomatic cables, was widely seen as a catalyst for Arab Spring in 2010, and Manning was viewed as both a 21st-century Tiananmen Square Tank Man, or an embittered traitor." Tank Man, the Unknown Protester, is the nickname of an anonymous man who stood in front of a column of tanks on June 5, 1989, the morning

Guy Fawkes mask worn by protester (author Pierre Selim - CC BY-SA 3.0)

after the Chinese military suppressed the Tiananmen Square protests by force.

Edward Snowden is a computer specialist who worked for the CIA and the NSA and leaked details of several top-secret United States and British government mass surveillance programs to the press. Daniel Elsberg, who leaked the Pentagon Papers in 1971, says Manning and Snowden are heroes and that we need more whistleblowers. Others believe the two are traitors.

The high side of Uranus energy is awakening, shedding light and utopian vision on outworn structures that need to be deconstructed and re-visioned. Rogue Uranus energy is like ungrounded electricity, a lightening strike, or a dangerous and unpredictable high voltage wire. Uranus represents radical change, invention, revolution and the capacity for idealism; its effect can be shocking and unpredictable. Uranus in the fiery sign of Aries sparks an irrepressible urge for freedom, an irresistible energy that breaks us out of self-imposed prisons.

Astrologer Isabel Hickey says Uranus can help us discover the undiscovered. Viewed in a positive light, this action is like spring cleaning, or perhaps moving, where old patterns are disrupted and a whole new structure or way of life replaces one that has been outgrown. If we are awake, and paying attention, this feels like positive change. If we have been asleep, or in denial, it can feel like a tornado or volcanic eruption.

Pluto represents destruction, transformation, and renewal, and unlike Uranus, its effect is slow and ruthless. Some might argue that Pluto's demotion to dwarf planet status has diminished his role in astrology and his potential for significance. Paradoxically, Pluto now seems to act in the manner of homeopathy where the more diluted solution increases the potency of the medium.

Uranus combined with Pluto forces change, and resistance only makes the explosion bigger. The underlying momentum of the pattern is an evolutionary thrust toward humanitarian change fueled by an intense desire for freedom—Aquarian Age impulses. As Uranus squaring

Pluto increasingly reveals information stored in the shadow, we can expect these upheavals to increase, both in number and intensity. Redemption is another of Pluto's themes. In the wake of what can seem like literal or symbolic death and devastation the intangibles that really matter can be revealed. How we use these energies is up to us.

Atlantis Rising #102 October 2013

23.GAIA: WHAT IS THE EARTH'S ROLE IN ASTROLOGY

"You cannot get through a single day without having an impact on the world around you. What you do makes a difference, and you have to decide what kind of difference you want to make."

Jane Goodall

Earth seen from Apollo 17 - NASA public domain

On February 22, 2017 NASA made a stunning announcement. The Spitzer Space Telescope revealed the first-known system of seven Earth-sized exoplanets (planets outside our Solar System) in orbit around a single star. This system is in the constellation of Aquarius and is about 40 light-years from Earth--relatively close in stellar terms. NASA believes three of these exoplanets may be in the habitable zone where a rocky planet is likely to have water.

In a radical departure from the opinion that "earths" are exceedingly rare, widely held only a decade ago, scientists are now realizing that Earth-like planets are common. This new awareness requires a radical shift in our paradigm relative to our place in the scheme of things. The reality is that the Universe is likely teeming with life, and this life may be diverse and "alien" in appearance and nature, or perhaps familiar, if evolution has proven templates of form. The implications are complex and far reaching.

Earth is the only planetary body in our Solar System, other than the Moon or dwarf planets in the Kuiper Belt, that wasn't named after a Greek or Roman god or goddess. In Greek mythology the personification of the Earth was Gaia, the very first deity. In the beginning Gaia emerged from a primordial void called Chaos and was the creator and great mother of all. Gaia brought forth Ouranus (Uranus) the sky. She mated with him and they had twelve children-- the original Titan gods. The sea gods were born from her union with Pontus, the ocean.

In heliocentric (Sun-centered) astrology the view of the sky is from the center of the Solar System with the Sun in the middle and the Earth as a circling planet interpreted in a similar manner to the other planets. However, most Western astrologers use a geocentric model (Earth-centered) where the Sun becomes a planet in a sign, and the meaning of Earth's placement is ignored. The Sun's apparent motion is viewed in the astrological sign that is appears to move through, even though we realize this is only a useful convention, since Earth's motion is what causes the appearance.

When the twelve zodiac signs are viewed in a sequential or linear fashion, beginning with Aries and progressing through Pisces, the experience represents an unfolding path and the soul's journey through time and space to gain experience. This circle of stars is formed by energies that alternate in gender or positive or negative polarity. The nature of the signs develops from a personal, and individual, orientation in Aries to a transpersonal and collective orientation in Pisces, the Fishes, which swim in the cosmic ocean.

A Russian proverb states that every road has two directions, and so it is with the highways we call the signs of the zodiac. The place of Earth is always 180 degrees opposite of the degree and sign of the Sun. If the Sun is in Aries, the Earth is in Libra. If the Sun is in Scorpio, the Earth is in the opposite sign of Taurus. The two ends of any spectrum are both polarized and complementary. Opposition can denote balance or imbalance, cooperation or conflict, depending on awareness. Between the extremes of black and white lie infinite shades of gray. Between hot and cold are varying degrees of temperature. Lying along the spectrum of wet and dry are degrees of humidity. The qualitative energy of the twelve signs are also six pairs of polarized expression, each operating like a continuum. Seen this way each duo of opposite zodiac signs forms a spectrum of energy with twelve signs and six pairs. Therefore, the sign on the opposite side of the circle of animals is also of opposite elemental polarity: fire-air and earth-water. So it is with the Earth and Sun.

Symbolically, the Sun is always casting light on the Earth. This highlights and emphasizes the polarity of the two signs. I believe the symbolic relationship between the Sun and the Earth represents a process of reorientation, shifting our awareness from what is familiar to what we must learn to balance the poles. Earth is literally the ground where we stand, while the Sun on the opposite side of the sky, is where we gaze and what we came to learn. The Earth is our inner identity, our deep needs, and how we are grounded. The Sun is the path we tread and our outer expression. Astrologically one of the keywords, or ways of understanding the aspect of polarity or opposition, is awareness. When we acknowledge and recognize what confronts or "opposes" us we begin to understand ourselves through what's reflected in the mirror of relationship.

Aries and Libra represent the continuum of personal expression. Mars-ruled Aries is the fiery sign of action while Venus-ruled Libra is the airy sign of partnership. Aries initiates and Libra responds. This polarity offers the extremes of domination or acquiescence, leading or following, with the higher ground pointing the way toward partnership and cooperation. As the energy moves back and forth along this continuum we shift from individual action to joint effort. The goal is the middle ground of taking turns and perceiving strength and talent based on specific situations. With Aries Earth (Libra Sun)

the inner urge is to be in charge and number one, so the lesson is to move from an emphasis on "me first" and learn to relate and let others lead. With Libra Earth (Aries Sun) there has been an over emphasis in the past of too much merging with others, resulting in a loss of personal identity. Therefore, the goal is toward more independence and self-sufficiency.

Taurus and Scorpio form the continuum of resources. Earthy Taurus gathers possessions while the deep waters of Scorpio desires intense experiences. This energy moves along the line of what we personally possess to how we spend or invest these resources. Taurus can hoard possessions like a miser while Scorpio can indiscriminately spend their resources for the excitement of it. The goal of this pair is knowing when and what to acquire and how to utilize our energy appropriately on every level. Money is "green" energy and sex is life energy. How we store, keep a savings, or pass the energy on, is the lesson of this polarity. Taurus Earth (Scorpio Sun). The lesson here is learning to let go of possessions and experience desire with non-attachment. The Buddhist practice of creating intricate sand mandalas and then letting them wash away in the river is an example. Scorpio Earth (Taurus Sun). This placement must learn to create things that last and have eternal beauty. In this case the energy must be materialized in form and "owned" before it is surrendered.

Gemini and Sagittarius are the continuum of mental exploration. Gemini is perhaps the quintessential air sign, darting mentally and physically in every direction, seeking stimulation. Fiery Sagittarius pulls back his bow and aims his arrow high, often without a target. Gemini tends to explore close at hand while Sagittarius roams far afield. This spectrum explores how we move out of our home base, familiar territory, and into the macrocosm. Do we shoot our arrows just for the fun of it? Synthesis is the key for this pair. Stop, look, and listen might be the motto for both. What is the purpose of the exploration and what is the value of the data collected? Gemini Earth (Sagittarius Sun). This placement must learn to move from pure curiosity without a purpose to a way to apply knowledge in a practical manner. Sagittarius Earth (Gemini Sun). Here the lesson is to learn to think closer to home and deal with matters that are within the reach of the hands. The motto "think globally, act locally" would be a perfect guide.

Cancer and Capricorn are the continuum of field of influence. This duo contrasts home and family with work and career. Cancer feels the pull of deep roots and heritage while Capricorn strives to climb the heights of power and position. This polarizes the personal domain of hearth and home versus making a mark in field and town. The goal is understanding our personal impact on our world and learning the consequences of our acts. Whether we are the nurturing influence to an Einstein or a Mother Teresa, or whether we go out into the world to make a fortune, this spectrum can teach us the relationship between our base of security and our ability to strive and overcome. Cancer Earth (Capricorn Sun). There has been too much need for comfort, resulting in a retreat into the "shell." This must be transformed into the ability to risk climbing the mountain to get a wider view. Capricorn Earth (Cancer Sun). Too much ambition without purpose must be transformed and channeled into taking care of the home front and understanding our base of support.

Leo and Aquarius represent the continuum of personal power. Symbolically, Leo represents the king and Aquarius the kingdom. This pair moves along a spectrum from potentially dogmatic dictatorship through rebellion for its own sake. Leo examines how authority is held and power over others is wielded, while Aquarius examines how we respond to impulses toward individuation and personal freedom. Even monarchs have to obey natural law, and everyone is ultimately subject to some authority. How we deal with authority, whether following orders or directing others, is the domain of this energetic couple. Is Utopia defined by an enlightened monarch or a conscious, contributing populace? The goal is true understanding of rulership and the concept of *noblesse oblige* as well as the role of the enlightened members of a democratic republic. Leo Earth (Aquarius Sun). A tendency to demand a constant spotlight and continuous applause must be transformed into an awareness of group process and community. Aquarius Earth (Leo Sun). The need for freedom at any price must be transmuted into an understanding that rules are necessary and a kingdom requires structure and judgment.

Virgo and Pisces are the continuum of assimilation. In the case of practical Virgo, the approach is to inspect the parts, isolating each unique snowflake or grain of sand. At the other extreme, Pisces is immersed in the ocean unaware of the solitary drops of water. Virgo analyzes details through a microscope while Pisces gazes dreamily through a telescope. The goal of this duality is knowing when to differentiate and when to blend. This combination of energies has the potential for a collective experience akin to the story of the Emperor's new clothes. Is there a collective illusion or the ability to see the naked truth? Virgo Earth (Pisces Sun). In this case, true compassion is born from the depths of the feeling nature and can be channeled into a form of service. Pisces Earth (Virgo Sun) With this placement an instinctual tendency to lose a sense of self in an ocean of togetherness must give way to a more objective awareness of the discrete components.

The priceless lesson we can learn from the placement of the Earth in our birth charts includes illuminating our blind spots, bringing sunlight into dark places. If we become aware of unconscious motives and instinctual urges, we can gain valuable perspective. The Earth moves in a spiraling dance of partnership with the Sun. Depending on the signs involved the dance may be a tango or a waltz. Learning the steps, and the nature of the partner, can set us free to move to the reciprocal rhythm of the music.

Atlantis Rising #123 April 2017

24. GEOMETRY OF TRANSFORMATION: WHAT CAN WE LEARN FROM POTENT ASTROLOGICAL ASPECTS FORMING THIS SUMMER?

"There is geometry in the humming of the strings, there is music in the spacing of the spheres."

Pythagorus

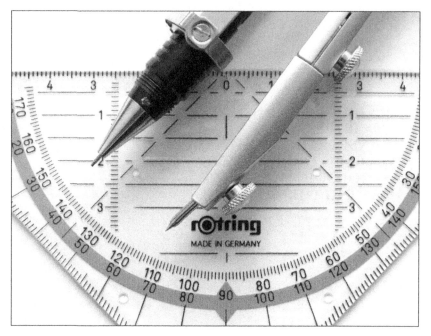

Geometry Set square (SnappyGoat.com 625155)

The summer of 2010 will witness some powerful planetary configurations. A Grand Cross will form in June at the full moon, and a Cardinal T-Square takes shape as July comes to a close. These astrological aspects may be the most intense in seven decades. Astrologers are watching, wondering, and trying to interpret their influence. Everyone on Earth will feel these energies, although the perceived effect will differ based on individual charts and states of consciousness. These configurations will also have a strong connection to the birth chart of the United States, presenting potentially transforming energies.

Astrology has been described as the study of cycles in which the real and apparent motions of the Sun, Moon, and planets are observed relative to Earth. People have gazed at the sky for countless ages, searching for meaning and purpose through the Law of Correspondences. This law is sometimes stated as the Hermetic Axiom, "As above, so below; as within, so without." The premise is that patterns in earthly affairs can be perceived by understanding the symbolic significance of repeating patterns in the heavens.

The Zodiac is a circular band of space above and below the ecliptic plane, the orbit of Earth and the planets, and the apparent path of the Sun. A horoscope in Western astrology is a circle with Earth at the symbolic center. The origin of the word is the Greek *horoscopus*, meaning "watcher of the hour." This refers to the Ascendant, or the sign rising in the east at the moment of birth. This idea seems to have emerged about the time of Alexander when the focus began to shift from watching portents in the sky solely on behalf of king and country, to looking at the astrological influences in the charts of individuals.

The three main factors in any astrological chart are the Sun, Moon, and Ascendant. The Ascendant is not a planet, or celestial body, but an angle--the eastern horizon. The Midheaven, the point directly overhead the birth place, is the other primary angle in a horoscope. The Tropical Zodiac, which is based on the seasons and the apparent cycle of the Sun, is used in most natal charts in Western astrology. The planets are placed within this symbolic wheel of the seasons, and their positions are calculated at the exact moment of birth.

In addition to a planet's position by sign and house, planets are also interpreted based on their angular relationship to one another; these are called aspects. An astrological aspect is the distance measured in degrees and minutes of Celestial Longitude along the ecliptic. Aspects are viewed from the Earth, and are computed between two or more planets around or across a horoscope.

Planets are the primary archetypes embedded in astrology, and their aspects are interpreted as focal points in the horoscope where combined planetary energies are given extra emphasis. The more exact an aspect is, the more its influence is felt. Usually, aspects are formed between two planets, although aspects between planets and the Ascendant and Mid-Heaven are also considered. Aspects are divided into major or minor, and harmonious or stressful. Generally, major aspects are more powerful than minor, but there are exceptions based on context. When the planets move within orb of the angle, the aspect builds, reaching maximum influence when the degrees of connection are exact. As the planets separate, the influence decreases, disappearing as they slip out of orb.

Each aspect has its own signature, or manner of expressing, and not all aspects combine planetary energy in the same way. When two planetary energies connect, they either blend harmoniously or produce tension according to the nature of the planets or the geometry of the aspects. Harmonious aspects are characterized as easy and positive, and tense aspects as difficult or hard. Challenging aspects bring difficulties that can result in great achievement, while harmonious aspects bring easy conditions that may lead to wasted opportunities.

Tense aspects cause friction, bringing psychological and environmental challenges, or a combination of both. Friction may be uncomfortable, but can stimulate growth. Coping with challenges may stimulate someone to overcome difficulties and develop their astrological potential. Individuals with only harmonious aspects may have plenty of potential but no drive to develop it, while those with only tense aspects may lack positive direction and forward momentum. A balance of friction and harmony produces a constructive mix in which to gain the most from life experiences.

To the ancients, certain aspects and planets were considered either good (benefic), or bad (malefic). Modern opinion is more philosophical and psychological and seeks to understand how the dynamics and synergy of the horoscope can promote soul growth through the exercise of the will and conscious choice. This approach is more in tune with research on astrological harmonics. John Addey was a major proponent of this view in England, and Johannes Kepler proposed similar ideas in his book *Harmonice Mundi* as far back as 1619.

Aspects can also be characterized by their harmonics, grouping them into similar numeric patterns, In this way, aspects may be understood through the principles of numerology. The nine aspects listed below are harmonic with the numbers 1-9 and are calculated by dividing the circle by those numbers. Among other aspects are the semi-sextile of 30 degrees, harmonic with the number 12. Its key word is tension. The semi-sextile offers a sort of reciprocal friction between alternate polarities. The inconjunct aspect is 150 degrees and is thought to demand adjustments in beliefs and behavior.

1 Conjunction: zero degrees. Combines two or more planets in a concentrated and blended energy.

2 Opposition: 180 degrees. Offers awareness through conflict or cooperation.

3 Trine: 120 degrees. Brings planets together in an easy flow that must be harnessed and channeled through the will.

4 Square: 90 degrees. Creates friction and blocks between planets that can fuel growth.

5 Quintile: 72 degrees. Bestows talent and innate gifts that must be harnessed and developed.

6 Sextile: 60 degrees. Offers balanced energies and opportunities.

7 Septile: 52 degrees. Reveals a healing challenge and often gives a "defining moment" in life.

8 Semi-square: 45 degrees, sometimes called octile. Brings growth-producing friction.

9 Novile: 40 degrees. Offers decisions and choices which have a quality of destiny.

Aspects can also combine the energies of planets into larger and more complicated groups. When a number of planets combine in this way, they form an energetic geometry--a three-dimensional signature. These patterns take on meanings of their own. Such geometry, like the square aspect formations of 2010, magnetize challenges and life lessons in a more dramatic and compelling manner, creating a potent archetype field. In a natal chart they bring lifelong lessons. When they appear by transit they offer unique growth opportunities.

This summer, the powerful energies of Pluto in Capricorn, Uranus in Aries, and Saturn in Libra are arranging themselves in the early degrees of the Cardinal Signs. This is like a vortex of strong wind currents. In this case, it's the winds of change that can be harnessed. Saturn and Uranus have seesawed in and out of five oppositions since 2008, and they will now move into Libra and Aries. In addition, Saturn will be joined by Mars in Libra, and as Jupiter enters Aries in June, he will conjoin Uranus.

These dynamic geometries hold the potential for personal and planetary transformation, according to where they activate horoscopes. Tension and stress focused constructively can bring a higher state of awareness and an openness to new paradigms. Positive expression can bring creative breakthroughs and quantum leaps and advances in science. Resistance to this energy clings to old and outworn patterns and beliefs.

Grand Cross -- A Grand Cross is composed of planets at the four arms of a cross. All are in square aspect, or 90 degrees, to each other. It's an intense geometry, like a crossroads, that can bring issues to a head and ask for choices and decisions about direction. June 26, 2010, at the full moon, a Grand Cross will form. Seven planets are involved. Jupiter and Uranus in Aries oppose Saturn in Libra. The full Moon and Pluto in Capricorn oppose the Sun and Mercury in Cancer. We are advised, individually and collectively, to take a hard look at what's not working. It may be time to choose a new way. The Sun and Mercury will overlay Venus and Jupiter in the chart of the United States, bringing a focal point of tension to our nation's relationships, both at home and abroad.

Cardinal T-Square -- A T-Square aspect is formed by an opposition of 180 degrees between two planets, both of which are square to a third. Additional planets may also be involved. Viewed another way, connecting the points from the outside, this angular relationship forms an isosceles triangle. We have the choice to focus on the blocked energy or to seek the insight within the energy pattern to release the flow. On August 1, 2010 five planets form this aspect. Saturn and Mars in Libra oppose Uranus and Jupiter in Aries. All four square Pluto in

Capricorn. In this case, the resolving energy flows to Pluto and the possibility of transforming structures of power.

If we examine this aspect geometry using the mythic language of archetypes inherited from the Greeks, both aspects square off three powerful gods. Pluto, Lord of the Underworld, is in Capricorn, offering the transformation of organizations. Saturn, principle of form, is in Libra, bringing hard work and challenges to relationships of all types. And Uranus, Lord of the Sky, is in Aries, presenting a focus on personal freedom with an influence of rapid change and unexpected shifts in circumstances. Together, the message might be stated simply as, face the shadow of the past (Pluto), reform outworn structures (Saturn), and rebuild the future according to a new and revolutionary vision (Uranus).

Astrology contains a paradox that is demonstrated in the words of the Roman philosopher, Seneca. "The Fates lead he who will. He who won't, they drag." The ancient system of wisdom called astrology is not meant to be an external process. An individual, or a nation, is not a passive bystander, or unwitting victim of circumstances beyond their control. Astrology isn't a Wheel of Fortune, spinning and stopping with no apparent pattern, and operating like a game of chance. This is an illusion that keeps us blind and feeling powerless. We always have our power of choice, even if it's only in how we respond to influences.

Rather, astrology is meant to be a powerful navigational tool. The deeper purpose is to learn to exercise choice, free will, and personal responsibility in order to grow and evolve our full potential. Astrology offers a map that reveals the terrain and enables us to make wise decisions on our life path. In some ways astrology is akin to weather forecasting. If we know gale force winds are expected, it's unwise to set sail in a small craft. Conversely, if we see that timing is optimum, we should take action and not languish on the shore.

I see our challenge in navigating the sea change of our times, and making the jump to light speed, as making choices that keep us grounded and balanced. I also believe it's wise to keep the objective of higher consciousness in our sites. We should strive to act rather than react, and not become caught up in polarized rhetoric or apocalyptic hyperbole, thereby confusing the school with the lesson. In other words, we should use common sense, and the wisdom of experience, to make decisions and chart our course for the future. These times of transformation have been foreseen by numerous and diverse cultures around the world. We can choose to move through them consciously and responsibly or be swept along in a maelstrom of negativity and confusion. It's up to us to choose.

Atlantis Rising #82 June 2010

25. CIRCULAR LOGIC: HOW CAN GEOMETRIC SHAPES HELP US UNDERSTAND THE PLANETS?

"Everything an Indian does is in a circle, and that is because the power of the world always works in circles, and everything tries to be round."

Wallace Black Elk (1863-1950)

Mandala pattern (SnappyGoat.com 1145821)

Symbols are a silent and potent language that reaches our conscious awareness through the agency of subconsciousness. A symbol is a representation, a mark, a picture or an image that stands for something else. All communication, or transmission of ideas, takes place through the use of symbols whether spoken or ideographic.

A symbol is generally a pictorial emblem for a concept or idea and acts like shorthand communication that bypasses linear, alphabetical language. For example, in a religious context, a cross has become the symbol for Christianity, a six-pointed star for Judaism, and a star in a crescent represents Islam. We recognize these symbolic linkages automatically without words or conscious thought.

Symbols are how we communicate whether through an inviting smile, a finger to our lips asking for silence, or through the words of the most exquisite prose. An arrow with the point on top means up and with the point on the bottom means down. A black circle with diagonal line through the center now says to the world, "No . . . smoking, entry," or fill in the blank. In America a bright red octagon means stop. Male or female figures on bathroom doors indicate which gender should use the room.

As the Chinese maxim states, "One picture is worth a thousand words." Pictures are emblems of ideas and demonstrate concepts that might take pages of words to explain. Symbols might be viewed like keys that unlock doors at different levels of our consciousness and provide access to previously concealed or separated rooms of our psyche. In a metaphorical sense, all of life can be experienced as a symbolic reflection, offering us wisdom and growth.

Occult or sacred symbols are meant to communicate an idea directly to our awareness, transcending the intellect and aiming straight for the heart. It might be said that all geometry is sacred because meaning and archetype are contained in the shapes in the same way archetypal principles are contained in numbers.

Although the names of the planets are derived from Greek and Roman gods, those humanized figures were meant to represent the archetypal natures of the planets that had been observed for thousands of years. Mythical tales of the exploits of the all-too-fallible gods provided a means of perceiving how their movements through different signs, and their angular relationships to one another, played out on the stellar stage. Their antics, foibles, and heroism showed through stories how humans might respond to these energies.

The language of astrology is symbolic and, in the case of the planets, all of the symbols are formed from different combinations of the circle, the crescent, or half-circle, and the cross, or two straight lines. In order to understand the planets in a purely symbolic way it is valuable to know how their glyphs have been constructed and what they represent.

The circle has no beginning or ending point and is therefore said to symbolize eternity, infinity, spirit and the never-ending cycles of manifestation. The circle also represents unlimited potential, like a blank canvas. The crescent or half circle is said to signify the soul and the receptivity implied by the chalice. The half circle also visually resembles a lens through which the light of spirit and the sun may be both focused and reflected.

A cross is formed by two straight lines that intersect and is said to indicate the domain of the material world and our self-conscious awareness. A cross enclosed within a circle is an ancient symbol of the four corners of the year, and the horoscope is laid out on this plan, showing the four corners of the day: dawn, noon, sunset, and midnight. A cross inside a circle is also the symbol of Earth.

In their purely archetypal roles the planets were seen by the ancients as immortal gods imbued with supernatural powers. They moved through the sky against the background of the stars, engaging each other in harmony or discord, and affecting mortal life in the process. By combining the symbolic meaning of the circle, crescent, and cross, the glyphs of the planets represent these complex spiritual ideas.

Planetary Symbols

Sun - Focused Power -- In the symbol for the Sun the circle of the infinite has been brought to a focus by a central dot, bringing a cycle of manifestation to a beginning through a point of concentration. This symbol also represents the faculty of superconsciousness. This is the center or heart of the astrological chart as the Sun is the center of the solar system. The
symbol for the Sun shows the central lesson, or focus of experience, revealed through the chart. To understand the Sun's significance we must know where power needs to be brought to bear in the life, and through what kind of experiences.

Moon – Receptivity -- The crescent is the symbol for the Moon, which plays the role of both reservoir and reflector in our lives, representing the lens through which the solar rays of spirit may be focused. The crescent also signifies the waxing and waning monthly phases of the

Moon and the idea that the Moon's ability to fully reflect the Sun's light is cyclical.

Although the Moon has no light of her own she does possess movement, and her monthly cycle produces phases of light and dark, representing the journey of the soul throughout cycles of expression. The Moon's crescent symbol signifies the faculty of subconsciousness as well as her capacity to receive and respond to impressions as well as the ability to reflect back what we have gained in experience and soul growth.

Mercury – Expression -- The glyph for the planet Mercury is a combination of the circle, cross and crescent. The half circle, or partial reflection, is above the circle of spirit, showing limitation of eternal expression, but both are above the cross of materiality. Mercury was the swift messenger of the gods and the only Olympian who could travel freely from the underworld to Mount Olympus. Contained within this symbol is the knowledge of right use of will and the power of the word.

Venus – Attraction -- The symbol for Venus is often described as a mirror for the goddess of beauty. This glyph contains the circle of spirit over the cross of matter, pointing us in the direction of the path to perfect reflection and embodiment of spirit in the material world. If our lives are a mirror of the divine we bring heaven to earth. The symbol for Venus closely resembles the Egyptian Ankh, symbol of life. The Ankh shows an oval, or elongated circle, above a cross. This ancient symbol was often shown held to the nostrils of a mortal monarch by the gods and offered as the gift of eternal life .

Mars - Energy -- The symbol for Mars is the reverse of the symbol of Venus. In the symbol of the war god the cross

of matter is oriented in a specific direction
and is exalted over the circle of spirit. The
more ancient representation of Mars was the
symbol for Venus inverted, the cross over the
circle, indicating that this planet has more to
do with earthly issues. The god of war tends
to show us our personal battlegrounds and

his arrow is often aimed toward physical conquest rather than spiritual
dominion.

Jupiter – Expansion -- In this planet's symbol
the crescent of receptivity, or the half-circle of
the soul, is rising in the East, or waxing
(increasing), and creates a focal point for the
cross of matter. Somewhat resembling the
number r, the symbol shows the potential for
growth and increase. Where will we optimize
our resources in order to learn the principle of growth and the
subsequent issue of stewardship?

Saturn – Concentration -- Saturn's symbol is
the reverse of Jupiter. The cross of matter is
elevated over the receptive crescent, now
placed in the west, or place of the past. This
designates Saturn's gravity-like pull and the
forces of limitation and concentration. The
cross of matter is slightly above the crescent,

revealing a focus on matter and the lessons of the material world. In a
sense, Saturn forces us to deal with the consequences and
responsibilities (Karma), of the abundance of Jupiter.

Uranus – Independence -- Although the symbol for Uranus is usually
shown as two straight lines with a cross surmounting a circle in the
center, I believe it is more appropriately seen as two crescents, back to
back. Seen in this way Uranus combines the energies of Jupiter and
Saturn and brings the full cycle of reflection into play as we learn the

lessons of the physical plane. Ronald Davison describes the symbol for Uranus as the cross of matter above the circle of spirit between the twin columns of good and evil.

Neptune – Sensitivity -- At its most obvious and familiar the symbol for Neptune depicts the trident of Poseidon, lord of the sea. The symbolic elements of this glyph are the crescent of receptivity, pierced by the cross of matter. In earlier times Neptune's trident was drawn as two crescents back to back with a cross piercing the middle. This resembles the older symbol for Uranus and indicates the cycles of the soul's expression crucified on the cross of material existence.

Pluto – Redemption -- Pluto's glyph shows the circle of spirit contained within the crescent of receptivity above the cross of materiality. The elements of this symbol alter the arrangement of the circle, cross and crescent in Mercury's glyph. In the case of Pluto the essence of spirit is now contained within the receptive image of the soul. This symbol embodies the ultimate goal of redemption at the end of the long journey on the Path of Return.

By studying the relative strengths and freedom of expression of certain planets in a horoscope, and likewise the challenges to expression of others, we can gain a sense of the symbolic thrust of the life. For example (and to oversimplify), if Mars is the dominant planet in a horoscope, the life will be characterized by the need to develop the right use of will and overcome fear of conflict by continuing battles which present themselves. By contrast if Pluto is the ruler of the chart the path may require renunciation of "earthly" concerns and a turning of mind and heart toward transforming the physical appetites and cultivating a more spiritual focus.

Atlantis Rising #55 December 2005

26. GEOMETRY OF THE SPHERES: ASTROLOGY, NUMBER & SACRED GEOMETRY

"Mathematics expresses values that reflect the Cosmos, including orderliness, balance, harmony, logic, and abstract beauty."

Deepak Chopra

Sunflower spiral center (SnappyGoat.com 94184)

I believe what we call time is an unfolded circle that we experience like a line in the third dimension. Our perception of reality is stepped down so what is happening all at once from one perspective, or higher dimension, is seen as linear and sequential from our limited 3-D awareness.

Everything spins and moves in circles, spirals, or ellipses. The Hindu god Shiva is often depicted within a circle, dancing the Universe into circular manifestation. Shiva is a vastly ancient deity, representing the power of the life force that enlivens and motivates everything in form. Shiva is always pictured with a flute, symbolizing the transforming quality of vibration and sound.

There are wheels within wheels, seasons and rhythms in the vast cycles of our galaxy that pour down through the planes of manifestation, impinging on the lives of nations and individuals. Astrology is the study of some of the smaller cycles, using an archetypal language to define twelve signs and ten planets. A skilled astrologer uses this language to translate the coded, energetic blueprint of interactions of the planets and the signs at birth and throughout unfolding and repeating cycles.

Author and astrologer Dane Rudyar defined Astrology as a technique for the study of cycles. In his book, *The Lunation Cycle, a Key to Understanding Personality,* Rudyar remarked "Its (astrology's) main purpose is to establish the existence of regular patterns in the sequence of events constituting an individual's inner and outer experience; then to use the knowledge of these patterns in order to control the genesis, development, and recurrence of experiences and achieve mastery."

Measure is the means through which matter manifests as form, and number is the agency by which multiplicity emerges from unity. It is through number and geometry that the Universe is generated and maintained. Number is both vibration and frequency, and geometric patterns underlie all of existence. All geometry is sacred because meaning and archetype are contained in the shapes in the same way archetypal principles are contained in numbers.

Music is sacred geometry. The Sufi master musician and teacher, Inayat Khan said, "The nature of creation is the doubling of one. And it is this doubling aspect that is the cause of all duality in life; one part is positive, the other negative; one expressive, the other responsive. Therefore spirit and nature in this creation of duality stand face-to-face."

Certain shapes communicate symbolic meaning. The circle is a symbol of infinity since its border has no beginning or ending. The round shape symbolically conveys infinite potential and carries the notion of a womb, pregnant with possibilities. The circle is what lies behind creation before a cycle of manifestation. Zero is "no thing" before expression. The Zodiac is both a circle and a cycle.

The triangle or pyramid is a symbol of the divine principle of trinity, or threefold aspect of of Creator. Pointing upward, the triangle is an emblem of the element of fire and aspiration toward the divine.

Pointing downward, the triangle represents the element of water and divine energy moving into manifestation. A triangle is also a geometric representation of the number three, connoting growth and multiplicity.

A square has four sides and is therefore the geometric equivalent of four. A square and the number four convey stability and the idea of being anchored in the Earth. A cube, or solid square, signifies the physical realm and represents aspects of walking the spiritual path. Masons use squares to build buildings and the symbolic temple within.

Because humans have five fingers and toes on each of our appendages, and because when we stretch out our arms and legs we resemble a five-pointed star, five is said to be the number of humanity. Five is the number of change. The pentagram symbolically represents the work and experience of the human condition. Five-pointed stars represented celestial deities, and perhaps the completed work, when they were carved into temples in Egypt.

A Hexagram is formed by two intersecting triangles and shows the idea of balance and the reciprocity of opposite energies. Sometimes called the Seal of Solomon, the name of this figure in Hebrew is *Mogen David*, or seal of David, the shield of love.

Cycles reveal unfolding patterns of energy and opportunity that recur at different times, depending on the circumference of the circle. Many cultures celebrate feasts, or holy days, performing ceremonies at critical symbolic moments of the moving year to honor the cycles and what each phase represents.

Like a "freeze frame" we stop the action and study the quality of a particular image. When a point in time is isolated from the flow it becomes oracular in nature and divinatory. Time is not a still photograph, but like a haunting picture, a powerful moment in time may yield an illuminating vision. Astrological charts are cast for captured moments and studied and interpreted like X-Rays.

As the planets move, shifting angular relationships form between them in a definable sequence, and different energetic formulas develop as the character of a planet is affected by the zodiacal sign it occupies and the tension formed with other planets. Aspects between planets, or their angular relationships, are based on divisions of the circle. The characteristic of the angle has a similar nature to the archetypal meaning of the number used to divide the circle, resulting in harmonic frequencies in a horoscope. Aspects convey the meaning of numbers by virtue of their geometry. In his book *Horoscope Symbols*, astrologer Robert Hand remarked, "The nature of aspects does not arise out of the relationships among the signs . . . the relationships among the signs arise from the numbers that divide the circle into aspects."

The most commonly used aspects are divisions of the circle by one, two, three, four and six. Also described here is one-fifth of a circle. Other numbers and aspects, including multiples of seven, eight and nine, are used less frequently.

∼

One - One is always first and stands alone. Symbolically one cannot be divided. Unity can only create by a process of addition. Meanings of the number one include initiation, unity, beginning, initiative, singleness, isolation, originality and self-conscious. In the vertical, linear form of the Arabic numeral one initiation of movement begins with the vertical line that connects above to below, showing the place where heaven touches earth. Two planets occupying the same degree is called a conjunction and divides the circle by one. A conjunction relates to the number one, embodying a union of planetary energies and a singular focus of combined energies. The result depends on the nature of the planets involved.

Two - In the expression of two the energy of manifestation moves from singularity to duality. Two is a perfect replica of one, created by addition, and is the first divisible number. Meanings of the number two include duplication, duality, reflection, replication, division, recreation, receptivity, dependence, polarity, division, double, twin, mirror image, antagonism, opposition, complementary, alternate, life force and sub-consciousness. One half of a circle is 180 degrees and two planets on either side is termed an opposition. The opposition gives the experience of polarity and standoff, but also potentially unites complementary energies, just like the number two.

Three - Three expresses the perfect outworking of the principles of one and two and grows through multiplication. Meanings of the number three include: multiplication, trinity, development, imagination, growth, creativity, unfoldment, pro-creation, and expression. One-third of a circle is 120 degrees and a trine aspect. The energy of a free-flowing trine brings ease, and like the number three gives growth and multiplicity of the planetary energies which relate in this way. Sometimes this ease creates a troubling inertia.

Four - The number four carries the memory of the order of manifestation and an understanding of the lay of the land, moving from the first three numbers. Meanings of the number four include: classification, order, reason, measurement, recording, planning, surveying, naming, tabulating, stability, geometry and topography. One-fourth of a circle is 90 degrees and a square angle. The square aspect is usually considered the most difficult. Squares place two energies at cross purposes and make it harder to see what's at work behind the scenes.

Five - The number five embodies the law that proceeds from the abstract order of the number four. Five stands in the middle of the numbers one through nine. Meanings of the number five include: mediation, change, adaptation, means, agency, activity, process, uncertainty, instability, transition and versatility. One-fifth of a circle is 72 degrees and is called a Quintile. Quintiles, like the number five, are a dynamic energy which carry the potential for genius if grasped and developed.

Six - One form of the number six is two interconnected triangles, forming a perfectly balanced symmetry. Six embodies the perfected union of opposites and rests in the center of the Qabalistic Tree of Life. Meanings of the number six include: equilibration, balance, symmetry, harmony of opposites, balanced polarities, reciprocity, love and complementary activities. Dividing the circle by six yields a slice of sixty degrees and is called a sextile aspect. Sextiles offer growth, but require work and choice. Effort is necessary to achieve the balanced polarities inherent in the meaning of the number six.

Drawing lines between aspects can also form a kind of "solid" geometry or harmonic resonance within a chart. Configurations called Grand Trines (three planets in trine to each other), Grand Crosses (two intersecting oppositions), T-Squares and Kites (a Grand Trine pierced by an opposition), contain more powerful impact because they are formed of multiple planets. Some of these configurations are somewhat common, while others, such as a Grand Sextile, may be seen only once in an astrologer's career. These geometric astrological formations can take on a significance that dominates the quality of the horoscope, vibrating like the powerful keynote of a number above all other influences.

A kaleidoscope is an optical instrument that uses a reflecting surface and bits of colored glass. Rotating the lens creates beautiful symmetric patterns in a series of unfolding designs. The geometry of astrology works in a similar manner. Depending on the planet, and the duration of its orbit around the Sun, we experience complete cycles of planetary geometry or portions of the pattern. Mercury speeds around the Sun three times in a year, but Pluto takes more than 240 years to make one circuit. Our experience and understanding of time can be deepened by a combined perspective of a single, beautiful but ephemeral, geometric expression or by seeing life like a kaleidoscope in constant motion. Paradoxically, if our conscious is focused in the "now," we experience both the magic of the moment and the mystery of the flow.

Atlantis Rising #41 August 2003

27. THE POLES OF THE ZODIAC: THE NATURE OF POLARITY

"You can never find yourself until you face the truth."

Pearl Bailey, American actress and singer

Dephi Greece - site of famous ancient pre-Hellenic Oracle (photo by author)

Above the doorway to the temple of Delphi in ancient Greece hung the admonition, "Know Thyself." Astrologically speaking, knowing ourselves, understanding the true nature of our "sign," depends in part upon embracing the opposite.

Modern magazines, newspapers and web sites are filled with astrological Sun Sign forecasts that eager readers consume, hoping for guidance and insight into their increasingly complex lives. Sun Signs are divisions of time and space based on the Sun's apparent annual journey through a circular band of sky called the ecliptic.

Astrologers divide the 360-degree circle of the year into twelve equal segments of thirty degrees each, resulting in the familiar twelve zodiacal signs. In this system Aries, the first sign, has the number one position. The Sun's annual journey begins in March at Spring Equinox in the northern hemisphere as Autumn begins down under. As the Sun seems to advance through the year its place in the sky and signs changes, progressing from Aries in Spring, to Cancer at summer solstice, through Libra at the beginning of autumn, and into Capricorn at winter solstice. The equinoxes are reversed in the southern hemisphere. The four arms of this axis are called the cardinal points of the year and form a conceptual frame or wheel of time.

Six pairs, or twelve of a kind?

The twelve signs of the zodiac can be viewed in a sequential or linear fashion, beginning with Aries and progressing through Pisces. Seen this way the experience of the signs represents an unfolding journey and an experience of the soul moving through time and space to gain experience. The nature of the signs develops from a personal and very individual orientation in Aries, the first sign, to a transpersonal and collective orientation in Pisces, the Fishes, which swim in the cosmic ocean. Moving from the Sun outward through the Solar System the planets are symbolically viewed the same way.

The word zodiac comes from Greek and means "circle of animals." A Russian proverb states that every road has two directions. So it is with the highways we call the signs of the Zodiac. This circle of stars is formed by energies which alternate in gender or positive or negative "charge." Beginning with masculine, projective Aries the signs alternate polarity every other sign.

The two ends of any spectrum are both polarized and complementary. Between the extremes of black and white lie infinite shades of gray. Between hot and cold are varying degrees of temperature. Lying along the spectrum of wet and dry are degrees of humidity. The qualitative energy of the twelve signs are also six pairs of polarized expression, operating as continuums. Therefore, the sign on the opposite side of the circle of animals is also of opposite polarity.

Since we view the position of the Sun, the Sun Sign, from our home planet, the opposite sign is where the Earth resides. In some circles knowing your enemy is as important as knowing yourself. Astrologically one of the keywords, or ways of understanding the aspect of polarity or opposition (180 degrees), is "awareness." When we acknowledge and recognize what confronts us we begin to understand ourselves. The opposition can denote both balance or imbalance, cooperation or conflict, depending on awareness.

Aries - Libra Continuum of personal expression -- Mars-ruled Aries is the fiery sign of action. Venus-ruled Libra is the airy sign of partnership. Aries initiates and Libra responds. This polarity offers the extremes of domination or acquiescence, leading or following, with the higher ground pointing the way toward partnership and cooperation. As the energy moves back and forth along this continuum we shift from individual action to joint effort. The goal is the middle ground of taking turns and perceiving strength and talent based on specific situations.

Taurus - Scorpio Continuum of resource -- Earthy Taurus gathers possessions while the deep waters of Scorpio desires intense experiences. This energy moves along the line of what we personally possess to how we spend or invest these resources. Taurus can hoard possessions like a miser while Scorpio can indiscriminately spend their resources. The goal of this pair is knowing when and what to acquire and how to utilize our energy appropriately on every level. Money is "green" energy and sex is life energy. How do we store, keep a savings, or pass the energy on?

Gemini - Sagittarius Continuum of mental exploration -- Gemini is perhaps the quintessential air sign, darting mentally and physically in every direction, seeking stimulation. Fiery Sagittarius pulls back his bow and aims his arrow high, but frequently without a target. Gemini tends to explore close at hand while Sagittarius roams far afield. This spectrum explores how we move out of our home base, familiar territory and into the macrocosm. Do we shoot our arrows just for the thrill of it? Synthesis is the key for this pair. Stop, look and listen might be the motto for both. Why am I exploring, and of what value is the data collected?

Cancer - Capricorn Continuum of field of influence -- This duo contrasts home and family with work and career. Cancer feels the pull of roots and heritage while Capricorn strives to climb the heights of power and position. This polarizes the personal domain of hearth and home versus making a mark in field and town. The goal of this polarity is understanding our personal impact on our world and learning the consequences of our acts. Whether we are the nurturing influence to an Einstein or Mother Teresa, or whether we go out into the world to make a fortune, this spectrum can teach us the relationship between our base of security and our ability to strive and overcome.

Leo - Aquarius Continuum of personal power -- In a sense, Leo represents the king and Aquarius the kingdom. This pair moves us along the continuum from potentially dogmatic dictatorship through rebellion for its sake. One end of this polarity examines how authority is held and power over others is wielded, while the other side examines how we respond to impulses toward Individuation and personal freedom. Even monarchs have to obey natural law, and everyone is ultimately subject to some authority. How we deal with authority, whether following orders or directing others, is the domain of this energetic couple. Is Utopia defined by an enlightened monarch or a conscious, contributing populace? The goal is true understanding of rulership and the concept of noblesse oblige as well as the role of the enlightened members of a republican democracy.

Virgo - Pisces Continuum of assimilation -- In the case of practical Virgo the approach is to dissect the parts, isolating each unique snowflake or grain of sand as an individual. At the other extreme, Pisces is immersed in the ocean unaware of solitary drops of water. Virgo analyzes details through a microscope while Pisces gazes dreamily through a telescope. Do we take everything apart into its component pieces or just swim in collective awareness, unaware of distinction? The goal of this duality is knowing when to differentiate and when to blend.

Principles in Action

Zodiacal signs represent qualities of experience while planets embody archetypal expressions of energy. Using the Leo-Aquarius polarity, we can examine a current planetary opposition to see how polarities operate. Jupiter in Leo will oppose Neptune in Aquarius for the second time on June 2, 2003 (the last time was Sep 11, 2002) . We will feel this influence building in April and peaking at the beginning of June.

Jupiter represents growth and abundance. The planet of expansion and lavish expression, operating in Leo, the sign of image, drama and outward display brings to mind the words of Fernando, a character from the Saturday Night Live program, "It is better to look good than to feel good." Appearance can become more important than substance and a great deal of roaring and posturing may mask inner feelings of doubt and lack.

Neptune, god of the sea, embodies idealism and mysticism but also brings deception, camouflage, and illusion. Neptune moving through Aquarius stimulates both idealistic imagination and blind faith. Neptune can signify the highest spiritual ideal to which we can aspire as well as a delusion of oneness and temporary ecstasy. Neptune holds up a magic mirror in which we see what we want to see, or bravely pierce the illusion, perceiving underlying truth behind appearances.

When these planets oppose one other in opposite signs we may experience conflicting urges of self-indulgence, struggling with impulses to act for the greater good. The issues are wisdom versus denial, truth versus illusion, and bombast versus substance. Powerful potential for wisdom and inspired rulership exist along side showy self-indulgence.

This combination of energies has the potential for a collective experience akin to the story of the Emperor's new clothes. Will we share a collective illusion or be able to see the naked truth? We may lean toward individual self-interest, blind to needs of unknown others who suffer as a result, or we may sense our connectedness and make choices that heal and benefit the whole. Patterns of thought and choice will play out in our families, our one-on-one relationships, and in the global arena.

Before the discovery of Neptune, Jupiter was considered to be the ruler of the sign Pisces, and Jupiter still holds influence over Pisces as co-ruler. A deep mystery of Pisces, embodied in the opposition of the two planets that hold rulership of this mystical sign, lies in the paradox of unity and diversity. Contained within this mystery is the path of sacrifice on behalf others. When we understand the unity of all things, an unselfish act becomes second nature because we see that there is no separation. In the interwoven web of life the choice of one of us can ultimately affects the condition of all of us.

Atlantis Rising #39 April 2003

PART IV

DWARF PLANETS, PLUTOIDS & ASTEROIDS

28. PLANET TO PLUTOID: PLUTO'S IDENTITY CRISIS

"The name of Eris was so appropriate, it's enough to make me almost start believing in astrology."

Dr. Mike Brown, Caltech Astronomy Team Leader

The Plutoids

Technology is dramatically expanding our Solar System as the light-gathering capacity of telescopes increases the number of objects we see in the sky to billions. The IAU, the International Astronomical Organization, brings together nearly ten thousand distinguished astronomers from all nations. In August of 2006, the IAU downgraded Pluto from a planet to a dwarf planet. According to new rules, which define a planet for the first time, a planet must meet three criteria: it must orbit the Sun; it must be big enough for gravity to make it round; and it must have enough mass to clear other objects from its orbital neighborhood.

The third measure knocked out Pluto, which orbits among the icy wrecks of the Kuiper Belt, along with Ceres, which is in the asteroid belt. It was the 2003 discovery of Eris -- a body bigger and farther from the Sun than Pluto -- that led to Pluto's demotion in a contentious international meeting.

In June of 2008 the IAU voted to establish a new class of substellar objects called plutoids. Pluto regains some dignity lost through his diminished status by becoming the prototype of a new category of Trans-Neptunian Objects, TNOs≥He now sets the standard by which all similar bodies will be measured. Astronomers expect more plutoids to be named in the future, but as of this writing there are officially four: Pluto, Eris, Haumea, and Make-make. Pluto is also a plutino--the unofficial, but nearly universally accepted, name for objects in a 2:3 orbital resonance with Neptune. For every two orbits around the Sun that a plutino makes, Neptune orbits three times.

By definition plutoids are "bright celestial bodies that orbit the Sun beyond Neptune and have sufficient mass for self-gravity to overcome rigid body forces so they assume a near-spherical shape, but they have not cleared the vicinity around their orbit." What is fascinating is that the defining criterion is one of brightness and not of size, as size is difficult to determine for such distant objects. For the present, plutoids are distinguished by the brightness of their reflected light, suggesting symbolically that they can illuminate our consciousness in a new way.

The term plutoid joins a list of other odd appellations -- plutinos, centaurs, cubewanos and SDOs -- that astronomers have created in recent years to define objects in the outer Solar System. This part of our Sun's domain grows more complex every year.

Between Jupiter and Neptune, minor planets which act like both asteroids and comets, are called Centaurs, after the mythical Greek creatures with dual natures. Chiron is the most famous. Trojans are asteroids that don't reside in the Main Asteroid Belt, but travel in lockstep with Jupiter, orbiting the Sun either ahead of or behind the gas giant.

Beyond Neptune astronomers now divide space in the extended Solar System into three sections, which extend in "bands," billions of miles into space: the Kuiper Belt, Scattered Disk, and Oort Cloud. A Trans-Neptunian Object, or TNO, is any object in the Solar System that orbits the Sun at a greater distance, on average, than Neptune within this broad expanse. TNOs are grouped according to their orbital characteristics and distance from Neptune. Since 1992 more than a thousand TNOs have been identified and numbered, and the list keeps growing.

The Kuiper Belt is a disk-shaped ring of debris, similar to the Main Asteroid Belt, but largely unexplored, which contains short-period comets, asteroids, and tens of thousands of other objects, including Pluto. Many of the largest Kuiper Belt Objects could soon be reclassified as dwarf planets. Many objects found in the Kuiper Belt orbit the Sun in a 2:3 ratio to Neptune, like Pluto; meaning it takes one and one-half times longer to circle the Sun. The Kuiper Belt itself can be roughly divided into two regions: the "resonant" belt, consisting of objects whose orbits are linked to Neptune, generally called plutinos. The "classical" belt is a relatively thin region of space that corresponds to the same plane in which most of the planets orbit and consists of objects that don't have any resonance with Neptune.

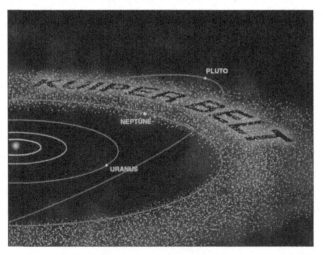

Kuiper Belt (image credit NASA)

Overlapping the Kuiper Belt, but extending much further outwards, is the Scattered Disk. Scattered Disk Objects, or SDOs, form their own ring of rocky, icy objects. These objects may still be influenced by Neptune's gravity, but their orbits are eccentric and inclined. An SDO's distance to the Sun varies enormously and can reach billions of kilometers.

The third division is the Oort Cloud, named for astronomer Jan Oort, who theorized its existence to explain the mysterious origin of long-period comets. The Oort Cloud is a thousand times farther from the Sun than the Kuiper Belt. The Oort Cloud is a hypothetical spherical cloud of rocky and icy debris, leftover material from the formation of the solar system, which suggests that the aura of our star is colossal. Scientists estimate that the distance to the Oort Cloud is one light year, a quarter of the way to the nearest star. Although located ten times closer than expected, astronomers believe dwarf planet Sedna is confirmation of the existence of the Oort cloud, revealing that this giant cloud extends much farther into the solar system than previously believed.

Plutinos -- A plutino is a Trans-Neptunian Object in 2:3 mean motion resonance with Neptune, like Pluto. Plutinos are the largest class of the resonant TNOs. The name refers only to orbital resonance and does not imply common physical characteristics. Plutinos form the inner part of the Kuiper Belt, closest to Neptune, and represent about a quarter of the known Kuiper Belt Objects. The largest plutinos include Pluto, Orcus, Ixion and several others with numbers but no names as yet.

Cubewanos -- 1992 QB1 was the first Kuiper Belt Object discovered sixty years after Charon, Pluto's Moon. During the intervening time our awareness of the Solar System was strangely static. QB1-0 was in the classical Kuiper Belt and not a plutino. As it happened the science fiction name of cubewano, phonetically based on the letters and numbers, stuck. Objects with similar characteristics are now collectively called cubewanos. Make-Make, Haumea, Varuna, and Quaoar are cubewanos.

Scattered Disk Objects -- SDOs are believed to have been ejected from the Kuiper Belt by the gravitational influence of the giant planets and thrown into erratic orbits in the outer fringes. Their orbits are highly inclined to the ecliptic plane, and are often almost perpendicular. SDOs are unlike plutinos which are locked into orbital resonance with Neptune. Eris, a new plutoid, is twice as large as Pluto and the largest Scattered Disk Object so far.

Plutoids -- To date, Pluto, Eris, Makemake and Haumea are the Trans-Neptunian Objects that have official Plutoid status. Plutoids are identified by their brightness and could appear in any part of the extended range beyond Neptune. Among those already named who are likely to join the group are Sedna, Quaoar, Varuna, and Orcus. As many as seventy may already have the required characteristics. Plutoids must be farther from the Sun than Neptune, so Ceres is a dwarf planet, but not a plutoid, as it is located in the main asteroid belt between Mars and Jupiter.

Pluto and 8 Dwarves -- The IAU has established guidelines for naming celestial objects under the auspices of the Committee on Small Body Nomenclature. Essentially, dwarf planets beyond Neptune are categorized by their orbital characteristics. Plutinos, objects with a similar size and orbit to that of Pluto, are named after underworld deities. Classical KBOs, those not in resonance with Neptune's orbit, are given names of mythical beings of creation. Mythically, we might say this addresses heaven and hell.

Dwarf planets can be used in astrology in a similar way as the so-called Fixed Stars. If a planet resides at a certain degree of Celestial Longitude, and a star or dwarf planet is at the same degree, then a deeper meaning can be explored in the horoscope. How might the myths of these dwarf planets blend with the energy of a traditional planet, adding a more subtle meaning? I've chosen the four official plutoids, and four who are likely to receive this status soon, to briefly examine mythically and astrologically. (Degrees of the Tropical Zodiac, converted from Celestial Longitude, were taken from Philip Sedgwick's site www.philipsedgwick.com, rounded the degrees).

Pluto - 29 Sagittarius – Transformation -- Pluto himself has been transformed and is the first plutoid and a plutino. In myth he is lord of the underworld where he rules over the souls of the dead. Pluto is all about the Shadow, the part of us that is unseen and unacknowledged. What lies buried in the depths of the underworld can be gifts, curses, wounds or legacies. We have to mine for precious gems and minerals. As Pluto moves into Capricorn in January 2009 many structures will be annihilated, transformed, and reformed.

Eris - 21 Aries – Discord -- Eris is the largest plutoid and a Scattered Disk Object. She was named after the Greek goddess of discord who myth says triggered the Trojan War. Eris is currently the largest known TNO. True to her nature, her discovery caused the demotion of Pluto. She asks where things need to be overturned and reexamined, questioning the status quo and not taking things for granted.

Haumea - 15 Libra – Renewal -- Haumea is a plutoid and a cubewano. She is a great Hawaiian mother-creator goddess who is embodied in the Makalei tree of Hawaii. She is the mother of many children, each of whom emerge from a different part of her body. Her nature is ever-renewing. Haumea is a nourishing source of life and teaches faith in the continual cycles of rebirth.

Ixion - 13 Sagittarius – Transgression -- Ixion is a plutino. In myth he was a mortal king but a descendant of the god Ares. Ixion is said to be the first human to shed kin's blood. He paid for this, but then offended Zeus by raping Nephele, a creature made of clouds, and thereby giving birth to the centaurs. As punishment, Ixion is eternally chained to a wheel of fire in the underworld. His lesson is the inevitability of paying for our sins.

Make-make - 25 Virgo – Fertility -- Makemake is the third largest plutoid and a cubewano. Makemake is the creator god of the bird cult of Rapa Nui island, better known as Easter Island. He created humanity and is revered as a bird with a human head, and is seen in sea birds of the area. He reminds us of our connection to nature and the sea, and the inherent wisdom of instinct.

Orcus - 1 Virgo – Retribution -- Orcus is a large plutino, and appears physically to be a "twin" of Pluto. Orcus is an Etruscan god, precursors of the Romans, from the area now called Tuscany. He was portrayed in tomb paintings as a bearded and hairy giant. He is a lord of the underworld whose specialty is punishing broken oaths. His lesson is the importance of honoring our vows.

Quaoar - 17 Sagittarius – Generation -- Quaoar is a large cubewano. He is the personified force of creation of the Tongva Indians of California near Los Angeles, also known as the Gabrielenos. Quaoar sings the Song of Creation and dances the world into existence out of primeval chaos. Quaoar shows us the power of joy in bringing forth new life.

Sedna- 21 Taurus – Reclamation -- Sedna is called an E-SDO, an Extended Scattered Disk Object, as she lives in the frigid outer reaches of the Kuiper Belt, perhaps on the fringes of the Oort Cloud. She is goddess of the Arctic deep of the Inuit people who were once called Eskimos. Her story is one of betrayal, sacrifice, and redemption. The Inuit beseech her permission to hunt the creatures of the sea on which their lives depend. Sedna teaches us to never take Nature for granted.

Varuna - 21 Cancer – Judgment -- Varuna is a large cubewano. In ancient myth he was a celestial Hindu god, a universal monarch, judge and guardian of cosmic law. Varuna created the three worlds of heaven, earth, and the space between. His name means "coverer" as in the starry canopy. Varuna reminds us that we cannot violate cosmic law without consequences.

For sixty years our Solar System has been a fairly static reality and now change is happening so fast it's difficult to keep pace. We live in a universe of mega proportions that changes even as we observe it and makes mystics of the most rational among us. Rather than losing Pluto, I believe astrologers have gained a growing number of enriching, new archetypal and mythical influences to consider, albeit "dwarves." As more deities from world mythologies step out of the darkness and reveal themselves to us we can learn more about ourselves and widen our consciousness horizons. We are invited to enhance the faculty of intuition, opening to the wisdom of a much grander vista of existence.

Atlantis Rising #73 December 2008

29.PLUTO'S ONGOING TRANSFORMATION

" A sking the proper questions is the central action of
transformation. Questions are the keys that cause the secret
doors of the psyche to swing open."

Clarissa Pinkola-Estes

Charon and Pluto's Moons (NASA public domain)

In July 2011 astronomers using the Hubble Space Telescope identified a fourth moon orbiting the icy world of Pluto, making the dwarf planet the first object in the Kuiper Belt to have more than one satellite. Temporarily dubbed P4 the tiny moon appeared in a survey searching for rings around Pluto. For now P4 is the smallest of Pluto's moons. Since three of Pluto's four moons have been identified in the last five years, scientists believe it's likely more will be discovered.

Charon, Pluto's largest and innermost moon, is thought to be about 650 miles in diameter, more than 1,000 kms. Charon is so massive relative to Pluto that the two actually mutually orbit a point that is outside Pluto's interior, like a dumbbell spinning in space. Although Charon is officially a moon of Pluto, the two are actually a binary system--a double dwarf planet. Charon is larger, compared to Pluto, than any other moon is to a planet or dwarf planet-- half its diameter and 1/8 its mass. Pluto and Charon are also unusual among planetary systems because they are tidally locked, so they always present the same face to each other. From any position on either body, the other is always in the same position in the sky.

Pluto's home is the Kuiper Belt, a region of the Solar System that extends from the orbit of Neptune at 30 AU (Astronomical Unit), to approximately 50 AU from the Sun. One AU is the distance from Earth to the Sun, approximately 93 million miles, or 150 million kilometers. The Kuiper Belt is similar to the asteroid belt, but far larger—20 times as wide and 20 to 200 times as massive. Like the asteroid belt, it contains mostly small bodies believed to be remnants from the formation of the Solar System. Since its discovery in 1992 the number of known Kuiper Belt objects (KBOs), has increased to over a thousand, and more than 70,000 KBOs over 62 miles/100 km in diameter are believed to exist.

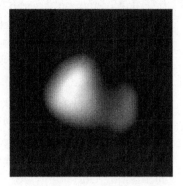

P4 is now named Kerberos (NASA public domain)

Studies since the mid-nineties indicate that the classical Kuiper Belt is dynamically stable, and periodic comets, those with orbits lasting less than 200 years, actually originate in the scattered disc. The scattered disc is an active region that scientists believe was created by the outward motion of Neptune 4.5 billion years ago. Scattered disc objects, such as dwarf planet Eris, have extremely eccentric orbits that take them as far as 100 AU from the Sun. The hypothesized Oort Cloud, home to dwarf planet Sedna, is a thousand times more distant than the Kuiper Belt. Objects within the Kuiper belt, together with the members of the scattered disc and Oort cloud objects, are collectively referred to as trans-Neptunian objects, or TNOs.

Pluto's origin and identity have long puzzled astronomers. Pluto's orbit is very elliptical, not circular like the other planets, and is also inclined relative to the plane where the other planets circle the Sun. One early hypothesis was that Pluto was an escaped moon of Neptune, knocked out of orbit by its largest moon, Triton. Pluto's true place in the Solar System only began to reveal itself in 1992, when astronomers started to find small icy objects beyond Neptune that were similar to Pluto, not only in orbit, but also in size and composition. Astronomers believe that Pluto is the largest member of the Kuiper Belt. Recent Hubble telescope photographs of Pluto have revealed a surprising yellow-black sphere with a surface that seems more dynamic than anything else in the solar system. In fact, dynamo seems like a good description of the Pluto-Charon system. Dynamo comes from the Greek word *dynamis,* meaning power, and is a device that generates electro-magnetic energy. Although it's not yet known for certain, Pluto may have a magnetic field. If so, the combined influenced of the unique double dwarf system with Charon would likely enhance this.

The origin of Pluto's moons is still a mystery. The currently accepted theory of Charon's formation is similar to the theory of the creation of Earth's Moon—another tidally locked dynamo. It's believed that an impact between two large Kuiper Belt Objects chipped Charon away from a proto-Pluto, putting the chunk of Pluto's mass into orbit. Over time, tidal forces slowed the pair and Charon settled into its present orbit. Although there are problems with the idea, one recent theory suggests that Pluto's moons Nix and Hydra might be a byproduct of this collision and are shattered fragments of the huge impact. Alternatively, Nix and Hydra may have formed from the rocky debris left over from the development of the Solar System, and this may hold true for the countless other Kuiper Belt Objects. It's hoped that the New Horizons mission, which was launched to the far reaches of the Solar System in January of 2006, will reveal answers to some of the questions that remain in the mysterious Kuiper Belt.

In myth, Hades, meaning "the unseen," was the ancient Greek god of the underworld. Hades was also called "Plouton," meaning "Rich One," who the Romans Latinized as Pluto. The Romans associated Pluto/Hades with their own underworld gods, Dis Pater and Orcus. The corresponding Etruscan god was Aita. In Chinese, Japanese, and Korean the name was translated as "underworld king star." Many other non-European languages use a transliteration of the name Pluto, and some Indian languages use of form of Yama, the Guardian of Hell in Hindu myth. Charon, Pluto's largest companion, was named after the ferryman from Greek myth who carried the souls of the newly deceased across the River Acheron, which divided the world of the living from that of the dead. In Christian theology, and in New Testament Greek, Hades is parallel to the Hebrew *sheol*, "grave," or "dirt pit," and also refers to the abode of the dead. The Christian concept of hell is more related to the Greek Tartarus, a deep, gloomy part of Hades that was used as a dungeon of torment and suffering. In belief systems such as animism it was seen as the place from which life originated and to which life returned at death, and it carried no negative undertones.

Hades was surrounded by a series of rivers: the *Acheron*, river of woe, the *Cocytus*, river of lamentation, the *Phlegethon*, river of fire, the *Styx*, river of unbreakable oath by which the gods swear, and the *Lethe* river of forgetfulness. Charon actually ferried the dead across the River Acheron, but it is now popularly believed that it was the River Styx. Styx was the Greek goddess of the river, and she was usually said to be the daughter of Nyx. The gods swore their oaths by the water of her river, which circled the Underworld nine times. Violating such an oath would result in the loss of their immortality. The rivers Styx, Phlegethon, Archeron, and Cocytus all converged at the center of the underworld on a great marsh, which was also sometimes called the Styx.

Hermes/Mercury led the souls of the dead to the entrance of the underworld and to the single ferry run by Charon, which carried the souls across the River Acheron. Only those who could pay the fare, with coins placed on their lips when buried, received passage. The rest were trapped between two worlds. Once across the river, the three-headed hound Kerberus guarded the entrance to the kingdom. Kerberus allowed all to enter through the strong metal gate but none could leave. According to Virgil's Aeneid (book 6), the Cumaean Sibyl directed Aeneas to the golden bough that was necessary to cross the river alive and return to the world of the living. Orpheus also made the round trip successfully.

Once inside, the souls appeared before a panel of three judges. The very good went to the Elysian Fields, while others were singled out for special treatment or punishment. Hades vast palace lay deep within the kingdom and was always filled with guests. Four months of the year his wife Persephone was required to be in residence. During this time the surface of the Earth was barren while her mother, Demeter grieved.

Nix, Pluto's second moon, was the primordial Greek goddess of darkness and night, and Charon's mother. Nyx, "night", Nox in Latin, was a shadowy figure who stood at or near the beginning of creation, and was also the mother of Hypnos "sleep," and Thanatos, "death." Nyx occupied a cave or *adyton*, where she pronounced oracles. Although her mythic references are few, they reveal her as a figure of exceptional power and beauty. Nyx took on an even more important role in several fragmentary poems attributed to Orpheus where she, rather than Chaos, appeared as the first principle of Creation.

Hydra, the third moon, was a many-headed, serpent-like water beast that guarded a back entrance to the underworld located deep below the surface of a lake. The monstrous serpent would periodically rise from the murky swamps of Lake Lerna and terrorize the city. In some stories the Hydra was born from the river Styx, and also appeared as the second in the twelve labors of Hercules. The number of heads varied in different versions of the legend, but most accounts agree on nine. If the heads were cut off, they would grow back, and severing one head resulted in two reappearing. The middle one was immortal and contained poisonous venom. Nine is a recurring theme in this context. Pluto was the ninth planet for a time; the Hydra had nine heads, the River Styx circled the underworld nine times, and there were nine hells in Mayan cosmology.

Moon P4 (now named for the three-headed guard hound Kerberos) orbits Pluto between Nix and Hydra, and is estimated to have a diameter of 8-21 miles, or 13-34 kilometers. It will be fascinating to see what name the tiny moon will be given and how that will enter the mythic blend of Pluto's family. Candidates for names might include one of the other underworld rivers, like Styx or Acheron. Styx would introduce the element of swearing an unbreakable oath, while Acheron would represent a permanent shift into another state of being.

Eventually, Hades came to designate the actual abode of the dead, the underworld itself, as well as its ruler, so in a symbolic and astrological sense, Pluto-Charon transports us to that realm. Likewise, the Kuiper belt can be seen like the river that separates the living and dead. As the largest object in the Kuiper belt Pluto may somehow collect and magnetize the energy and significance of the whole belt. And, with the effect of its unique double-dwarf nature, Pluto-Charon may represent how we can be transported across a river of consciousness to this deeper, and usually hidden, aspect of our psyche. Similar to the Earth-Moon symbolism, Pluto-Charon may hold a key to unlocking knowledge and shadow material that ordinarily remains concealed beneath conscious awareness.

Currently, dwarf planet Pluto-Charon in Capricorn, and Uranus in Aries, are forming a square aspect. They will move in and out of this 90-degree angle for the next four years, making seven exact hits—the most connections possible. Astrologically this creates a potent tension between Pluto's powers of transformation in the sign of structure and the awakening and potentially shattering energy of Uranus. This may serve to topple power structures that no longer serve the greater good and to awaken us to higher forms of expression. We can also examine this aspect in light of Pluto's changing significance. Pluto is no longer a planet, but he is unique, and his dynamic relationship with Charon intensifies this. Although it is counter-intuitive, astrologers still experience Pluto as powerful. This strong, and somewhat puzzling influence, may be related to the double-dwarf planet relationship between Pluto and Charon.

I believe the ongoing square aspect between Uranus and Pluto has the potential to reveal what needs to be awakened and redeemed within individuals and the collective. This can be seen as a stunning wake-up call at the cusp of a new age, revealing how we use, abuse, or abdicate power in our lives. Our work over the next four years, if we choose, is to undertake a shamanic journey deep within our own underworld and discover what's been buried that needs to be resurrected, released, redeemed or consciously integrated. This symbolic journey could result in profound personal and planetary healing.

Atlantis Rising #92 February 2012

30. TWELFTH PLANET, PLUTINO, OR PLANET X?

"Your theory of a donut-shaped universe intrigues me, Homer."

Dr. Stephen Hawking, guest-voicing on the popular, long running, animated television series *The Simpsons*

Artist's impression of size comparison of Quaoar with other objects (NASA/JPL Caltech)

From the relative proximity of the Moon to the vast distance of the heart of our galaxy astronomy is making CNN headline news. Recent reports include: confirmation of a Black Hole at the center of our own galaxy, discovery of large Kuiper Belt Objects (KBO), location of a Jupiter-sized planet in a binary star system, and sighting of a Near Earth Object (NEO) that was at first dubbed Earth's second Moon. Our paradigm of the Solar System and galaxy is being radically altered. Some of these discoveries may challenge traditional astrology.

In October 2002 astronomers announced confirmation of a colossal black hole at the center of our galaxy based on observations of the star closest to the heart of the Milky Way. Rainer Schoedel, at the Max Planck Institute for Astrophysics in Garching, Germany said, "We can now confidently say that a black hole does indeed exist at the center of our galaxy."

Closer to home, in a story reminiscent of *Star Trek, The Motion Picture*, a surprising object was discovered on September 3, 2002. Thought at first to be an asteroid, astronomers realized the object was orbiting Earth, not the Sun. The NEO (Near Earth Object), christened J002E3, has yet to be clearly identified. Experts at NASA's Jet Propulsion Laboratory (JPL) believe it could be the third-stage booster of the Saturn V rocket which propelled Apollo 12 astronauts to the Moon in November 1969. (The object was confirmed to be the S-IVB third stage of Apollo 12 Saturn V rocket).

Our Sun is in the minority as a solitary star. The majority of Milky Way stars have companions. On October 6, 2002 CNN announced discovery of the first-ever planet in orbit around one star in the binary star system Gamma Cephei. The implications are that many more planetary systems may exist within our galaxy than previously believed.

Atlantis Rising readers will be acquainted with the work of Sumerian scholar Zecharia Sitchin and his ground-breaking work. Sitchin decoded Sumerian creation myths and demonstrated that advanced astronomical knowledge was contained there. Images on cylinder seals depict what seem to be twelve planets in our solar system. He believes the myth is a form of cosmogeneis, explaining creation of the asteroid belt (a collision between the invading "Twelfth Planet" and another planet), and formation of Earth's Moon due to a catastrophic collision caused by the twelfth planet in ancient times. Called Nibiru this planet supposedly has a long elliptical orbit of 3,600 years.

At present nine known objects orbit between Jupiter and Neptune, including Chiron and Pholus. These objects have been designated as Centaurs. Their orbits are unstable, and these objects are believed to be refugees from the Kuiper Belt. If Chiron is ever "perturbed" by the gravity of the larger planets it will become a truly spectacular comet as it races toward the Sun. It is my belief that such an event in the distant past may be the source of the information decoded by Sitchin from Sumerian cylinder seals since the long, elliptical orbit described is more likely to belong to a long-period comet.

The term "Planet X" has a different history than Nibiru, Zecharia Sitchin's Twelfth Planet. Astronomers have searched for planets beyond those already known since 1841. Pluto itself was an illusive Planet X for a time. Certain websites have muddied these waters, claiming that an imaginary Planet X is Nibiru, and casting Sitchin's important work in a bad light with unsubstantiated apocalyptic predictions of a rogue planet striking the Earth.

Quaoar, a new world beyond Pluto - Shifting back to the outer reaches of the Solar System, in a region beyond the orbit of Neptune, a new object has recently been identified. Half the size of Pluto, and one-tenth the diameter of Earth, this new "world," has been named Quaoar (kwah-o-wahr), after a native American creator god. Quaoar orbits the Sun every 288 years in a region of the Solar System called the Kuiper Belt. Quaoar is also not Planet X.

Beyond Neptune is the Kuiper Belt (pronounced like viper), named for the astronomer Gerard Kuiper who predicted its existence. The Kuiper Belt is a disk-shaped ring that contains short-period comets, asteroids and tens of thousands of other objects, including Pluto and newly-discovered Quaoar. Some astronomers have dubbed these objects "plutinos." Many objects found in the Kuiper Belt orbit the Sun in a 3:2 ratio to Neptune, including Pluto; meaning it takes one and one-half times longer to circle the Sun.

The Oort cloud, named for astronomer Jan Oort, is an immense, spherical cloud of rocky and icy debris that surrounds our Solar System beyond the Kuiper Belt. This cloud is leftover material from the formation of the Solar System and is now believed to be the source of long-period comets. Comets are "dirty snowballs," rocky, icy objects which produce spectacular tails of dust and gas if they approach the Sun.

From an astrological perspective, Quaoar, and other objects in the Kuiper Belt, have the most immediate potential to alter common astrological wisdom. Even before Quaoar's discovery Pluto's status as a planet was being called into question because of growing awareness of large objects within the Kuiper Belt, Pluto's neighborhood. Many astronomers already believe that Pluto is not actually a planet but just another KBO—Kuiper Belt Object. (Pluto was officially demoted to dwarf planet in 2006). So how will astrologers adapt to the changing image of the smallest planet?

Before Herschel discovered Uranus in 1781, there was a convenient relationship between the known planets and their relationship with the twelve Zodiac signs. Astrologers speculated about other planets that would ultimately fill out rulership of the twelve signs. Planet Vulcan and the dark Moon Lilith were popular candidates.

Esoterically astrologers didn't miss a beat and defined the discovery of Uranus as an evolutionary step in humanity's unfoldment. When Neptune (1846), and Pluto (1930), in turn were "discovered" astrologers perceived that our collective consciousness as a human race had evolved to the point where we could recognize and respond to these higher planetary frequencies on a conscious level. Symbolically we were ready to move beyond the limiting rings of Saturn. Astrologers speak of the outer planets as "higher octaves" of Mercury, Venus, and Mars respectively, acting to raise our thoughts, feelings and actions above the realm of ordinary pursuits.

Pluto was discovered in 1930 by Clyde Tombaugh, who continued the work of Percival Lowell. Pluto's rocky composition, tiny size and atmosphere contrast dramatically with the four gas giants at the outer limits of the solar system. Pluto's orbit is highly elliptical, taking 248 years to cycle around the Sun. During this time the orbit's eccentricity causes Pluto to venture inside the orbit of Neptune for a period of twenty years.

Pluto's moon, Charon, is nearly half its size and was named after the mythical boatman who ferried souls across the river Styx to Hades. Astronomers believe that the Pluto-Charon system resulted from a collision with another small planet in the ancient past. At present this is also the most accepted scenario for the Earth-Moon system which agrees with Sumerian myth.

Pluto's origins were considered a mystery for a long time because of its small size relative to the other planets. Pluto orbits in the Kuiper Belt among tens of thousands of smaller objects orbiting beyond Neptune. Many astronomers now believe Pluto and Charon are merely the largest KBOs (Kuiper Belt Objects). Similarly, Triton, Neptune's largest moon, may have been a captured KBO. Quite a furor erupted in 1992 when a consideration of giving Pluto a dual status as small planet and KBO was discussed. Some astronomers believe more than a dozen objects larger than Pluto exist, and feel it's just a matter of time until a Pluto-sized object is detected in the Kuiper Belt. For the moment however, Pluto is a sentimental favorite and keeps its planetary status, albeit the smallest and coldest in our solar system family.

Pluto was named for the mythical god of the dead, Hades in Greek. He was an Olympian who was given rulership of the Underworld, called the House of Hades. Hades name meant "the Invisible," and was not spoken aloud for fear of arousing his anger. Instead he was most commonly called Pluton, "the Rich," signifying the wealth of mines cultivated beneath the Earth. He was often depicted with a horn of plenty.

Since Pluto's discovery astrologers have witnessed the paradox first hand that Pluto's small size is no indication of its influence. His astrological significance is viewed as an agent of transformation through annihilation. He rules the deep and complex sign of Scorpio. Astrologically and archetypically Hades, the Invisible, and Pluton, the Rich, fit well with the deep, psychological issues that must be mined when the influence of Pluto presents itself.

I believe we are at the brink of a shift with implications as profound as Copernicus's gift in showing us that Earth was not the center of the Universe. These new discoveries have the potential to impact and expand how astrologers interpret symbolic and archetypal content of the Solar System. Like the discoveries of Uranus, Neptune, and Pluto heralded new awareness, technology and transformation, so too will further discoveries take us to the next level in our unfolding pattern.

As new objects are discovered within the Kuiper Belt it is possible that we will experience an entirely different psychological mechanism. If Pluto is seen in a new light his symbolic significance may expand rather than diminish. Perhaps Pluto engages the collective energy of this second "hammered bracelet," like focusing sunlight through a magnifying glass, in an energetic manner we don't yet understand. Pluto's physical presence may come to be be seen as a gatekeeper, guarding access to the vast region of the outer solar system?

The Kuiper Belt itself may archetypically prove to be like the River Styx, and crossing the outer reaches of the Solar System will lead us to the dark and icy realm of the Oort cloud, an underworld containing potential riches to be mined. What will it then mean if a comet is released from this region, flaring brilliantly in the sky? As we pass the outer limits of the Solar System we begin to engage the galaxy itself; the largest unit most of us can conceive. Potential new interpretations can represent evolution in our conscious, defining an expanded way of understanding and delving into the deeper levels of our consciousness.

Atlantis Rising #37 December 2002

31. CERES: GODDESS OF THE ASTEROID BELT

"Ceres was the first to turn the earth with the hooked plowshare; she first gave laws. All things are the gift of Ceres; she must be the subject of my song."

Ovid, *Metamorphoses*, Verses 341-344

Dwarf planet Ceres, Vesta, Pallas, and Hygea, three largest asteroids
(NASA/JPL Calthech)

On January 1, 1801, Giuseppe Piazzi pointed his telescope in the
direction of the rocky objects that orbit the Sun between Mars and
Jupiter and discovered what he thought at first was a new comet.
Piazzi named the object Ceres, after the Sicilian goddess of grain, and
Ceres became a planet for fifty years. Three other objects were
discovered in the next few years: Pallas, Vesta, and Juno, which were
also considered to be planets. Later, William Herschel, discoverer of
Uranus, argued that they were too small to be planets, and when the
fifth, Astraea, was identified they were all re-classified as asteroids,
which means "star like." By the end of the 19th century several
hundred had been spotted, and at present, several hundred thousand

asteroids have been given provisional designations. Thousands more are discovered every year.

Most planetary astronomers believe that the planets of our Solar System formed from a nebula of gas, dust, and ices that coalesced around the developing Sun. Although some have suggested that the asteroids are remains of a proto-planet that was destroyed in a massive collision long ago, and there is considerable mythic evidence to support this view, the prevailing scientific opinion is that asteroids are leftover rocky matter that didn't become a planet. It's believed that insufficient mass, and Jupiter's strong gravitational influence, caused collisions and captured many small bodies, perhaps placing the Trojan asteroids that precede and follow Jupiter i the positions. Instead of sticking together, the planetesimals shattered, preventing them from becoming a larger planet. Astronomers believe that most of the main belt's mass has been lost since the formation of the Solar System.

In 1930, 129 years after Ceres appearance, Pluto was discovered, and he was also a planet for seven decades. But in 2006, after the discovery of Eris, who was the tenth planet for a brief time, Pluto was demoted, becoming the first in a new class of objects called plutoids—objects in a 2:1 orbital resonance with Neptune. These events also caused a planet to be defined for the first time. Ironically, it was Pluto's change in status, and the creation of new categories of objects in our Solar System, that resulted in a promotion for Ceres. She was reclassified as a dwarf planet in September 2006, placing her on a level playing field with Pluto, and making her unique (so far) in the Solar System since she is the only dwarf planet in the Main Asteroid Belt. Asteroid Vesta may also be a candidate once the Dawn spacecraft gets a closer look at her in 2011. Dawn will then visit Ceres in 2015.

The combined mass of all the asteroids in the Main Asteroid Belt is less than that of the Moon, and Ceres contains approximately one-third of the total. Unlike the lumpy, potato-like objects with lower gravity we normally expect to see, Ceres is spherical, and with a diameter of about 950 km, she is by far the largest and most massive object in the asteroid belt. Ceres appears to be differentiated into a rocky core and ice mantle with a surface that is probably a mixture of water, ice, and various hydrated minerals like carbonates and clays. Ceres may contain a tenuous atmosphere with water vapor and also harbor an ocean of liquid water that makes her a target in the search for extraterrestrial life.

Ceres and Pluto share several correspondences. They were both the first objects to be discovered in their respective belts, and both have the distinction of being the first of their kind in recent nomenclature. Both were considered planets for decades, and both occupy highly populated belts of objects orbiting the Sun. There's a symmetry between the Main Asteroid Belt and the Kuiper Belt, Pluto's home, where four planets precede each belt; Ceres follows the terrestrial planets, and Pluto comes after the gas giants.

Ceres and Pluto are also profoundly linked in myth. In the earlier Greek stories their names were Demeter and Hades. Demeter was the ancient Greek mother goddess of the greening of the Earth. She oversaw cycles of life and death as well as preserving sacred law. Demeter taught humanity the arts of agriculture: sowing seeds, plowing, and harvesting. In the Homeric Hymn to Demeter, dated to about the seventh century BCE, she is invoked as the "bringer of seasons." According to Isocrates, an Athenian rhetorician, the greatest gift that Demeter bestowed was grain, the cultivation of which elevated humans above the animal kingdom and freed people from the seasonal migrations of the hunter-gatherer.

In myth, Demeter's daughter Persephone (Prosperpina in Latin), was picking flowers in a field when she was abducted and raped by her uncle Hades/Pluto, god of the underworld. This violent act occurred with the complicity of her father, Zeus/Jupiter, which also mythically describes the abduction of the feminine principle that occurred as the patriarchy rose to power.

Demeter grieved for her daughter, or her own lost innocence, and withdrew to search for her. Without her the Earth became barren, and people risked starvation. Zeus sent gods with gifts to influence her, but it was not in his power to command her to make the Earth green. Nor could the king of heaven order the crops to grow on his own, as the nature of her feminine fertility was not within his domain. This strongly suggests that Demeter was an earlier and more powerful goddess. In fact, when Demeter was given a genealogy, she was the daughter of the Titans Cronos and Rhea, and therefore Zeus's elder sister, even though Persephone was said to be his daughter. Their mother, Rhea, finally intervened, and Zeus agreed to bring Persephone back. Meanwhile, Hades/Pluto had tricked Persephone into eating pomegranate seeds, which meant she had to remain part of the year with him. At the end of the tale, Demeter taught humanity the secrets of wheat and cultivating grain, pointing toward the deeper meaning of the story.

Demeter and Persephone were the central figures of the Eleusinian Mysteries that predated the Olympian pantheon. These were the most important rites of initiation in ancient Greece and are believed to have originated in Minoan goddess worship in Crete nearly 4,000 years ago. The road between Athens and Eleusis was called the Sacred Way as thousands of pilgrims from all levels of society, from Greece and beyond, made their way to celebrate the mysteries. The only requirements were never having committed murder and not being a "barbarian," that is, unable to speak Greek.

A binding vow of secrecy was required, and the penalty for breaking this oath was death, so we can only speculate from clues and indirect evidence what actually occurred. But tradition says that the high point of the ritual was a eucharist where a "sheaf of grain was reaped in silence." What little is known about the exact nature of the rites bears similarity to the Egyptian mysteries of Isis and Osiris, and Syrian and Persian mystery cults, which have similar themes.

It's said that the secret mystery ritual of Eleusis held the symbolic key to immortality and the principle of resurrection. Ancient writers asserted that the rites of Demeter promised the initiate a better life on Earth and happiness in the afterlife. The Eleusinian Mysteries were seen as deeply spiritual and inspiring--a far older and more elevated approach than the intrigues of the battling and scheming Olympians-- and offered an alternative religion well into the Christian era, as did the worship of Isis in Egypt.

Demeter's emblem was the poppy, a bright red flower that grows among barley, or grain, which links her to altered states of consciousness as well as themes of death and resurrection. Scholars say that the great Mother Goddess, who bore the names Rhea and Demeter, brought the poppy from Crete to Eleusis, which means "arrival," or "advent," and assert that in the Cretan cult, opium was prepared from poppies. In a clay statue, which resides at the Heraklion Museum on Crete, the Minoan poppy goddess wears the seed capsules in her diadem, source of both nourishment and narcosis.

The pomegranate played a key role in Persephone's journey. Hades tricked Persephone into eating the red seeds, which tied her to the underworld. The number of seeds varies from four to six, but determined the number of months she had to spend as queen of the underworld. The pomegranate has been a symbol of life and death, rebirth, resurrection and eternal life, fertility and marriage, abundance and prosperity throughout history and in almost every religion. The abundant seeds held the promise of cyclical resurrection. Almost every aspect of the pomegranate, its shape, color, seeds, juice, has come to symbolize something.

Dwarf planet Ceres rotates on her axis in nine hours, orbits the Sun in 4.6 years, and stays in an astrological sign about 4.6 months, creating an intriguing harmonic resonance with the number of months Persephone spent in Hades. Ceres astronomical symbol is the sickle, or barley hook, an ancient harvest implement and instrument of reaping. It seems natural that Ceres should be astrologically aligned with Virgo. Virgo is the only female among the zodiacal constellations, and other than the Gemini twins, Castor and Pollux, she is the only human figure. Virgo is depicted as a maiden, holding a palm branch in her right and a single ear of wheat in her left. Her brightest star is named Spica, "ear of wheat." The symbolic eucharist of Eleusis is the perfect symbol of Virgo, and of the mysteries of alchemical transmutation, that occur in the intestines, the area of the body ruled by that sign.

Virgo is one of the oldest constellations and over time has been equated with every important feminine deity, including Ishtar, Isis, Demeter, Persephone, Medusa, Artemis, and Urania. Richard Hinkley-

Allen says, "Those who claim very high antiquity for the zodiacal signs (15,000 years ago), assert that the idea of these titles originated when the Sun was in Virgo at the spring equinox, the time of the Egyptian harvest." Astrologer Bernadette Brady has remarked that, "Whatever image is chosen across time and cultures, what is contained in Virgo is the archetype of the harvest-bringing goddess, pure and good, independent of the masculine. She gives the four seasons and is the source of the fertile Earth."

Earth is the womb of the Goddess, and her mysteries of generation and regeneration include the seeds that are planted, germinated and the subsequent harvest that results. We reap the harvests of our lives according to the seeds that we have sown, and the manner in which the garden has been tended, carefully winnowing the wheat from the chaff as we learn our lessons.

When the sickle is wielded, the crop is severed from the stalk and its connection to the Earth is terminated. As the fruits of the Earth are gathered and consumed, the promise of another harvest is implicit.

The symbolic themes of Ceres and Virgo are roots, fertility, plenty, crops, renewal, cultivation, nourishment, substance, eucharist and communion. Astrologically, I believe Ceres/Demeter represents reclamation and renewal and can reveal what needs to be uncovered deep in the underworld of our consciousness. Examining Ceres place in a natal chart we can ask, what is hidden, lies fallow, or is imprisoned in the underworld of our psyches that needs to come to the surface so our fertility returns and our personal gardens flourish?

Ceres reemergence as a planet, albeit a dwarf, is similar to her myth. Her energy is reappearing from the underworld of our awareness and coming into her own. I believe this also represents the resurgence of the feminine principle, which must be reintegrated into humanity's psyche. The resolution involves a restitution and restoration of balance.

Pluto is seen as the astrological agent of transformation, but he must remain in the underworld. Persephone/Proserpina, daughter of Ceres/Demeter, was his wife and queen, and each year she journeyed from above to below and back, reuniting with her mother to make the world green again. What might the Persephone in each of us bring back from her annual journey to the underworld? Her mother as "bringer of the seasons" teaches us that nothing really dies, but a cyclical descent to the underworld of our own psyche may be required for real growth to occur. Bravely undertaken, this passage leads us toward a Sacred Union with the Goddess, revealing the "knowledge of the gods," the superhuman qualities that reveal the true nature of immortality.

Atlantis Rising #86 February 2011

32.CERES: IS THE ANCIENT GODDESS OF GRAIN THE RULER OF VIRGO?

" And the day came when the risk it took to remain tight in a bud was more painful than the risk it took to blossom."

Anais Nin

Goddess Ceres Antoine Watteau 1717 (Wikimedia; National Gallery of Art

Before telescopes astronomers defined objects in the sky as Sun, Moon, and stars. Mercury, Venus, Mars, Jupiter and Saturn, the five planets visible to the unaided eye, moved against the backdrop of the seemingly "fixed" stars. Today, knowledge of our Solar System and beyond is expanding at an exponential rate, and the picture is more vast and complex than we ever imagined. Scientists now speak of a Multiverse where an infinite number of universes may exist.

Astrology was also less complex before the discovery of Uranus, Neptune, and Pluto. A simple and elegant system assigned the visible planets as rulers of the twelve astrological signs. The Sun and Moon, called "luminaries," each ruled one sign. The Sun ruled Leo and the Moon ruled the adjacent sign Cancer. Moving backward and forward in the zodiac circle the rest of the planets ruled two signs each.

Mercury was said to rule Gemini and Virgo, Venus ruled Taurus and Libra, Mars aligned with Aries and Scorpio, Jupiter ruled Sagittarius and Pisces, and Saturn ruled Capricorn and Aquarius.

When Uranus and Neptune were discovered, Uranus became the ruler of Aquarius and Neptune was aligned with watery Pisces. When Pluto was discovered he was seen to connect with Scorpio and the shadowy underworld of Hades. This made logical and mythical sense, but upset the previous symmetry. Since there aren't enough planets to assign to the twelve signs, Venus is still said to rule both Taurus and Libra, and Mercury still governs Gemini and Virgo. In 2006, after the discovery of dwarf planet Eris resulted in a demotion for Pluto, and a promotion for dwarf planet Ceres, the mythical apple cart was upset again.

In the 18th century, Emanuel Swedenborg, Immanuel Kant, and Pierre-Simon Laplace developed a model for the formation of our Solar System known as the nebular hypothesis. Since the beginning of the space age, and the discovery of extra solar planets, the model has been challenged and refined. The Solar System has evolved considerably since its formation. Moons have formed from circling disks of gas and dust around their parent planets. Other moons are thought to have formed independently and been captured by planets. Still others are likely the result of collisions between bodies that have occurred continually and been central to the evolution of the Solar System. Positions of planets have often shifted, and planets have switched places. In fact, planetary migration is now thought to be responsible for much of the Solar System's early development.

Also in the 18th century, astronomer Johann Titus perceived a pattern that predicted the spacing of the planets in the Solar System. In 1778, J. E. Bode did the math and predicted the existence of a planet between Mars and Jupiter in what is now known as the Main Asteroid Belt. This mathematical relationship is known as Titus-Bode's Law. In 1800 twenty-five astronomers, called the Celestial Police, each searched fifteen degrees of the zodiac for the missing planet. However, the discovery of the first body in this region came from an outsider, Italian astronomer Giuseppe Piazzi. He named it Ceres, after the Roman goddess of grain, whose Greek counterpart is Demeter. A second body,

Pallas, was found a little over a year later, and for fifty years Ceres and Pallas were considered planets. By the beginning of the 19th century, more than 100 objects had been found, and scientists realized they were too small to be planets; they were dubbed asteroids, meaning, "star like."

Mainstream astronomers believe that the Asteroid Belt is a collection of objects that never coalesced as a planet. Although dismissed by mainstream science in the same manner as Atlantis itself, there is considerable lore, including the well-known work of Zechariah Sitchin, describing a planet that once existed in what is now the Main Asteroid Belt. The planet has been variously called Malona, Maldek, Marduk, and Phaeton. Although explanations differ, sources agree that the mythical planet suffered a violent destruction either from a doomsday weapon or a collision with another object in space.

The combined mass of millions (perhaps billions) of tiny asteroids in the Main Asteroid Belt is less than that of the Moon, but dwarf planet Ceres contains approximately one-third, and is a quarter the size of our Moon. Although Ceres is the smallest (known) dwarf planet in the Solar System, she is closest to Earth, and the largest object between Mars and Jupiter. Unlike other potato-like objects with lower gravity, Ceres is spherical, with a diameter of nearly 600 miles (950 km). Ceres may be the remnant of a once vital planet, holding both powerful memories and symbolic meaning.

Researchers at the European Space Agency in Spain, and the *Observatoire de Paris* (Paris Observatory), used the Herschel space telescope to detect two "geysers" on the surface of Ceres, blasting plumes of water vapor into space. Further analysis indicated that some of the water falls back onto the dwarf planet's surface. Michael Küppers, lead author of a paper published in the January, 2014 issue of *Nature* said, "This is the first time water vapor has been unequivocally detected on Ceres, or any other object in the Asteroid Belt, and provides proof that Ceres has an icy surface and an atmosphere." This makes Ceres a "world" rather than just a barren rock. In 2015 the Dawn spacecraft, which has already visited asteroid Vesta, the second largest object in the Belt, will get a close up and detailed look at Ceres.

Ceres —NASA Space Exploration; Dawn spacecraft public domain

In myth, Ceres is the Roman equivalent of the Greek goddess Demeter, who was the ancient Greek mother of the greening of the Earth. She regulated cycles of life and death and preserved sacred law. Demeter taught humanity the arts of agriculture: sowing, plowing, and harvesting. In the Homeric Hymn to Demeter, dated to about the seventh century BCE, she is invoked as "bringer of seasons." According to Isocrates, an Athenian rhetorician, the greatest gift that Demeter bestowed was cultivation, which elevated humans above the animal kingdom and freed people from the seasonal migrations of the hunter-gatherer.

Demeter's daughter Persephone (Proserpina in Latin) was picking flowers in a field when she was abducted and raped by her uncle Hades/Pluto, god of the underworld. Demeter grieved for her daughter, or her own lost innocence, and withdrew to search for her. Without the daughter the Earth became barren, and people risked starvation. Zeus sent gods with gifts to influence Demeter/Ceres, but it was not in his power to command her to make the Earth green. Nor could he order the crops to grow, as her feminine fertility was not within his domain. Meanwhile, Hades/Pluto had tricked Persephone into eating pomegranate seeds, which meant she had to remain part of the year in the underworld. At the end of the tale, Demeter taught humanity the secrets of wheat and cultivating grain, pointing toward the deeper meaning of the story.

Demeter and Persephone were the central figures of the Eleusinian Mysteries that predated the Olympian pantheon. These were the most important rites of initiation in ancient Greece and are believed to have originated in Minoan goddess worship in Crete nearly 4,000 years ago. The road between Athens and Eleusis was called the Sacred Way as thousands of pilgrims from all levels of society, from Greece and beyond, traveled to celebrate the mysteries. The only requirements were never having committed murder and not being a "barbarian," that is, unable to speak Greek. A binding vow of secrecy was imposed, and the penalty for breaking this oath was death, so we can only speculate what actually occurred from clues and indirect evidence. Tradition says the high point of the ritual was a Eucharist where a "sheaf of grain was reaped in silence." What little is known about the rites bears similarity to Egyptian mysteries of Isis and Osiris, and Syrian and Persian mystery cults.

Virgo, Latin for "virgin," is one of the oldest constellations. Virgo has been equated with every important feminine deity, including Ishtar, Isis, Demeter, Persephone, Medusa, Artemis, and Urania. The constellation is the second largest after Hydra, the Water Serpent. The Greeks and Romans associated Virgo with Demeter and Ceres.

The Babylonian Mul.Apin, dating from 1000–686 BCE, says this constellation was known as "The Furrow," representing the goddess Shala's ear of grain. The alpha star Spica, which is Latin for "ear of grain," retains this meaning. Richard Hinkley-Allen (*Star Names, Their Lore and Meaning*), says "Those who claim very high antiquity for the zodiacal signs, 15,000 years ago, assert that the idea of these titles originated when the Sun was in Virgo at the spring equinox, the time of the Egyptian harvest." Astrologer Bernadette Brady says, "Virgo is the archetype of the harvest-bringing goddess, pure and good, independent of the masculine. She gives the four seasons and is the source of the fertile Earth."

Virgo is the only female among the zodiacal constellations, and other than the Gemini twins, Castor and Pollux, she is the only human figure. Virgo is depicted as a maiden, holding a palm branch in her right hand and a single ear of wheat in her left. The symbolic Eucharist of Eleusis is the perfect symbol of Virgo, and of the mysteries of alchemical transmutation that occur in the intestines, the area of the body ruled by that sign. The secret mystery ritual of Eleusis is said to have held the symbolic key to immortality and the principle of resurrection through cyclical renewal.

I believe there is a strong link between Ceres and Virgo. Although Mercury is a perfect match with the mutable air sign Gemini, a more appropriate ruler of Virgo is dwarf planet Ceres, the largest object in the Main Asteroid Belt. The astronomical symbol for Ceres is the sickle, or barley hook, an ancient harvest implement and instrument of reaping, linking Ceres to Virgo. The symbolic themes of Virgo and Ceres are roots, fertility, crops, renewal, cultivation, nourishment and substance. Ceres reemergence as a dwarf planet is similar to her myth. Her energy is coming to light from the darkness of the underworld of our awareness.

Astrologically, I believe Ceres represents reclamation and renewal and can reveal what is hidden, lies fallow, or is imprisoned in the underworld of our psyches and needs to come to the surface so our personal gardens can bloom. As a failed or possibly exploded planet Ceres might point the way toward what needs to be "re-membered" and requires spiritual will to coalesce. Ceres might also indicate patterns of poor choices with disastrous consequences that need to be reexamined. Orbiting the Sun between Mars and Jupiter Ceres might have significance related to the meaning of the terrestrial planets versus the gas giants beyond.

The harvests of our lives are reaped according to the seeds we have sown, and the manner in which our gardens have been tended, carefully winnowing the wheat from the chaff as we learn our lessons. When the sickle is wielded, the crop is severed from the stalk and its connection to the Earth is terminated. As the fruits of the Earth are gathered and consumed, seeds contain the promise of another harvest.

Ceres as "bringer of the seasons" also teaches us that nothing really dies, but a cyclical descent to the underworld of our own psyches may be required for real growth and personal transformation. As our window to the Universe continues to widen, revealing new knowledge and wonders, we have to be willing to open our own minds to expanded meaning.

Atlantis Rising #105 April 2014

33.DWARFING PLUTO: ERIS, GODDESS OF DISCORD, UPSETS THE PLANETARY APPLE CART

"There are no rules anywhere. The Goddess Prevails."

The Discordian Society, page 00032

Eris and Moon Dysnomia (NASA public domain)

The Solar System hasn't had such a jolt since 24-year old Clyde Tombaugh, continuing the work of Percival Lowell, found Pluto on February 18, 1930. Lowell died in 1916 unaware that his photographic plates had captured Pluto. For a long time that was the final word on planets.

Our word for planet comes from the Greek *planates*, meaning "wanderer," and was meant to distinguish the moving stars (planets), from what seemed to be fixed stars. That seemed self-evident until now, but life in the Solar System is becoming more complex. Burgeoning discoveries of planets orbiting other stars, as well as planetoids and comets that keep popping up, created a classification dilemma. In the face of mounting demand the International Astronomical Union (IAU) formed a committee to define a planet.

Eris, Greek goddess of discord, has upset the apple cart. Officially dubbed 2003 UB313, Eris was identified on January 5, 2005 and is for now the largest object found in orbit around the Sun since Neptune was discovered in 1846. Eris is a spherical body larger than Pluto residing in the Kuiper Belt, the icy ring that separates the planets from the deeper parts of space. Pluto is no longer the solitary object it was once thought to be but rather the brightest of a large class of Kuiper Belt Objects.

True to her name Eris stirred up a tempest of controversy at the August meeting of astrophysicists in Prague. According to reports the scientific discussion about her proper designation became a "raucous" debate that ended with Pluto and newcomer Eris both being relegated to dwarf planet status, leaving the Solar System with eight newly-defined planets. As even more objects may be discovered in our solar neighborhood the astronomers voted that Pluto couldn't remain a planet without doing scientific disservice to other "real" planets. It had to be a blow, but at least Pluto is now considered first in the new class of trans-Neptunian dwarf planets, along with Eris, Quaoar, called plutoids.

Eris is also the most distant object ever found in orbit around the Sun, further than Sedna, which was discovered in 2004, and has an oval orbit of 560 years, more than twice as long as Pluto's. Eris apparently looks similar to Pluto, but while the lord of the underworld is red, Eris is white, reflecting more sunlight from her surface than any body in the Solar System except Saturn's moon Enceladus. Scientists believe her great distance from the Sun causes methane and nitrogen to freeze solid and her atmosphere is therefore more reflective. She is visible through a telescope in the constellation of Cetus, the Whale, or Sea Monster. According to my colleague Philip Sedgwick, Aries currently resides at 20 Aries 54 in the Tropical zodiac.

Some exquisite mechanism appears to act within collective consciousness to result in the naming of archetypal influences. The naming of Eris further confirms my belief that astronomers are just as fascinated by this process as story tellers. Naming something imbues it with power, and once a celestial body has a name its existence comes alive in our consciousness.

Myth transmits truth through the ages even when it seems to contradict history. Troy for example was only myth for a time. Eris was Xena the warrior princes for awhile but is now a full-fledged goddess. Mythically there's not much to draw on but some sources say Eris was the daughter of Zeus and Hera, twin sister of Ares (Roman Mars), and said to be his constant companion. So Eris is an Olympian in her own right. The Greeks generally disliked Ares as a trouble maker, and likely his sister by association, but the later Mars was held in high esteem by the imperial Romans.

Eris seems to be mischievous with lots of attitude. One of her artifacts is a golden apple of immortality, brilliant, shining and fatally attractive, which hints at a deeper meaning to her nature. Anyone who saw the shining orb desired it. It's not clear from mythic fragments how she attained this priceless artifact, but in the old stories it was always a goddess who conferred immortality on a hero. That apple instigated the Trojan War. Legend says Eris was angered after not being invited to a wedding on Mount Olympus. She crashed the party and threw her apple (or one of them), into the midst of the revelers. The apple had a note attached that said, "For the fairest." Naturally, three mighty goddesses each thought they should have the apple: Hera, Aphrodite, and Athena. They summoned a mere mortal, Paris, a poor but royal shepherd, to choose between them. Paris, who wanted Helen of Troy, chose Aphrodite goddess of love. The result triggered the Trojan War as Helen was inconveniently married to someone else.

How will astrologers adapt to the demotion of the smallest planet and the addition of a new Olympian, albeit a dwarf planet? Before Herschel discovered Uranus in 1781, there was a convenient relationship between the known planets and their relationship with the twelve Zodiac signs. Astrologers speculated about other planets that would ultimately fill out rulership of the twelve. Planet Vulcan and the dark Moon Lilith were popular candidates. There is actually some talk of returning to the classical rulerships, but I think this is unlikely.

Esoterically astrologers adapted and defined the discovery of Uranus as an evolutionary step in humanity's unfoldment. When Neptune (1846), and Pluto (1930), in turn were "discovered" astrologers perceived that our collective consciousness as a human race had evolved to the point where we could recognize and respond to these higher planetary frequencies on a conscious level. Symbolically we were ready to move beyond the limiting rings of Saturn.

These new discoveries have the potential to expand how astrologers interpret symbolic and archetypal content of the solar system and our psyches. Like the discoveries of Uranus, Neptune, and Pluto heralded new awareness, technology, and transformation, so too will further discoveries take us to the next level in our unfolding pattern. As new objects are discovered within the Kuiper Belt and Oort Cloud it is possible that we will experience an entirely different psychological mechanism.

Pluto was named for the mythical god of the dead, Hades in Greek. He was an Olympian who was given rulership of the Underworld, called the House of Hades. Hades name meant "the Invisible," and was not spoken aloud for fear of arousing his anger. Instead he was most commonly called Pluton, "the Rich," signifying the wealth of mines cultivated beneath the Earth, and he was often depicted with a horn of plenty. Pluto has guarded the gates to the underworld for nearly a century, but we have lost the deeper meaning of Pluton and what it means to mine the depths. There are wonders waiting beyond the artificial limits we have enforced and we must summon courage to dive.

Since Pluto's discovery astrologers have witnessed the paradox first hand that Pluto's small size is no indication of its influence. Astrologically and archetypically Hades, the Invisible, and Pluton, the Rich, fit well with the deep, psychological issues that must be mined when the influence of Pluto presents itself. Whatever we call Pluto his influence will still be felt. If we doubt that look at the ruckus tiny Eris has stirred up.

The Kuiper Belt itself may archetypically prove to be like the mythical River Styx, and crossing the outer reaches of the Solar System will lead us to the dark and icy realm of the Oort cloud, an underworld containing potential riches to be mined. As we pass the outer limits we begin to engage the galaxy itself; the largest unit most of us can conceive.

Strange forces are at play in collective unconsciousness that Freud never dreamed of. In 1958 a new religion was created. Called Discordianism it is a modern, chaos-based religion. The deity of Discordianism is none other than our new dwarf planet, Eris, who the Romans identified with their goddess Discordia. Described as both an "elaborate joke disguised as a religion, and as a religion disguised as an elaborate joke," it has also been called "Zen for round eyes." Discordianism is evidently the code of computer hackers.

Although most religions revere the principles of harmony and order in the Universe, Discordianism can be interpreted as a recognition that disharmony and chaos are equally valid aspects of reality. The tenets of this discordant religion can be found in their guide book, *Principia Discordia,* which often hints that Discordianism was founded as a dialectic antithesis to more popular religions based on order. The book describes, often with humor, chaos as a much more underlying impulse of the Universe. Perhaps the intent was to balance the creative forces of order and disorder, but the focus is certainly on the more disorderly aspects of the world — at times the forces of order are even vilified. It's fascinating that Eris was worshiped as embodying disorder half a century before she reentered the Olympian arena. How might we examine the purpose of strife, or competition, in an Olympic game for example?

Serious students of myth notice that the tenor of the stories began to change after destruction of Thera by a volcanic eruption and the corresponding culture in Old Kingdom Egypt. Symptoms of this shift in Greek myths included an increasing glorification of war accompanied by a deteriorating value of agriculture and cyclical time. This coincides with the end of the age of Taurus and the beginning of the age of Aries. We are approaching the end of the age of Pisces and the dawn of the age of Aquarius, and it's time for the paradigm to shift again.

In October 2002, based on observations of the star closest to the heart of the Milky Way, Rainer Schoedel, at the Max Planck Institute for Astrophysics in Garching, Germany announced, "We can now confidently say that a black hole does indeed exist at the center of our galaxy." As recently as the Middle Ages Galileo was imprisoned for advancing Copernicus's view that Earth circled the Sun, not the other way round. In some ways our awareness has come a long way in several hundred years.

The Solar System hasn't changed has not fundamentally changed—we just see it differently. We shouldn't be surprised. As accounts of Near Death Experiences, After Death Communications, angelic visitations, and encounters with extraterrestrials increase dramatically it is becoming clear that the once impenetrable borders of the underworld, described like a veil between the worlds, is thinning and revealing more denizens from that realm.

These discoveries challenge traditional astrology to widen the lens and deepen the interpretation. I expect that astrologers will grab the golden apple that Eris offers, expanding the symbolic view of our collective consciousness without asking permission from the IAU.

Atlantis Rising #61 December 2006

34.ERIS IN ARIES — 1926 - 2048

"Truly, Eris is a goddess to fear."

Euripides, *Phoenician Women*

Eris & moon Dysnomia - NASA, ESA, A. Schaller for STScl

Pluto was discovered in 1930 and was considered to be a planet for seventy-six years. Then, along came Eris. At first, she was heralded as the tenth planet, since she is larger than Pluto. But the net result was Pluto's demotion, the IAU defining a planet for the first time, and the creation of a whole new category of objects in our Solar System--dwarf planets. Astronomers suspect that at least another forty known objects in the Solar System are dwarf planets, and estimate that another 200 dwarf planets may be found as the Kuiper Belt is explored.

Eris is the largest known dwarf planet beyond Neptune and the ninth-largest body known to orbit the Sun directly. Eris was first identified in January 2005 by a Palomar Observatory based team led by astronomer Mike Brown. For a while she was dubbed Xena, the warrior princess. Eris is also a trans-Neptunian object (TNO) native to a region of space beyond the Kuiper Belt known as the Scattered Disk. Eris and her moon Dysnomia are currently the most distant known objects of significance size in the Solar System apart from long-period comets and space probes.

Unlike the eight official planets, whose orbits are fairly circular and lie roughly in the same plane as the Earth's, Eris orbits above and below the other planets. Like Pluto, she can range from being a great distance from the Sun, to being almost as close to Sun as Neptune. The reason she had not been noticed before is most searches for large outer Solar System objects have concentrated on the ecliptic plane.

In myth, Eris, pronounced Ee-ris, is a Greek goddess who was the personification of discord or strife. Sometimes she is the daughter of the powerful Olympians Zeus and Hera, and brother to Ares (Roman Mars), the god of war. Her name was translated into Latin as Discordia. Her Greek opposite is Harmonia, whose Latin counterpart is Concordia. Homer equated her with the violent war-goddess Enyo, but I believe this is misleading and misrepresents the true nature of Eris.

The Greek poet Hesiod describes two very different goddesses named Eris, or strife, in his *Works and Days.* "So, after all, there was not one kind of Strife alone, but all over the earth there are two. As for the one, a man would praise her when he came to understand her. But the other is blameworthy, and they are wholly different in nature." The archaic definition of strife was "earnest endeavor," which seems more like honest striving and healthy competition. It is also like the friction that promotes growth. Seen in this way, the principle of discord, or strife, is the motive force of growth that yields the pearl in the oyster.

Eris appears with a different lineage in Hesiod's *Theogony* as the daughter of Nyx, "night," where she and some of her siblings were born "parthenogenetically" without a father. There is a much richer mythic trail to follow here. Nyx, Nox in Roman translation, was the primordial goddess of the night, "a veil of dark mist drawn forth from the underworld that blotted out the shining light of the upper atmosphere." A shadowy and primeval figure of great beauty and power, Nyx stood at the beginning of Creation, making her one of the first beings to emerge from the void. In several fragmentary poems attributed to Orpheus, it is Nyx, rather than Chaos, who is the first principle of creation.

In ancient art Nyx was portrayed as a either a winged goddess, or charioteer, sometimes crowned with an aureole of dark mist. In the cosmogony of Hesiod she mated with Darkness *Erebos,* and produced Light *Aither* and Day *Hemera,* which were the first components of the primeval universe. Alone, she gave birth to the three Fates, Sleep, Death, Strife (Eris), and Pain.

Goddess Eris depicted on Greek pottery (public domain)

The goddess Eris, daughter of Nyx, is depicted in art with black wings and was thought to haunt battle fields. Eris shares iconography with winged goddesses from other cultures. In Egypt, the vulture goddess Nekbet was one of the deities on the *uraeus* headdress of the pharaoh. The Celtic goddess Morrigan could take the form of a raven, a fierce war bird. Morrigan played a key role in the downfall of the hero Culcannon because he rejected her in her Crone aspect, revealing a lack of respect for feminine wisdom. The Celtic Branwen could assume the form of a white raven. The Norse goddess Freya either wore a cloak of falcon feathers, enabling her to fly, or assumed the form of a falcon. The Greek Harpy was once a beautiful maiden called Virgin Eagle but were transformed into ugly avian sisters. Eris also bears a similarity to one of the oldest goddess archetypes. Six thousand years ago in Sumeria, Inanna was the goddess of love and gifts, but also of war.

One of Eris's artifacts is the brilliant, and fatally attractive, Golden Apple of Discord. Anyone who saw the shining orb desired it. It's not clear from mythic fragments how she obtained this priceless artifact, but in old stories around the world it was always a goddess who conferred immortality to a questing hero, usually by virtue of an apple.

Eris is best known for her role, in a plan hatched by Zeus, at the wedding of Peleus and Thetus, who became parents of the hero Achilles. Eris tossed her apple, marked "For the most beautiful one," into the celebration. *Kalliste* is the ancient Greek word that was inscribed on the Golden Apple of Discord. In Greek, the word means "beautiful." Naturally, three mighty goddesses each thought they deserved the golden fruit: Aphrodite, goddess of love, Hera, Queen of the Olympians, and Athena, grey-eyed goddess of wisdom and war.

Zeus appointed Paris, Prince of Troy, to judge. Hera offered him political power; Athena promised skill in battle; and Aphrodite tempted him with Helen, the most beautiful woman in the world; who was already married to Menelaus of Sparta. Paris chose to award the apple to Aphrodite, thereby dooming his city, and triggering the Trojan War.

It is telling that the story is called The Judgment of Paris. A human man is asked to choose the most "beautiful" from three potent feminine archetypes. In the older stories, it is mortals who must prove themselves, and magical gifts are bestowed by the gods to those who are deemed worthy. Since Euripides, this story concerns a choice among the gifts that each goddess embodies. The subtext of their bribery of Paris was added later.

Do we simply believe that the goddesses were vain and quarrelsome, or is there a deeper lesson contained in this myth? What are the intrinsic qualities of beauty, strength, and wisdom that these goddesses characterize and represent? And, what is the cost of looking only at surface appearances? Most importantly, how does the emergence of Eris into our collective psyche impact how we look at feminine archetypes?

The classic fairy tale of *Sleeping Beauty,* made famous by Disney, was partly inspired by Eris's role at the wedding of Peleus and Thetis. In the Disney version, there are three good fairies, representing the three Fates, and one "bad" fairy who wasn't invited to the christening. The fairy named Malificent cursed the princess, but the curse was altered from death to a sleep of one hundred years after she pricked her finger on a spinning wheel. The Fates were also daughters of Nyx and were the spinners and weavers, always the domain of the elder Crone.

The orbital plane of Eris is so inclined that her journey around the Sun takes her above and below the orbits of the other planets, so she doesn't actually move through all of the zodiacal constellations on the ecliptic plane. Symbolically therefore, she moves beyond the realm of linear time. However, because the signs of the zodiac are measures of time and not space, corresponding to degrees of Celestial Longitude, Eris does visit each of them in turn, spending decades in each sign.

Eris is estimated to be 27% larger than Pluto, and filled with potent meaning, so it seems she deserves to be considered in the tool box of astrological interpretation. Eris, like Uranus, shakes up the status quo and seems to upset existing structures. Strife can be a great teacher. She challenges us to look at issues that have been ignored. Eris represents what I think might be called the unpleasant truth. She forces our denial out into the open, pointing out that the emperor isn't wearing any clothes.

Paris, the mortal in the myth, contemplated the powers of goddesses and chose physical beauty for his own selfish purposes. We are called to look beneath surface appearances and to find inner beauty, strength, and wisdom. This may require disturbing the delicate balance of a long-held illusion. Therefore, in a natal chart, the house Eris occupies may reveal our hidden gifts, which are brought into expression through "strife" or friction, creating a pearl.

The orbit of Eris is long, twice as long as Pluto. Therefore, her influence by transit is multi-generational. Eris is currently at the furthest point from the Sun in her 557-year orbit, roughly three times farther than Pluto, so it's likely our awareness of her will grow as she heads back around. Eris entered the astrological sign of Aries (not the constellation), early in 1927, in the midst of the Roaring Twenties.

At present, Eris occupies 21 degrees of Aries and will remain in Aries until spring of 2048. Aries, ruled by Mars, is a good place for a goddess who likes to disrupt the status quo. In 1929, after a long battle, the 19th amendment of the Constitution extended the right to vote to women. (In 1948 women's right to vote was introduced into international law by the UN.) Eris may in fact represent the Women's Movement in modern times.

Eris has changed the order of things in the Solar System, and she is poised to ask some hard questions. The gods have placed us in the role of Paris. What systemic order needs to be deconstructed in our lives and nations? Where do we bring the hard questions to a conscious level? How do we come to praise the strife that Eris represents, as Hesiod has suggested?

I believe the symbolism of Eris corresponds to the deeper meaning of *Sleeping Beauty*. The Divine Feminine has slumbered for thousands of years. Until the advent of the asteroid goddesses, there has been an imbalance of planetary gender. Only Venus and the Moon represented the feminine. But this is changing, and as Eris passes through Aries, her apples of discord will likely facilitate a chain reaction as feminine energy is once again arising to bring back balance. If I am correct, and Eris in Aries has helped to facilitate a reawakening of the feminine, then we have two more generations of this influence to experience, observe, and integrate. Hopefully, the human race will become more balanced, conscious, and humane.

Atlantis Rising #80 February 2010

35. ASTEROID VESTA: WILL OUR SOLAR SYSTEM GAIN ANOTHER DWARF PLANET?

"It is through the world of the imagination, that takes us beyond the restriction of provable fact ,that we touch the hem of truth."

Madeleine L'Engle, *A Circle of Quiet*

Asteroid Vesta — NASA taken by New Dawn spacecraft (public domain)

The Titius-Bode "law" is a rough rule that predicts the spacing of the planets in the Solar System. The relationship was first noted by Johann Titius in 1766 and was formulated as a mathematical expression by J.E. Bode in 1778. This led Bode to predict the existence of another planet between Mars and Jupiter. On New Year's Day of 1801, Giuseppe Piazzi pointed his telescope in this direction, hoping to find a planet, and discovered what he thought was a comet. Piazzi named the object Ceres, after the Sicilian goddess of grain, and Ceres did become a planet for fifty years.

Three other objects were discovered in the next few years: Pallas, Vesta, and Juno. They were named after Roman goddesses who corresponded to the remaining Greek Olympians, and these four have become part of astrological interpretation. Later, William Herschel, discoverer of Uranus, argued that they were too small to be planets, and when Astraea, the fifth, was identified they were all re-classified as asteroids, which means "star-like." That is really a misnomer--the term planetoid would be more appropriate. By the end of the 19th century several hundred asteroids had been spotted. At present several hundred thousand have been given provisional designations, and thousands more are discovered every year.

In 1930, 129 years after Ceres' appearance, Pluto was discovered, and he was a planet for seven decades. In 2006, after the discovery of Eris, Pluto was demoted and became the first in a new class of objects called plutoids--objects in a 2:1 orbital resonance with Neptune. These events also caused a planet, and dwarf planet, to be defined for the first time. Ceres was reclassified as a dwarf planet, placing it on a level playing field with Pluto, and making Ceres unique (so far) in the Solar System since it is the only dwarf planet in the Main Asteroid Belt. However, some scientists are now advocating that asteroid Vesta be reclassified as a dwarf planet, which would further complicate planetary interpretation for astrologers. The current need to revision astrological interpretation is similar to the dilemma of incorporating the meanings of Uranus and Neptune into the astrological pantheon after their discoveries.

Einstein thought that quantum entanglement was impossible, calling it "spooky action at a distance." Newton would have thought that non-locality was impossible. Galileo was imprisoned for echoing Copernicus and suggesting that the Earth revolved around the Sun. Physicists now speak of the effect of the observer on an experiment. As we learn more about the Universe, our science and philosophy must also expand to include new meanings.

NASA's Dawn spacecraft entered orbit around Vesta in July of 2011 for a one-year exploration and left orbit in September 2012, heading for an expected arrival at Ceres in 2015. Dawn's mission is to completely map Ceres and Vesta, two of the biggest worlds in the Main Asteroid Belt. According to astronomers on the Dawn team, Ceres and Vesta are huge worlds, planet-scale objects that are more appropriately compared to Mercury, the Moon, and outer planet moons. There is high interest in this mission as Ceres is a possible destination for human colonization since it has abundant ice, water, and minerals.

Vesta, sometimes Vestia, is translated as "hearth" in English. The Latin word for hearth is *focus*, indicating the central importance of her role. She was *mater* in Latin, "mother" and was the literal hearth of Rome. Vestal Virgins, *Vestales*, tended a sacred and perpetual fire in her temples and were the only full-time priesthood in Rome. Their vow of chastity was so binding they were burned alive if it was broken. Ovid said Vesta was the Earth itself, the sacred sphere that makes life possible. Scholar Georges Dumezil compared Vesta to Agni, the Hindu god of fire, and saw parallels in the sacrificial rituals in Vedic India that offered smoke to heaven as a prayer. Sacred fire was thought to connect the ordinary world to the divine.

Hestia was the earlier Greek goddess, "first born of the Olympians," and the Roman Vesta followed suit with the same mythology. The root of both names in Greek and Latin conveys fire and burning. Hestia, "hearth" or "fireside," was a virgin goddess of Greek architecture, right ordering of domesticity, the family, and the state. Hestia was the daughter of the Titans Cronus and Rhea and one of the twelve Olympians. Her name means "home" and "hearth", the *oikos*, which included the household and its inhabitants. An early form of the temple was the hearth house. Early temples at Dreris and Prinias on Crete are of this type as is the temple of Apollo at Delphi, which always had its inner *hestia*.

Hestia received the first offering at every sacrifice in the household. In the public domain, the hearth of the *prytaneum* functioned as her official sanctuary. She was the *metropolis*, the "mother city," and when a new colony was established, flame from Hestia's public hearth was carried to the new settlement. Hestia sat on a plain wooden throne with a white woolen cushion and did not have an emblem, as she was the embodiment of the fire of life. The Greeks said, "Start with Hestia," meaning begin at the beginning.

Tens of thousands of asteroids congregate in the Main Asteroid Belt that is a vast, doughnut-shaped ring located between the orbits of Mars and Jupiter but closer to Mars. It's estimated that if the total mass of all the asteroids now present in the Main Asteroid Belt were combined, the result would comprise a body less than half the size of

the Moon. Asteroids range in size from Ceres, roughly the size of
Texas, down to pebble-size bits of rock. Sixteen asteroids have a
diameter of 240 km or greater. Asteroids are not visible to the naked
eye (except for Vesta under the right conditions), but many can be seen
with binoculars or small telescopes. Vesta is the brightest asteroid and
can be seen with the naked eye when it is at opposition and perihelion
simultaneously. Some asteroids have moons while others orbit in
binary pairs. Most asteroids have slightly elliptical orbits that range
from about three to six earth years. The strong gravitational force of
Jupiter shepherds the Asteroid Belt, pulls the asteroids away from the
Sun, and keeps them from careening into the inner planets.

Astronomers were surprised by Vesta's complexity, calling it the
"smallest terrestrial planet." Vesta has a rich metal core that constitutes
40% of its diameter and 80% of its mass and has a mean diameter of
525 kilometers (326 mi). Vesta has an orbital period of 1,325 days, or 3.6
years, that lays entirely inside that of Ceres whose solar circuit is four
years. Vesta is the second-most-massive asteroid after dwarf planet
Ceres and comprises an estimated 9% of the mass of the Main Asteroid
Belt while Ceres boasts 30%.

Vesta is the only known asteroid to have an earth-like structure with a
core, mantle, and crust. Images taken by the Hubble Space Telescope
revealed a basaltic surface that suggests ancient lava flows originating
from a molten interior and two large, overlapping impact basins at the
South Pole. Its largest crater is thought to have resulted from a
collision with another celestial body, tearing out large chunks that
formed a distinctive class of small asteroids; some of which have
reached earth as meteorites. In October 2012, data from *Dawn* revealed
that the origin of anomalous dark spots and streaks on Vesta's surface
were likely deposited by ancient asteroid impacts. In December 2012,
NASA reported that flowing liquid water had eroded gullies on Vesta's
surface, like on Mars.

Most planetary astronomers believe that the planets of our Solar
System formed from a nebula of gas, dust, and ices that coalesced
around the developing Sun. Likewise, asteroids are thought to be
composed of proto-planetary material that was prevented from

accreting into a planet-sized body by Jupiter's strong gravity. NASA scientists believe Vesta to be the "last of its kind," the only remaining example of the large planetoids that came together to form the rocky planets.

Alternatively, the Exploded Planet Hypothesis (EPH) holds that all the asteroids, comets, and meteorites in our Solar System originated from one or more planetary explosions. This would explain the relatively small amount of remaining material in the Asteroid Belt. This theory is the work of American astronomer Dr. Tom Van Flandern, who accumulated an impressive body of evidence from the late 1970s. Prior to his death in 2009 Van Flandern authored numerous scientific papers on the EPH and the book *Dark Matter, Missing Planets, and New Comets.* Van Flandern believed that what is now the Asteroid Belt was once a large planet that exploded due to phase changes, natural fission reactions, or gravitational heat energy. He also believed that Mars was originally a moon of the destroyed planet.

There is also mythic evidence to support this view, including the story of the Greek god Phaeton, son of Helios the sun god, who perished in a fire while driving the sun chariot. Later writers assigned Phaeton's name to either Jupiter or Saturn since a planet no longer existed in the location we now know as the Asteroid Belt. Some writers assumed the story referred to a star, but the Greeks certainly knew the difference between a planet and a star; in fact our word planet comes from the Greek *planates*, meaning "wanderers."

The myth of Ceres (Demeter in Greek) tells of the abduction Ceres' daughter by Hades/Pluto, god of the underworld, who took her to his kingdom. She was violently "severed" from her mother, and the world became barren. The mother remained on the surface of the earth grieving while the daughter became queen of the underworld for part of the year. Pluto, the dwarf planet of our modern world, resides in the Kuiper Belt, which can be seen as the icy underworld of the Solar System. It's also the location of many comets and other rocky debris.

A large amount of matter exists in the orbital zone predicted by Titius-Bode whether a planet did not coalesce or one exploded. How do we account for this symbolism in astrological terms? Whether it was a failure to form, or a shattering fragmentation, the mythos is one of synthesis through reclamation and reintegration. What triggers symbolic or literal explosions within us, and how would we bring about healing?

How might the influence of dwarf planets like Pluto and Ceres differ from a larger body, and should a singular object among thousands be interpreted differently than a unitary planet in its own orbit? How might the harmonic intervals themselves that are predicted by the Titius-Bode formula factor into astrology? Might there also be alternating polarities as we move outward from the Sun? There may even be yet undiscovered planets in the Solar System.

Ceres is the principle of reaping and harvest. Vesta represents the sacred fire that kindles life and the holy sphere upon which life exists and unfolds. If a planet had exploded in some ancient time, these worlds are large remnants of a once thriving planet that may contain vital memories and messages. Might their symbolic significance represent a fracturing of our psyches from some early, or even past life, wounds? What if we had once lived on that planet, and our souls are still recovering from the loss of that distant world? These are questions with uncertain answers but may suggest how astrologers will search for new meaning in a discipline that is expanding before our eyes.

Atlantis Rising #109 December 2014

36. HAUMEA AND MAKEMAKE: WHAT DO SANTA, HIS REINDEER, AND THE EASTER BUNNY HAVE TO DO WITH DWARF PLANETS?

"Any darn fool can make something complex; it takes a genius to make something simple."

Pete Seeger, American folk singer and activist

Haumea (credit Ann Field, Space Telescope Science Institute
ESA/NASA

Makemake - MK2-400 NASA, ESA, A. Parker Southwest Research
Institute

About two decades ago astronomers began to understand that Pluto was just the most visible member of the Kuiper Belt, a vast ring of tens of thousands icy, rocky debris circling the outer solar system. Other small, planet-like bodies, called Trans-Neptunian Objects (TNOs), joined the Sun's family, and when a world named Eris was found in this region, and seemed to be larger than Pluto, astronomers reluctantly decided to define a planet for the first time. Since 2006, a planet is defined as a body in orbit around the Sun with sufficient mass to achieve a nearly-round shape, and to have "cleared the neighborhood" around its orbit.

The International Astronomers Union (IAU) then reclassified Pluto as a dwarf planet and later as a "plutoid." The term was officially announced in June 2008 and provided a greatly simplified definition: all trans-Neptunian dwarf planets are plutoids. Pluto is now also recognized as the prototype plutoid. This new category was then applied to other dwarf planets that met the conditions of being like Pluto in terms of period, inclination, and eccentricity. Plutoids orbit the Sun like the planets at a distance greater than Neptune, and are "round," but have <u>not</u> cleared the neighborhoods around their orbits.

Satellites of plutoids are not plutoids. Dwarf planet Ceres is not a plutoid because it is located in the main asteroid belt between Mars and Jupiter and not beyond Neptune. Although forty more plutoids are expected to be identified, as of the summer 2013, the official plutoids are: Pluto, Eris, Haumea, Makemake, Sedna, Quaoar, Orcus, and "Snow White," which has yet to receive a permanent name. Haumea and Makemake are the subject of this article.

Santa & Haumea - In September 2008 the IAU named the fifth dwarf planet and plutoid after Haumea, the Hawaiian creation goddess. Prior to that the Caltech discovery team had used the nickname "Santa," as they discovered the object on December 28, 2004, just after Christmas. David Rabinowitz of Yale University, one of the co-discoverers, chose her name. Among a variety of reasons, the goddess is associated with stone, and the dwarf planet appears to contain more rocky material than most Kuiper Belt Objects, perhaps being made almost entirely of rock; most KBOs contain more ice. Haumea is the third-brightest object in the Kuiper Belt after Pluto and Makemake, and easily observable with a large amateur telescope. Although estimated to be one-third of Pluto's mass, Haumea is elongated like a football and is similar to Pluto in length. Haumea's extreme elongation makes it unique among known dwarf planets as it spins rapidly end-over-end at a rate of once every 3.9 earth hours. Haumea has an orbital period of 285 earth years, about forty years longer than Pluto.

Haumea is the mother and creation goddess of Hawaii, where the Mauna Kea Observatory is located, and where members of the discovery team used the observatory's telescopes. Haumea is also identified with Papa, goddess of the earth and wife of Wakea (space). Haumea is a goddess of fertility, childbirth, food, and nurturing. She gave birth to many children, sometimes even turning herself into a young woman to marry her children and grandchildren. Each of her children emerged from a different part of her body, symbolizing a profoundly nourishing source of life. Haumea also acts as a divine midwife to human mothers, teaching women the mysteries of childbirth. Her nature is constantly renewing, representing the cycles of women's lives. Her legends say she first lived as a mortal woman named La'ila', who gave birth to the Hawaiian island chiefs. She is the ancestor of all indigenous Hawaiians who are said to be descendants of the ancient civilization of Mu. Haumea is the elder in a trinity of Hawaiian goddesses that includes Hina and Pele.

Author Martha Beckworth, whose collection resides in a Hawaiian museum, suggests that the name Haumea actually comes from Hanaumea, which means "sacred birth." Haumea is thought to inhabit the *Makalei* tree, a Tree of Life on the island of Oahu, whose mystical branches and deep roots yield infinite amounts of food. Like a cornucopia, the tree symbolically provides many staples to the Hawaiian people such as coconut, bamboo, taro root, breadfruit, and sugar cane. When the goddess shakes a sacred branch of the miraculous *Makalei* tree over water, she attracts abundant fish. Her nature, like Santa's, is a generous giver of gifts.

Haumea's moons were named after two of her daughters, Hi'iaka and Namaka. Astronomers think Haumea may have crashed into another large object a long time ago, and it is possible that pieces left over from this collision came together to form Haumea's moons. If so, the children did indeed spring forth from the body of their mother. Hi'iaka, at first nicknamed "Rudolph" by the Caltech team, is mythically said to have been born from Haumea's mouth and was carried as an egg by her older sister Pele from their distant home to the Hawaiian Islands. Hi'iaka danced the first Hula on the shores of Puna and is the patron of hula dancers. The smaller moon Namaka, first nicknamed "Blitzen," is named after the water spirit born from Haumea's breasts. When fiery Pele spews her volcanic wrath, sending her burning lava into the sea, Namaka cools it and creates new land.

Easter Bunny & Makemake - Makemake, discovered in 2005 and named in 2008, is a small, red-tinged world in the Kuiper Belt that is among the largest objects in the outer solar system. This dwarf planet was discovered soon after Easter in 2005 and was first nicknamed "Easter Bunny." Although Makemake is smaller, probably two-thirds the size, and dimmer than Pluto, it's also bright enough to be seen by a high-end amateur telescope. When Mike Brown, who headed the Caltech discovery team, selected an official name, he chose the chief creator god from the South Pacific island of Rapa Nui, whose English name is Easter Island. The island was "discovered" by white people at Easter in 1722 and is famous for its 887 monumental stone heads called *Moai*, which are now known to have bodies below the ground.

Mike Brown remarked, "We consider the naming of objects in the Solar System very carefully. Makemake's surface is covered with large amounts of almost pure methane ice, which is scientifically fascinating, but not easily relatable to terrestrial mythology. Suddenly, it dawned on me: the island of Rapa Nui. Why hadn't I thought of this before? I wasn't familiar with the mythology of the island so I had to look it up, and I found Makemake, the chief god, the creator of humanity, and the god of fertility. I am partial to fertility gods. Eris, Makemake, and

Haumea were all discovered when my wife was three to six months pregnant with our daughter. I have the distinct memory of feeling this fertile abundance pouring out of the entire Universe. Makemake was part of that."

Visually, it is the second brightest trans-Neptunian object, after Pluto. Makemake has no known satellites, making it unique so far among KBOs. Makemake follows an orbit very similar to that of Haumea but is slightly farther from the Sun. Its orbital period is nearly 310 years, a bit more than Pluto's 248 years and Haumea's 283 years. Makemake is a classical Kuiper Belt object, which means its orbit lies far enough from Neptune to remain stable over the age of the Solar System. Astronomers consider Makemake to be a member of the "dynamically hot" class of classical KBOs, meaning that it has a high inclination compared to others.

Makemake was the chief god of the Tangata-Manu birdman cult at Orongo and was worshipped in the form of a sea bird. Petroglyphs of Makemake, which look like a man with a bird's head, can be found on Rapa Nui. Like his first code name Easter Bunny, he was connected with eggs. In earlier times islanders competed in an annual ceremony to be the first to capture a sea swallow egg from a precarious breeding site at the tiny islet of Moto Nui. Contestants traversed dangerous cliffs and swam through shark-infested waters, and not all of them survived. The winner was honored with the title Tangata-Manu, "bird man," and became chief of the Rapa Nui people for a year. The last bird man competition took place in 1867.

Through the magic of naming and the power of myth, these new Solar System objects will acquire a symbolic significance that can be integrated into a much richer, albeit more complex, system of astrological interpretation. As new archetypal figures emerge in our awareness, they will begin to influence our collective consciousness. Astrologers will be challenged how to incorporate these new planetary bodies into their interpretation. But I believe plutoids such as Haumea and Makemake must be considered along side Pluto since they are so similar. We might also ask if the Kuiper Belt itself symbolizes a sort of threshold to the outer Solar System, and whether objects in the Kuiper Belt might act together in some collective way based on their synchronous orbits?

The IAU has chosen to divide the expanse of the Kuiper Belt into two sections, inner and outer, with naming protocols. Plutoids identified in the inner half, closer to Neptune, must be named for creation deities. Those discovered in the outer Kuiper Belt, like Pluto, must be named for gods and goddesses of the underworld. Haumea and Makemake are both creation deities who emerged in the mythos of islands, while Pluto is lord of the Greek underworld. In astrological interpretation Pluto is said to represent the principle of transformation, so perhaps Haumea embodies the idea of regeneration through the re-creation and "sacred birth" of new forms. Aligned with a planet in an astrological chart, she might reveal where a whole new form, or approach to life, is required to take shape. Makemake's symbolism involves a metamorphosis into a hybrid creature, a "bird man," allowing the new creature to experience multiple elements. His connection to a planet might show where courage is required, a seemingly life-threatening contest, that will utterly change the person's life.

If the number of plutoids increases to four-dozen as expected, it will be impossible to use them all at once. The meaning of the dwarf planets may become like the bright and named stars, having significance only if they closely aspect a planet or an angle. As more outer Solar System inhabitants reveal themselves and astrology becomes more complex, it's also possible that planets will come to have one kind of influence and dwarf planets another. Smaller terrestrial planets such as Venus and Mars may assume a role that's different from gas giants like Jupiter and Saturn. A planetary body's influence may be related to its class as a planet.

Astrology has been rewritten before as science has expanded our view of the universe. After telescopes revealed the existence of Uranus and Neptune two new planetary archetypes had to be added to the astrological pallet. With the advent of increasingly powerful telescopes, a wider window to the Solar System, and the Universe, continues to open. As we learn of more Pluto-like worlds beyond Neptune, and of earth-like planets in orbit around other stars, our paradigm has to widen. The Universe is bigger than we can imagine, and an open mind is the key to embracing its mystery.

Atlantis Rising #101 August 2013

37.SEDNA: WHAT'S IN A NAME?

"Perhaps they are not stars, but rather openings in heaven where the love of our lost ones pours through and shines down upon us to let us know they are happy."

Inuit proverb

NASA/JPL Caltech R. Hurt, artist's conception of Sedna

As recently as the Middle Ages Galileo was imprisoned for advancing Copernicus's view that Earth circled the Sun, not the other way round. Then along came Uranus, Neptune, and Pluto, further upsetting the apple cart. Today, most people probably still think of the Solar System as the Sun and nine planets (eight since 2006) that orbit our star. But that picture is changing dramatically as technology reveals other members of the Sun's extended family.

In March of 2004 astronomers announced the discovery of a planet-like body in the far reaches of our Solar System, three times farther from Earth than Pluto. Officially dubbed 2003 VB12, the object was discovered in November 2003 at Caltech's Palomar Observatory as part of a three-year project. The team who discovered this planetoid named her Sedna, after the Inuit goddess who lives at the bottom of the frigid, Arctic ocean.

Sedna is the largest, coldest, and most remote body orbiting the Sun identified since Pluto's discovery in 1930. The red-colored newcomer is three-fourths the size of Pluto, and travels in an enormous, narrow ellipse. The orbit is unlike anything astronomers have seen and lasts a whopping 12,000 plus years. Sedna is currently approaching its closest orbital position to the Sun, getting closer and brighter over the next seventy-two years, before turning back toward the far reaches of the Sun's domain. The last time Sedna came this close Earth was coming out of an ice age. It's intriguing to contemplate what our home planet might be like twelve thousand years from now when she makes a return engagement.

Beyond Neptune is the Kuiper Belt (pronounced like viper), an icy asteroid belt named for Gerard Kuiper, the astronomer who predicted its existence. Evidence strongly suggests that the Kuiper Belt has a fairly sharp edge, terminating at 50 AU (Astronomical Units). Beyond this is an immense, hypothetical, spherical cloud of rocky and icy debris called the Oort cloud (named after astronomer Jan Oort), which surrounds our Solar System. The diameter of the icy sphere that defines the physical, gravitational, and dynamic orb of influence of the Sun is three light years, or thirteen billion kilometers (eight billion miles). This cloud is the birthplace of proto-comets that loosely orbit the Sun at a distance nearly halfway to the closest star. Scientists believe that the Oort cloud may contain more total mass than the Kuiper Belt and Asteroid Belt combined.

Although located ten times closer than expected, astronomers believe Sedna is confirmation of the reality of the Oort cloud, revealing that this giant cloud extends much farther into the Solar System than previously believed. According to the team at Caltech who discovered her, Sedna is a new class of object. She does not reside in the Kuiper Belt (where Pluto and Quaoar live), but cycles through what is now called the "inner Oort cloud." Sedna's discovery has also shed light on the origin of our Solar System. Caltech team leader, Dr. Michael Brown, speculated that this "inner Oort cloud might have been formed billions of years ago when a rogue star passed by the Sun, nudging some of the comet-like bodies inward."

Our word for planet comes from the Greek *planates*, meaning "wanderer," and was meant to distinguish the moving stars (planets), from what seemed to be "fixed stars." Strangely enough, that seemed self-evident until now, but life in the Sun's neighborhood is becoming more complex. Sedna's discovery has reignited a heated debate over what constitutes a planet, and suddenly, defining the nature of a planet has become as tricky as describing the nature of the gods they represent. Burgeoning discoveries of planets orbiting other stars, as well as planetoids and comets that keep popping up, have created a classification dilemma. The International Astronomical Union (IAU) now has a committee dedicated to defining a planet.

Planet-like bodies are being discovered almost routinely in orbit around other stars. These gas giants (most like Jupiter) are thought to be Brown Dwarfs. These massive bodies are failed stars, enormous orbs of star-making material that did not manage to catch fire. Although the ingredients were present, the alchemy did not occur. They radiate some light of their own, but do not blaze like stars.

Pluto's hold on planetary status has again become tenuous. Dr. Brown asserts that "if we discovered Pluto today, knowing what we know about other objects in the Kuiper Belt, we wouldn't even consider it a planet." Planets are round, but asteroids and comets are rocky and irregular. Planets have stable orbits, while planetoids may move at angles to the ecliptic and travel in odd, elliptical orbits around the Sun. One way to define a planet is a body orbiting the Sun that is more massive than the total mass of all other bodies in a similar orbit. Technically Pluto is not a planet, just the largest body in the Kuiper Belt, but astronomers expect it's just a matter of time until a KBO (Kuiper Belt Object), larger than Pluto is discovered. What then?

Scholars and researchers have suggested that myth serves a profound purpose that is not limited to story telling. Myth transmits knowledge beyond dogma as well as conveying difficult concepts through archetypal characters and principles. Those who live in closer harmony with the cycles of planting and harvest have myths to honor the forces of nature and often perform ceremonies to keep the scales in balance.

As is typical with myths, versions of Sedna's story differ. Sedna was a beautiful young Inuit (previously called Eskimo) girl who scorned all human suitors. Instead, she flew off with a sea bird—sometimes a raven. Her marriage was not happy and ultimately her father came to rescue her. She tried to escape in her father's boat, but her husband caused a huge storm on the ocean. Selfishly frightened for his own safety, her father pushed Sedna overboard, and when she tried to climb back into the boat, he gouged out one of her eyes and chopped off her fingers, which clung to the sides of the boat. When she ultimately succumbed to her fate, she drifted to the bottom of the sea. Her broken fingers became seals, walruses, and whales; the sea animals the Inuit hunted. Sedna then became goddess of the deep Arctic ocean, and like a petulant child, meted out life or death based on her mood.

Sedna's myth tells us that she must feel satisfied that humanity is keeping their part of the bargain before she will release her creatures to human hunters. Shamans are required to journey to the icy depths of her realm as intermediaries. Sedna's ultimate message is one of respect for the means of survival. She can be seen to reward respect and punish greed. Her own sacrifice resulted in her transformation. We are cautioned to respect this life-giving being and to honor her. Her nature will demand respect for the oceans, the biological origin of life on Earth. At a time when Earth's oceans are increasingly polluted and warming, she brings a harsh message about survival and quality of life.

A kind of magic seems to be at work in myth. Some exquisite mechanism appears to act within collective consciousness to result in the naming of archetypal influences. It is my observation that astronomers are just as fascinated by this process as the story tellers. Naming something imbues it with power, and now that this celestial body has a name her existence will come alive in our consciousness.

Sedna is a new order of being in our Solar System and the first queen of a new archetypal domain. She occupies the inner Oort cloud, living in frigid and distant "waters." She is a stark contrast to her "planetary" predecessors. Her mythic origins make her a New World goddess rather than Old World. She is a child rather than adult, and is female not male. Her mythic themes are sacrifice, betrayal, abandonment, and redemption. Like Persephone and Demeter, her presence and grace affects cycles of growth or greenness on earth, and she controls the ability of hunters to feed their families. The goddess of the Arctic deep deals with the cyclical relationship between humanity and the benevolence of Earth's bounty or the withholding of her gifts.

As a new class of being Sedna represents a new facet of our collective awareness. That she is a goddess bodes well for the return of the divine feminine. Uranus, Neptune, and Pluto (and Quaoar) are all decidedly male. Just as technology enabled us to perceive Uranus, Neptune, and Pluto, once again science will escort us into a domain that was beyond our imagining just a short time ago.

I wrote earlier that the Kuiper Belt might become like the River Styx, acting like a metaphorical barrier to a deeper understanding (AR #37 Chapter 30 in this volume). Sedna, and her counterparts, which may yet be discovered, will take us to another level of cosmic understanding. What kind of evolutionary leap in the unfolding of our consciousness will the new symbolic barrier of the inner Oort cloud represent? Perhaps we will see the Sun and its family more holistically.

Because it is our nature, astrologers will incorporate Sedna into the interpretative mix. It's early in the game to speculate, but I believe she will strongly resonate with the sign of Virgo, as well as the great goddesses of agriculture, and the cyclical give-and-take of hunting, growing and replenishment. Like the Black Virgins, whose milk is both miraculous and transforming, she also carries deep secrets of alchemical transmutation. The icy depths of Sedna's realm contain the paradox of the divine feminine in all cultures, which is seen as both giver of life and destroyer. Like the Hindu Shakti, She is the power itself, and the Path is learning to wield that power.

With another nod toward the magic of myth and symbolism, astrologer Philip Sedgwick informed me that Sedna is transiting 18 degrees (plus something) of Taurus. In a lovely synchronicity, the Sabian symbol (visual representation), for this degree of the zodiac is "a new continent rising out of the ocean." Here too is recognition of a very different, and as yet unrecognized, reality.

Astrologically, the outer planets are said to act like "higher octaves," taking an archetypal energy to a potentially expanded expression of energy. Uranus, Neptune, and Pluto are the higher octaves of Mercury, Venus, and Mars, respectively. In this vein, it's tempting to see Sedna as a higher octave of the Moon, with the potential to transmute the earthly concerns of food, shelter, and caring for our young into a pursuit for spiritual sustenance; searching for soul food. Seen this way, Sedna could open a previously-veiled gateway to eternity.

Atlantis Rising #46 June 2004

38.LILITH: GODDESS, DEMON, OR EARTHS DARK MOON?

"Light is the left hand of darkness and darkness the right hand of light. Two are one, life and death, lying together like lovers in kemmer, like hands joined together, like the end and the way."

Ursula K. Le Guin, *The Left Hand of Darkness*

Lilith - author Aiwok, CC BY-SA 3.0

Our concept of the Solar System is in a state of flux, and it's a challenge for astrologers to keep pace with the discoveries and their potential significance. We lost Pluto as a planet, and Dwarf Planet Eris, who upset the apple cart, has an even larger mass, added insult to injury. In 2001 an asteroid was identified that may be larger than Ceres, the first discovered. Ceres itself is now believed to be a "mini-planet," boasting pure water beneath its round and icy surface.

Lilith is an enigmatic figure with multiple identities in astronomy and divergent interpretations in astrology. She is just as mysterious in myth and legend. Astronomically, Lilith has four distinct identities: She is a bright star in the constellation of Perseus, an asteroid in the Main

Asteroid Belt, a controversial second moon of Earth, and an abstract mathematical point in space.

Lilith is believed to have emerged from Baalat, Lady of Gebal, at the ancient site of Byblos. One of the oldest continuously inhabited cities in the world, The Lady, as she was called, was worshiped 7,000 years ago. Lilith also appeared more than 4,000 years ago in the Mesopotamian *Epic of Gilgamesh*, a poem carved on twelve tablets. Sumerian king lists identified Gilgamesh as the first king of the first dynasty of Uruk. Lilith was said to live in a tree with a dragon at the roots and a nesting bird at the top, linking her with intrinsic symbols of the sacred feminine that appear in cultures around the world. Gilgamesh chopped down the tree because the goddess Inanna wanted the wood for a throne. Gilgamesh killed the dragon and caused Lilith and the bird to flee. Lilith, like the later Cannanite Asherah, who was the consort of Yawheh, was nothing less than the Tree of Life itself. Mythically destroying the Tree of Life presaged what has happened to human nature and our sense of the feminine.

Lilith is also identified with Ki-sikil-lil-la-ke, which is sometimes translated as "Lila's maiden, companion," or the "beloved" of Gilgamesh. She is described as the "Gladdener of All Hearts," and "Maiden Who Screeches Constantly," which might relate to the owls who like the Greek Athena, are her constant companions. Lilith echoes through the ages like the Crone goddesses from many cultures who guard the portals of life and death. As an archetype, she is similar to the goddesses Persephone, Hekate, Athena, Minerva, and the Hindu Kali, to name a few. Lilith is usually depicted with owls, nocturnal hunters, which like serpents, are symbols of hidden wisdom.

To solve the problem of two contradictory creation stories, the Hebrew Talmud portrayed Lilith as the first wife of Adam. Lilith refused to submit to Adam as she insisted they were created equal and simultaneously. She left the garden, seeking her own way. God sent three angels to bring her back, but she refused. According to the rabbis, she was punished for her independence by being turned into a bloodsucking demon.

Lilith has been a popular subject in art, frequently appearing with a serpent, suggesting her connection to the serpent in Genesis. John Collier's 1892 painting of her, embraced by a giant snake, is evocative of primal female sexuality. Sometimes Lilith is envisioned as a woman with a serpent's tail. Lilith is believed to be depicted in a Sumerian relief, now owned by the British Museum, and acquired as a jewel for their collection to celebrate the museum's 250 year anniversary. (the image appears at the beginning of the chapter). Originally called the Burney Relief after its original owner, this priceless artifact is now called Queen of the Night. Lilith is depicted with owls, and having bird's talons instead of feet. This links her to the goose-footed queen, *Le Reine Pedauque,* and suggests mythic links to the Egyptian Nile Goose, the "Great Chatterer," who created the universe. Also included in this mythic stream are European Black Virgins, the legend of the Queen of Sheba, also sometimes shown with webbed feet, and the greatly diminished Mother Goose of children's nursery rhymes.

Lilith, the Star -- Algol, the second brightest star in the constellation of Perseus, was called Lilith by Hebrew sky watchers. Algol was named *Ras al Ghul* by the Arabs, which means "head of the demon." The English word ghoul is derived from this name. Algol is an eclipsing binary star, a pair of stars that blink dramatically. When pictured in art, Algol, or Lilith, is at the brow of the severed head of Medusa, who Perseus beheaded in Greek myth. Medusa's name derives from the earlier *medha,* which means "feminine wisdom." Astrologer Bernadette Brady says, "Algol contains immense female passion and power." Algol is one of the most powerful stars in the sky, and how this energy is directed makes all the difference. Algol's Celestial Longitude is 26 degrees of the sign of Taurus.

Lilith, the Asteroid -- Asteroid #1181 is named Lilith and orbits the Sun in the Main Asteroid Belt, a ring of rocky planetoids between Mars and Jupiter. It was discovered in February of 1927 by Benjamin Jekhowsky and has an orbital period of about four years. Some astrologers use this asteroid in horoscope interpretation where it is believed to represent relationship difficulties and how conflict is resolved. It's glyph looks like an upturned hand.

Dark Moon -- Dark Moon Lilith is believed to be an actual satellite of Earth, orbiting in a stationary position on the back side of the Moon. This renders the Dark Moon invisible except when it crosses the face of the Sun, visible as a black spot moving across the Sun's surface. French astronomer Frederic Petit, Director of the Toulose observatory, claimed to see this object in 1846. There have been reported sightings by several astronomers, but the illusive Dark Moon has yet to be confirmed. Jules Verne's 1865 novel *From the Earth to the Moon* popularized this idea. The Dark Moon also captured the imagination of the famous astrologer Walter Gornold, better known as Sepharial, who created an ephemeris for this aspect of Lilith. Books have been written on the subject, one by the legendary astrologer Ivy Goldstein, and the Dark Moon is used by some astrologers who believe it represents the dark side of the feminine.

Black Moon -- This facet of Lilith's multiple personality is a mathematical point that is defined by the structure of the Moon's orbit. The Black Moon refers to the Moon's apogee, the point in the Moon's orbit where she is farthest from Earth. An ephemeris exits for this point too, but there are differing opinions about the calculation and interpretative value of "true" versus "mean"" apogee, as the Moon's orbit is an ellipse rather than a circle. The Black Moon represents the feminine shadow, what's hidden or repressed. The interpretation is metaphysical in nature, providing a deeper look at the dark side, the symbolic shadow of the Moon, where much is hidden from normal view.

The Black Moon is a deeper aspect of lunar astrology and is therefore related to the Moon's Nodes, the points in the sky where the Moon's orbital path crosses the ecliptic, or the Sun's apparent path through the sky. The Moon's Nodes have attained the status of planets in Indian Vedic astrology and have also been used for millennia in Chinese astrology. The Moon rotates only once on its axis during its orbit around Earth. Therefore, the same side is always visible to us and the other side is always in darkness, adding to the fertile ground of shadow work. Perhaps Black Moon Lilith connects us to what is unseen.

~Dancing with the Dark Side~

The word myth comes from the root word for "mouth," as storytelling was originally an oral tradition. Myths are sacred stories, and have been the way people transmitted their most sacred truths, their understanding of our relationship to the divine, for thousands of years. Myths, legends, and fairy tales, which contain principles and morals, are structured in the symbolic language of archetypes. Swiss psychoanalyst Carl Jung observed that archetypes, the intrinsic patterns of human consciousness such as Maiden, Mother, Crone, Queen and Princess, do not cease to exist if we ignore or devalue them. Rather, they become submerged in what Jung termed the Collective Unconscious, hiding underground and becoming strong forces that emerge in dreams, complexes or even psychoses.

Western culture has devalued, even demonized, aspects of the feminine for nearly 4,000 years, effectively pushing these archetypes beneath our conscious awareness. Serious scholars of myth have noticed that the tenor of the stories began to change nearly four thousand years ago. Symptoms of this shift in Greek myths included an increasing glorification of war, accompanied by a deteriorating value of agriculture and cyclical time.

Psychologically, in all her aspects, Lilith seems to represent facets of the feminine that have been suppressed. Her nature acts like a Multiple Personality Disorder where aspects of the feminine have been splintered, and some of the parts are now labeled good and others evil. How this shows up, individually or collectively, depends on the context. Lilith can be a righteous, avenging angel or a wrathful demon. Sometimes she is angry and vengeful, and sometimes she is empowered to regain her rightful status as an equal partner. Astrologers who use Lilith, in any of her forms, believe she reveals wounds related to feminine power in both men and women. Recognizing what has been disenfranchised is a first step toward restoring balance. One wonders what the fate of humanity might have been if Adam and Lilith had worked things out.

Lilith left the garden and subsequently her nature and uncontrolled power became feared and was declared evil. Lilith's story embodies what occurred in myths over time as earlier goddess worshiping cultures were eclipsed by the emerging patriarchy. Once the Tree of Life, Lilith is an example of how many powerful feminine deities became demonized. In modern times, as the pendulum swings back, Lilith has become an icon of feminine strength and the women's movement.

There were two trees in the Garden of Eden. Eve, created to replace Lilith as the Tree of Life, took fruit from the other one, the Tree of Knowledge. She has been blamed by the Church, along with all women, for the sins of the world. Decoding the symbolic significance of the serpent, ancient and pervasive symbol of feminine wisdom, is central to understanding the deepest levels of humanity's story. In Qabalah, the mystical tradition of Judaism, the serpent climbs the Tree of Life to return to the Source.

Lilith's fragmented and confusing nature in myth and astrology may reflect the ways our choices have fractured the human psyche, and she may hold a key that could unlock healing insights. Piercing the veil of Lilith's enigmatic persona may offer modern men and women empowering energy that is much needed in today's world. Some symbolists have suggested that the Age of Aquarius will be symbolized by gardens and the greening of the Earth. As human consciousness expands I believe we would all benefit from redeeming our separated natures. Integrating all the parts of femininity, including sexuality and the mysteries of old age and death, could make us stronger and wiser as we face current environmental challenges.

Atlantis Rising #71 August 2008

39. CHIRON: WISE CENTAUR OR ROGUE COMET?

"There is no power on earth that can neutralize the influence of a high, pure, simple and useful life."

Booker T. Washington

Chiron teaching young hero Achilles (Roman fresco - public domain)

I have often observed that Astronomers have a keen sense of myth.
Chiron was the first-known member of a new class of icy, dual-natured
planetoids called Centaurs after the mythical race of horse/man
beings. Astronomically, centaurs are comparable in size to asteroids,
but similar to comets in composition and behavior. Based on their
composition, Centaurs are either blue like Chiron or very red like
Pholus. Due to their erratic orbits Astronomers believe these unusual
objects are exiles from the Kuiper Belt. The Kuiper Belt is a
hypothetical disk-shaped reservoir of objects ranging in size from tiny
particles to dwarf planets like Pluto, Eris, and perhaps even larger
bodies.

If objects are expelled from the Kuiper Belt and gravitationally
attracted to the orbit of Neptune they become centaurs. At some point
they may further transition to become short-period comets. Phoebe,
one of the moons of Saturn, is now believed to be in this category.

Chiron was discovered in November of 1977 by Charles Kowal of Caltech. Kowal was searching for distant galaxies when the moving light of an unknown object appeared on his screen. He assumed it was a comet, but further examination revealed the object was more than one hundred times larger than known comets, placing it in the category of the largest asteroids. This was problematic since there are thousands of asteroids, and they are almost always located in the main asteroid belt between the orbits of Mars and Jupiter. The asteroid belt acts like a dividing line between the terrestrial-sized planets and the gas giants beyond. Chiron was a solitary traveler outside the asteroid belt, orbiting instead between Saturn and Uranus.

Chiron is composed of ice with a dark crust of carbon, has 50,000 times the characteristic volume of a comet, and is believed to have a diameter of nearly 200 kilometers. The celestial centaur travels in a quasi-circular but erratic and unstable orbit lasting fifty-one years, and if Chiron is ever seriously "perturbed" by the gravity of the larger planets it will become a truly spectacular comet as it races toward the Sun.

To further complicate Chiron's unusual nature, since 1988 he has displayed comet-like behavior, undergoing an outburst in brightness, and by 1989 Chiron had developed a cometary coma (cloud of gas and dust), caused by evaporation from its surface. Officially called Minor Planet #2060, Chiron is now classified as both a comet and an asteroid. He has since been joined by other Centaurs, several of which have also been named.

Chiron was set apart from the other Centaurs by both lineage and character. The rest of the mythical Centaurs were descended in an unfortunate episode from King Ixion and Nephele. Stories often vary in myth and Chiron's own wife, Chariklo, was said to be the daughter of Apollo. Chiron's parents were Saturn (Cronus), who disguised himself as a horse during the seduction and mating of the beautiful Oceanid, Philyra, in order to avoid detection by his wife Rhea.

As a result of his father's disguise Chiron was born half human and half horse. His mother was horrified by the entire affair and Chiron was abandoned at birth by both parents and left in a dark cave on Mount Pelion in Thessaly. His brother Apollo, the sun god, occupied the light side of the same cave, representing a vastly different mythic theme that is echoed by the parentage of Chiron's centaur wife, Chariklo.

Since Chiron's father was a god he was immortal and therefore didn't die as a result of his abandonment. Rather than becoming bitter at his fate he poured his energy into learning and grew in wisdom. He became a master musician and renowned teacher whose pupils were the great heroes of myth such as Jason, Achilles, Hercules and Asclepius. In fact the infant Jason was raised by Chariklo who was known for her grace and utter truthfulness.

Chiron was reputed to be the wisest of the Centaurs. As a race they were said to be wanton and reckless, typically exhibiting the "animal" side of their nature. He was markedly different from his brethren since he was highly cultured and kind. He was a great healer, a respected oracle, and in early Greek myth Chiron is credited with fashioning the constellations and teaching humanity how to interpret the meaning of the starry pictures. In other words, Chiron was the father of astrology to the Greeks.

An unfortunate incident involving wine occurred during one of Hercules's visits, which triggered a Centaur attack. While Chiron's student and friend fought the battle, the wise centaur was accidentally wounded by one of his defender's poison arrows. Again, because of his immortal nature, he didn't die but lived in constant and horrible pain. Although Chiron was an extraordinary healer, he couldn't heal his own wound and ultimately required the intercession of another.

He beseeched Zeus to let him die rather than suffer forever. He offered to trade places with Prometheus, who was being subjected to daily torture as a punishment for stealing fire for humanity. For reasons that aren't clear Zeus agreed to this bargain. Chiron's sacrifice achieved liberation from his own agony and allowed humanity to keep the gift of fire. Zeus honored Chiron's noble spirit and granted him another form of immortality by placing him in the sky as the constellation

Centarus, the only star group to possess two first-magnitude stars. The zodiacal constellation of Sagittarius is also a centaur but represents the process of transformation from instinctual to divine nature rather than the wisdom and enlightenment that Chiron embodies.

Although astronomers speculate that Chiron may one day journey elsewhere he has been in our conscious awareness for more than forty years and many astrologers have incorporated his influence into their interpretative practice. Astrologically Chiron's unique and dual nature, and his early abandonment, can reveal where in our own lives we don't fit in and where we will be forced to stand alone.

He began his life as an outcast and outsider, and examining his position and prominence in a horoscope shows the area of life where we may feel a profound sense of alienation. The work involved in learning these hard lessons enables us to reclaim lost or hidden parts of ourselves. Astrologers who have researched Chiron's influence have observed that on the extreme negative side of the ledger he seems to have a prominent place in the charts of rapists and serial killers, suggesting the damaging power of early abandonment. This is supported by clinical research in this area that has demonstrated that these individuals are characterized by early abandonment or estrangement from their mothers. Not surprisingly, on the positive side, his prominence is often revealed in the charts of healers.

Chiron was a teacher of heroes--those who also walk a solitary path. The mechanism that drives our spiritual growth is at times similar to the story of the ugly duckling who viewed his differences as a deformity until he saw the beauty of his true reflection and embraced his own identity. Chiron's presence in our astrology chart can teach us the nature of our response to betrayal. Each of us may have received some defining wound, which ever afterward shapes how we view the world. Do our experiences impel us to take the higher ground and grow in wisdom, or do we pursue a path of resentment and revenge?

Although in astrological symbolism Chiron is often viewed as an archetype of the wounded healer, it seems important to distinguish his early experiences from the point of time of his woundedness as the arrow pierced him later in life. Chiron was not damaged by his early emotional wounds. In fact it was these experiences that shaped his accomplishments. His solitary alienation forged the potential of his character and may therefore point the way to where we must find strength in isolation.

Recently several new objects have emerged into our awareness in the Solar System, including Sedna, Quaoar ,and dwarf planet Eris. They've been there all along but now our consciousness and our technology are ready to perceive them. Astrologers believe the "discovery" of new objects indicates that we've grown enough in consciousness to incorporate their archetypal meaning. What does Chiron's astronomical nature and place in the Solar System tell us about our own evolving consciousness as a human race? What was externalized in our awareness when Chiron was "discovered?" What does he represent in our collective consciousness, and how do we perceive the nature of reality? At the most elemental level I believe he represents how we are defined by our choices and not ruled by our circumstances.

He walked a path that carried themes of sacrifice and redemption, indicating that his symbolism shows how we can move out of wounds into healing. His archetype teaches us to look for the lesson or gift in our own pain. Ironically, in the end his wound brought liberation from an endless physical existence where all his mortal relationships ended in further isolation. Purely physical immortality may be overrated.

In 1977 Voyager I took the first picture of the Earth and Moon together in space, a portrait of our home and her satellite. Also in 1977 Voyager II launched its first ever flyby of Jupiter, Saturn and Uranus, heading toward Chiron's path, and the Space Shuttle took the first crew into space the same year. These events can be seen as shifts in our collective awareness from an earthbound focus to a wider perspective. Before space travel Earth too was in isolation.

Our awareness as a species is expanding and new objects such as Centaurs, Sedna, Quaoar, and Eris entering our consciousness reflect that expansion. The next step is recognition of their significance and integration of these principles into humanity's group soul. Whether they are interpreted in their own right or used as categories of connection to the outer reaches of our Solar System, I believe they offer glimpses into humanity's evolutionary unfoldment and gateways to higher consciousness.

In May of 2009 an alignment will occur between Jupiter, Neptune, and Chiron in the sign of Aquarius. This conjunction certainly holds the potential for profound healing and could be seen as a an aspect of nobility.

Atlantis Rising #67 June 2007

40. VULCAN: BLACKSMITH OF THE GODS

"Of the four elements, air, earth, water, and fire, humans stole only fire from the gods. And with fire forged mortal will upon the world."

Anonymous

Leonard Nimoy as the character Spock, the Vulcan on Star Trek 1975
- public domain

For a time, Vulcan was a small planet, or large asteroid, proposed to exist between Mercury and the Sun. Its astrological significance is still part of esoteric astrology, having a deep and hidden relationship to the sign of Taurus, the Bull. Attempting to explain peculiarities in Mercury's orbit, 19th-century French mathematician Urbain Le Verrier hypothesized that these anomalies were the result of another planet, which he named Vulcan after the Roman god of fire.

A number of reputable investigators joined the search; among these was Henry C. Courten of Dowling College, New York. Studying photographic plates of the 1970 solar eclipse, he and his associates detected several objects that appeared to be in orbits close to the Sun.

Even accounting for artifacts, Courten felt that at least seven of the objects were real. The appearance of some of these objects was confirmed by an observer in North Carolina and another in Virginia. Courten believed that an intra-Mercurial planetoid between 130 and 800 kilometers (80-496 miles) in diameter was orbiting the Sun at a distance of about 0.1 AU. Other images on the eclipse plates led Courten to postulate the existence of an asteroid belt between Mercury and the Sun.

Searches by NASA's two STEREO spacecraft failed to detect asteroids between Mercury and the Sun that might have accounted for the claimed observations. Most astronomers abandoned the search, but a few remain convinced that not all of the alleged observations were unfounded. Some of these—and other intra-Mercurial objects—may actually exist, being unknown comets or small asteroids. In recent years some astronomers have offered convincing logic for so-called *vulcanoid* asteroids, and the data from the SOHO satellite, a cooperative venture between NASA and ESA, which is examining the Sun for other reasons, will search for these objects. If found, one will of course be named Vulcan.

The Roman Vulcan, or *Vulcanus,* was the lame god of fire, crafts, and blacksmiths. His domain included the fire of volcanoes, and the word comes from his name. Gerard Capdeville traced the origin of Vulcan back to a young god from Crete named *Velchanos,* who also had a mastery of fire and was a companion, rather than son, of the Great Goddess.

In myth, Hephaestus, the Roman Vulcan, was the Greek god of blacksmiths, sculptors, metallurgy, fire, and volcanoes. He was portrayed with a hammer, anvil, and pair of tongs. He was a master craftsman who forged armor and weapons for the gods from metals found in the depths of the Earth. Hephaestus accomplished numerous feats of craftsmanship, such as marvelous palaces built for Olympian deities and Achilles's armor during the siege of Troy.

According to the epics of Homer, the Iliad, and the Odyssey, Hephaestus was the son of Zeus and Hera. In one account, Hera threw

Hephaestus from Olympus after he was born because he was crippled. However, Hesiod informs us that Hera bore Hephaestus alone—parthenogenetically—without a father. In this story Hephaestus tried, and almost succeeded, in freeing his mother when Zeus punished her for this by hanging her on a golden chain between heaven and earth. Angry at his son's interference, Zeus hurled him from Olympus, causing his injury and disability. Either way, as a heroic figure, Hephaestus had to deal with rejection, abandonment, and being crippled.

Most sources claim that Hephaestus landed in the sea near the island of Lemnos and was washed onto the shore where his body lay broken until he was rescued by the Nereids, the famous sea nymphs Thetis (mother of Achilles) and Eurynome (mother of the Three Graces). Hephaestus lived in secret with these goddesses, working in a cave deep within the Earth for nine years, awakening his creative energy, and becoming a master craftsman.

He was later accepted back to Olympus, becoming craftsman of the gods. He was married to Aphrodite/Venus, ruler of Taurus in astrology, which is a mythic hint of the deeper relationship between Venus, Vulcan, and Taurus. The spiritual path is often characterized as molding the noble self out of the denseness of earth through the fires of aspiration. It is a paradox that works of greatest beauty sometimes arise from the healing and transformation of our deepest wounds.

In the modern mythos of TV and film, Vulcans are a fictional extraterrestrial humanoid species in the *Star Trek* franchise, who originate from the planet Vulcan. They are noted for their attempt to live by logic without interference from unruly emotions. They were the first extraterrestrial species in the *Star Trek* universe to observe "first contact" protocol with Humans. Vulcans later became founding members of the United Federation of Planets. Science and science fiction had a happy collaboration related in the July 1991 issue of *Sky & Telescope*. The article reported how Gene Roddenberry, creator of *Star Trek*, and three Harvard-Smithsonian Center for Astrophysics scientists, chose an actual star (40 Eridani) as the fictional planet Vulcan's sun because of its characteristics.

Metaphysics has long held that what we can see is a fraction of what exists. According to the Planck mission team (the spacecraft measures Cosmic Microwave Background) and based on the standard model of cosmology, the total mass-energy of the known universe contains 4.9% ordinary (baryonic) matter, 26.8% dark matter, and 68.3% dark energy, a mysterious and invisible force that seems to be the opposite of gravity. Dark matter plus dark energy constitutes 95.1% of the total mass/energy content of the universe. The barely 5% that's left is the visible universe—including Earth, the Sun, other stars, and galaxies— that are made of protons, neutrons, and electrons bundled together into atoms.

Dark matter (not to be confused with anti-matter) is a hypothetical kind of matter that can't be seen with telescopes and neither emits nor absorbs light, or any other electromagnetic radiation at any significant level. It doesn't interact with "ordinary" matter, and is completely invisible. Dark matter has not been detected directly, making it one of the greatest mysteries in modern astrophysics. Its existence and properties are inferred from its gravitational effects on visible matter, radiation, and thus on the large-scale structure of the universe. Dark matter accounts for discrepancies between the mass of large astronomical objects determined from their gravitational effects, and their mass as calculated from the observable matter (stars, gas, and dust) they contain.

Many physicists and astronomers think dark matter is composed of exotic particles that don't interact with normal matter or light but still exert a gravitational pull. These particles have so far eluded detection during particle accelerator experiments or discovery among cosmic rays. Several scientific groups, including one at CERN's Large Hadron Collider, are working to generate dark matter particles for study.

According to standard physics, stars at the edges of a spinning, spiral galaxy should travel much slower than those near the galactic center, where a galaxy's visible matter is concentrated. Astronomer Vera Rubin discovered that stars orbit at more or less the same speed regardless of where they are in the galactic disk. This puzzling result makes sense if the boundary stars are feeling the gravitational effects of an unseen mass—dark matter—in a halo around the galaxy.

Dark energy is even more enigmatic than dark matter, and its discovery in the 1990s was a shock to scientists. Dark energy originated from efforts to understand the observed accelerating expansion of the universe. Unlike dark matter, scientists have no plausible explanation for dark energy. Dark matter attracts while dark energy repels. Previously, physicists assumed that the attractive force of gravity would gradually slow down the expansion of the universe, but when two independent teams tried to measure the rate of deceleration, they found that the expansion was accelerating.

Scientists now think the accelerating expansion of the universe is driven by dark energy, a repulsive force generated by quantum fluctuations in otherwise "empty" space. This force seems to be growing stronger as the universe expands. Perhaps dark energy hides portals to, or borders between, parallel universes or veils hidden gateways that lead to unseen realms?

According to another idea, dark energy is a fifth and previously unknown type of "fundamental force" called quintessence, which fills the universe like a fluid. The idea was first presented by R.R. Caldwell, Rahul Dave, and Paul Steinhardt. Science borrowed the term quintessence from ancient wisdom and alchemy where quintessence is the fifth and highest element that permeates all nature. According to ancient science and Medieval philosophy *aether,* quintessence in Latin, is the material that fills the region of the universe above the terrestrial sphere. In Homeric Greek *aether* means "pure, fresh air" or "clear sky" and was thought to be the essence breathed by the gods.

In the alchemist's hierarchy the *Supreme Architect* caused a division within itself into two principles, and from these the four elements resulted: Fire, Earth, Air, and Water. The four elements, with the addition of *Aether,* formed the *Quintessence of Matter.* The alchemist combined the four elements by way of Sulfur, Salt, and Spirit (Mercury) and sought to transmute metals, especially gold. Sulfur is "the stone that burns" that characterized the principle of combustibility, and Mercury contained the idealized principle of metallic properties. Over time quintessence has become synonymous with elixirs, medicinal alchemy, and the Philosopher's Stone itself.

Alchemy is also a metaphor for refining the personality into the "gold" of the spiritual nature. Vulcan/Hephaestus was an alchemist in the truest sense. He was thrown from the lofty heights of Olympus, losing his birthright for a time, but he worked deep in the earth, transforming buried metals into beautiful objects with the fire of his forge. Instead of the destructive force of revenge, he used his experience in constructive ways. The message is to discover what's buried deep within us, learn how to mine the riches, and transform the potential into priceless gifts.

In *Esoteric Astrology* by Alice A. Bailey, the Tibetan Master DK stated, "Vulcan is veiled by the potency of Mercury and hidden behind the planet. Vulcan can go into the depths of sub-consciousness and reveal obstructions upon the spiritual path." Alan Oken says in *Soul Centered Astrology*, "The sign of Taurus has two planetary rulers: Venus and Vulcan. Venus is the personality ruler, and Vulcan is both the soul ruler and the hierarchical ruler. Both are considered to be sacred planets, while Vulcan is a "hidden" planet. The fact that both ruling planets are sacred (and one is hidden) hints that the inner journey of Taurus is deeply hidden, mysterious, highly significant, and sacred."

This inquiry links chemistry, physics, and metallurgy with the radical and exploratory area of meta-materials and superconductivity at the frontier of modern science. The noble metals of the platinum series that includes silver, gold, and platinum, achieve seemingly inexplicable states at certain phases. One of the amazing properties of these noble elements is they become invisible in their super-conductive states. For humans these states move into the realm of spiritual mastery and immortality.

Science now believes that 95% of the universe is invisible, and our understanding of dark matter and dark energy is still preliminary and certainly just as inconclusive and mysterious as the idea of a "veiled" planet in Esoteric Astrology. As technology peers deeper into space we see the borders between astrophysics, alchemy, and esoteric astrology blurring. The ancients understood much that we are only rediscovering. We may come to understand Vulcan as a symbol for the priceless gold that alchemists have sought for millennia.

Atlantis Rising #116 February 2016

ACKNOWLEDGMENTS

Thanks to my husband Ted who unselfishly offers tireless editorial input and astrological advice that always improves my efforts. He also provides encouragement when my faith in myself falters. My immense gratitude goes to friends, students, and clients for giving life deeper meaning. There are so many who have encouraged me over the years. Your support has been a priceless gift.

Thanks to brilliant artist and graphic designer Sue Lion for the exquisite covers of these two sky lore volumes and the logo images that appear at the beginning of each section. And a shout out goes to bestselling author Sylvia McDaniel, who introduced me to Vellum software.

My heart is full of thanks to all who shared this journey.

ABOUT JULIE LOAR

Julie Loar has pursued a lifelong interest in angels, dreams, mythology, space travel, and other dimensions through an intensive study of metaphysics, while climbing the corporate ladder in two major companies. Focusing on symbols, mythology, Astrology, Tarot, Qabalah, and dreams, Julie has been a spiritual teacher and counselor since 1975. She has led thirteen sacred journeys to Egypt. She is the author of *Messengers*, co-author of *The Hidden Power Of Everyday Things*, and the award-winning, *Tarot & Dream Interpretation*.

Ancient Sky Watchers & Mythic Themes, Volume One in this series, was released in April 2020. Her latest book, *Goddesses For Every Day: Exploring The Wisdom & Power Of The Divine Feminine Around The World,* has won five national awards. Her books have been translated into several languages. Julie is a frequent speaker, radio guest, and workshop leader and is the co-creator of the multiple award-winning board game *Quintangled*.

Her popular astrology column appeared for two decades in *Atlantis Rising* magazine, and was the the genesis of these two volumes. She contributes regularly to SatiamaPublishing.com and was also featured on John Edward's *InfiniteQuest.com*

Visit her at www.JulieLoar.com

ALSO BY JULIE LOAR

Ancient Sky Watchers & Mythic Themes

Goddesses for Every Day

Quintangled: A Games of Strategy, Chance & Destiny

The Five Star Series with Ted Denmark PhD

Star Table Trance-Missions

Star Family Excursions

Star World Ascension

Star Time Convergence

Published as Julie Gillentine

Messengers: Among the Stars, Stones & Legends the Ancient Wisdom Dwells

The Hidden Power of Everyday Things

Tarot & Dream Interpretation

Visit Julie's author page on Amazon

Julie Loar author page

www.JulieLoar.com

Made in the USA
Monee, IL
10 May 2021

67113681R00204